The Language
of Everyday Life

The Language
of Everyday Life

An Introduction

Judy Delin

SAGE Publications
London • Thousand Oaks • New Delhi

ISBN 0-7619-6089-9 (hbk)
ISBN 0-7619-6090-2 (pbk)
© Judy Delin, 2000
In Chapter 2, *Road rage victim stabbed to death* (3 12 1996, Sarah
Boseley), *News in Brief: Road rage fiancée in hospital* (7.12.1996, staff
piece) and *'Rage victim' charged with murder* (20.12 1996, Vivek
Chaudhary) © The Guardian, 1996
First published 2000

SAGE Publications Ltd
1 Oliver's Yard, 55 City Road
London EC1Y 1SP

SAGE Publications Inc
2455 Teller Road
Thousand Oaks, California 91320

SAGE Publications India Pvt Ltd
B–42 Panchsheel Enclave
PO Box 4109
New Delhi 110 017

British Library Cataloguing in Publication data
A catalogue record for this book is available from the British Library

Printed digitally and bound in Great Britain by
Lightning Source UK Ltd., Milton Keynes, Bedfordshire

In memory of my grandfathers

Charles Dzialoszinsky
1902–1936

John Hughes
1899–1992

Contents

PREFACE

While there is a considerable literature on most of the kinds of texts that are discussed in this book, much of it is neither brief nor introductory. My own students' experience has been that there is a need for a book that will open up texts without requiring a huge theoretical apparatus to be assembled beforehand: they wanted to get their hands dirty and get *into* texts, learning the necessary terms and concepts along the way. What was needed, then, was a book that would dive straight in, providing a first introduction to several different text types, and laying the foundations for further study of a more advanced and extended kind.

The aim of this book, therefore, is to give an overview of a wide range of everyday texts at a consistent level of linguistic sophistication. Through an accessible theoretical approach, the book provides a jumping-off point for further and deeper analysis of the kinds of texts covered. I hope this book will prove to be a useful starting-point in the linguistic study of not only the text-types explicitly introduced here, but a wide range of others.

I am grateful to students at the University of Sussex and the University of Stirling for trialling various versions of the material contained in the book, and for the valuable feedback they have given.

ACKNOWLEDGEMENTS

I would like to thank all those who have generously given help and advice during the writing of this book, including Bethan Benwell, whose comments greatly improved the chapters on news reporting and magazines in particular, Jurgita Dzialtuvaite for her work transcribing sports commentaries, Susana Murcia-Bielsa for her insights about instructions, Malcolm Macdonald for references on medical interviews, Ian McGowan for advice on copyright, Martin Mellor for careful reading and comments, Ken Turner for his references on politeness, Tony Hartley and Donia Scott for years of collaboration on rhetorical structure and instructions, and John Bateman, Mick O'Donnell, and Mike Stubbs for sharing their ideas. All this input has been invaluable. Any remaining mistakes are, of course, my own.

Many thanks to Richard Coates and Max Wheeler from whom I inherited the first version of the *Language in Public Life* course at Sussex, and Lynne Cahill with whom I first worked on the idea for this book. Thanks too to seven years of students at Sussex and Stirling including, most recently, Emma Freedman, Joanna Young, and Emily Wilson, who gave valuable comments on the draft, and especially Rebecca Garner for sharing her data. My thanks too to those who agreed to be tape-recorded for the chapter on interviews, who must remain anonymous – Peter, Keith, Beth and Monica know who they are.

Mica Allan, Pat Allen, Bethan Benwell, Emily Carvill, Robert Dale, Martin Davies, Neil Keeble, Alex Lascarides, Peter McCourt, Stef Newell, Jon and

Vina Oberlander, Jeremy Olsen, Nick and Kati Royle, Will Steel, Johnny Tenn, Naomie Thompson, Sandra and Jack Uttley, Karen Valley, Tina Webberley, and especially Annie, Martin, and my parents for all their different kinds of support and inspiration in the process.

I would also like to thank the Department of English Studies and members of the Communication Seminar at the University of Stirling for their support, Julia Hall at Sage for her advice and encouragement, and Stirling Writer's Group for asking if I'd written anything.

1   Introduction

The aim of this book is to raise awareness of the richness of the language that plays such a central role in everyday life. By examining a small number of selected text types, the book presents concepts and ways of going about looking at language that will, it is hoped, expose some of the intricacy of human linguistic behaviour and its role in shaping and reflecting society. If the resulting understanding thereby invokes a sense of wonder at what we do through and with language day by day, then so much the better.

The book is also intended to be empowering. This may be on a practical, 'life skills' level: it is useful to know, for example, how advertising messages influence us, or situations of unequal power affect us in a job interview. In addition, however, the book aims to provoke independent research on language in everyday life, where so much remains to be discovered. There is a fascinating diversity of social situations in which language plays a role. This leaves ample room for projects that, even if the researcher is new to this kind of work, can yield genuinely interesting and even novel findings about how humans interact and how we use language.

LANGUAGE AND EVERYDAY LIFE

Myers takes the view that everyday talk is a distinct discourse type, and draws a distinction between this and 'other' text types such as advertising:

> Everyday life is not institutional – not politics, or church services, or courts. . .talk in everyday life is man to man, or woman to woman, or woman to man or whatever . . . everyday talk is created out of a contrast with advertising talk. (1994: 108)

If we take his view, this book is mistitled. On Myers' approach, the kinds of language we are looking at are not everyday, but are trying to either evoke the everyday (as in advertising, trying to use conversational devices in order to seem 'ordinary' and believable) or to avoid it (as in interviewing, where the 'ordinary' kinds of responses of interest and approbation towards what another is telling you have to be withheld). However, I have quite consciously adopted the title *The Language of Everyday Life* because the text types examined here are so common that they constitute an important part of our everyday experience, and the features of all of them overlap substantially with the features of everyday language. If everydayness is confined to face-to-face conversations between equals, it is surprising how much of our everyday life would have to be described as not everyday. However, it will be clear from much of the discussion in the book that face-to-face conversations between equals are a very useful touchstone for comparison of the text types that are examined. For example, the kinds of instructions a step aerobics instructor gives to her class are usefully contrasted with how people ask one another to do things when they are in an equal relationship. I have not devoted a chapter to face-to-face interaction between equals, although by the end of this book readers should find themselves well armed with terms and concepts with which to describe it. There are many good introductions to casual conversation: I recommend Eggins and Slade (1997) in particular.

CHOICE OF TEXTS

The book is organized around types of texts that we all intuitively know to exist, and expect to have different properties. Sports commentary, for example, will predictably be different from the language used in an interview, and the language of advertising will be different from that of instructions. This much is obvious. Given this observation, however, it is not always easy to see what can be said to pin down what makes a text of a particular type identifiable as such a text, and what can be said about how it achieves its purpose. What this book does is provide a survey of the more significant characteristics of each text type, providing the reader with a set of terms and ideas, taken from an eclectic range of linguistic theories and approaches, that can be used as a toolkit to open up the text, and, it is hoped, many other texts after that.

This book does not attempt to describe exhaustively the differences, or even the characteristics, of the different text types, and does not pretend to present text examples that can be guaranteed to be representative of their types in any formal way. The suggestions presented are not based on large bodies of text, but on relatively short, closely analysed, selected examples. These are all from real texts, not constructed ones. The texts discussed in the book were chosen because they are interesting, and display many of the characteristics that might normally be found in texts of their type. There is, therefore, an attempt to present informally what might be thought of as *normal* texts. I have not deliberately gone for the weird. The important point is that the texts presented here could easily have been found by the reader, and the skills, ideas and approaches described herein could easily be adapted to those texts. To reinforce the point, the final chapter of the book is dedicated to describing how just such a project in text description could be designed and carried out by someone who had read the book, with a view to illuminating his or her own texts in a similar way.

Following Christie (1990: 238), the book seeks to introduce a skill: 'the skill . . . in identifying those elements of the grammar which most usefully illuminate the particular text in hand'. We should be careful to interpret the term 'grammar' very inclusively: the whole system of choices that language presents. This is not a use of the term grammar as it is conventionally understood, referring to the way words are combined into the constituent parts of clauses, and clauses into sentences, but many other levels of description (here we use the term 'syntax' for referring to sentence structure). Levels of description used in the book include:

Production values	The way in which texts of certain types are constructed around expectations of what they will, and will not, contain.
Rhetorical structure	The constituent parts of texts, such as summaries, descriptions, narrative, warnings, step-by-step directions, etc.
Conversation structure	How a dialogue is constructed in 'turns' between speakers, and how these are formed, begun, and ended.
Syntax	The way certain syntactic constructions – different sentence types – are used.
Lexical choice	The way words are chosen, and used in relation to one another.
Semantics	The way meaning is conveyed by certain grammatical and lexical choices.
Pragmatics	The way meaning is retrieved through inference and through the use of shared knowledge and context.
Sound	The way audible elements such as intonation and stress contribute to meaning.

We also look at the ideological 'work' a text does as it is interpreted by its intended audience, and how this and all the levels listed above are orchestrated together to make a text work. This eclecticism of description illuminates not only the text, but the relationship it has with its producer, its consumer, and its situation.

TYPES OF TEXTS?

What is it that makes us feel that there are different 'types' of text? I noted above that most of us have quite secure intuitions about what texts are of the 'same kind', and which are of different kinds. A useful and widely used system for describing different kinds of text is the notion of **register**. The idea of register is meant to capture 'differences in the type of language selected as appropriate to different situational features' (Halliday et al., 1964: 77, cited in Leckie-Tarry and Birch (1995: 6)). On this approach, language is seen as arising from its context of situation, and different situations will predictably give rise to different language features. As Leckie-Tarry and Birch (in Halliday et al., 1964: 7) argue, both linguistic and situational features need to be captured in a proper account of the register of a text. Typically, the description of register is divided into three categories (see, for example, Halliday and Hasan, 1976):

Field	Characteristics of the nature of the situation (institutional or non-institutional; its location; participants; purpose) and domain, subject matter, or content.
Tenor	Characteristics of the social relationships of the participants; formality or informality; social identity; age; sex; power relations.
Mode	Means of transmission: spoken or written; planned or unplanned; the possibility or impossibility of feedback; closeness of relationship to some activity; distance over time and space.

We can see the description of register in action through applying it to a piece of text used later in this book. In the following extract, two presenters are commentating a football match between England and Romania. The 'main' presenter is Brian, but every so often an ex-footballer, Kevin, makes his own comments. The extract begins at the end of a long contribution by Kevin about England's performance in a previous match against Colombia, who tired in the last 20 minutes of the game:

Kevin	the Colombians did it in the last twenty minutes and we're good enough to do it
	We've just just got to believe and we've got to push forward and we can cause them problems
Brian	Le Saux – from Campbell – but it was difficult to take and there were too many Romanians round him
	And it's Popescu on the break
	Ilie

While the statement of field, tenor, and mode is not an exact science, the outline features of each category given above should give sufficient pointers for what to look for. Here is a suggested register description of the discourse. It is somewhat complicated by the fact that Kevin and Brian seem to be doing rather different things: Brian is doing play-by-play commentary to the television audience, while Kevin tends to address his more evaluative and conversational remarks to Brian.

Field	Institutional, football, evaluative, informative; TV station representative and ex-footballer to co-presenter, Kevin 'overheard' by home audience; Brian speaking directly to audience.
Tenor	Casual, unplanned, more knowledgeable than home audience but one presenter more powerful than the other.
Mode	Television, live broadcast, spoken to Brian/to camera, impossibility of feedback from audience but possible between presenters; Brian closely related to action of the game, Kevin less action-linked.

The next step is then to go on to look at what features of the language or its organization reflect, or make us perceive, these situational factors. For example, elements of the mode become clear in the **turn taking** behaviour of the two presenters and how they address one another (Kevin talks to Brian, Brian talks to the camera). Field is indicated by specific vocabulary such as players' names, phrases like 'difficult to take' and 'on the break' and the distinctive syntactic constructions, including elements such as 'from Campbell' and 'and it's Popescu . . .' that we might not expect to find in everyday conversation. The evaluative nature of some contributions and an obvious bias towards the perspective of the English team come through in Kevin's 'we're good enough to do it' and 'we can cause them problems', and in Brian's 'too many Romanians' (presumably not too many from the Romanians' point of view) and the tendency to perspectivize the action from the England players' point of view. Tenor is created partly through the 'unplanned' characteristics of the speech, leading to repetitions and utterances that look, on paper, ungrammatical or incomplete, and through certain informal vocabulary choices, such as 'causing them problems' as a metaphor for gaining an advantage in the game, and referring to winning as 'doing it' and progressing in the game as 'pushing forward'. There are many more features to comment on, but these few should give an idea of how we can relate various aspects of linguistic choice and organization to the three register features.

A consideration of the register of a text can highlight some features of its relationship with situation, and therefore its language, which may otherwise be overlooked, often because they are obvious. Using a technique like this, moreover, can provide a means of stating more carefully the relationship between texts of very disparate types, and therefore finding ways of comparing language features that might otherwise be confusing and difficult to approach.

Somewhat overlapping the notion of register is the notion of genre. Some theorists have seen genre to be a subdivision of register, and others as a super-category. Because of its difficulty of definition, the term is not used in this book, although Swales' definition of genre as a 'socially recognized communicative event' (1990: 13) may suggest, as Leckie-Tarry and Birch (1995: 10) point out, that a genre may be a complete communicative event, such as a church service or a coffee-break, while the notion of register can be used to describe segments or sections of such events. Register might change, therefore, as a text or discourse progresses, while genre would remain constant. For a very useful and readable discussion of the interrelationship between the two notions, see Leckie-Tarry and Birch (1995, Chapter 1).

Readers will also be aware throughout the book of the influence of researchers who see the use of language as an **ideological** activity. That is, language use and understanding require certain sets of assumptions to be in place in both speaker (or writer) and hearer (or reader). As Fairclough (1989: 2) argues very clearly, even when we feel these assumptions to be simply 'common sense', they actually reflect, enshrine, and even create differential relationships of power in society. To give a concrete example, when an advertiser suggests in an advert that such and such a shampoo gives a healthy shine to the hair, the advertisement is appealing to a 'common sense' assumption that shiny hair is desirable. If a reader or viewer does not have that assumption already, the advertisement may cause them to construct it for themselves and store it away for future use. Now, it may be difficult to imagine a situation in which shiny hair is not desirable, but this may be seen as testimony to how hard it is to examine one's own common sense and see it as a potentially ideological construct. To make this easier, recall that it is not currently constructed as desirable to have shiny *skin*: indeed, cosmetics are sold that are intended to banish just this effect. These values are entirely cultural. What the advertisement does is construct a wish or common-sense need for shiny hair (or matt skin), and present the product as the answer to the need. This creates a consumption role for the onlooker, and a powerful role for the shampoo or cosmetic company as a provider and adviser. It is often the case that advertising communication will fit into a whole slew of similar communications (magazine features, TV programmes, films) in which similar values are adopted, and so individual advertisements will not stand out as abnormal in terms of the assumptions they require and communicate. In the following chapters, many uses of language will be examined that make a particular contribution to the conveying of assumptions, or that appear to require certain assumptions to be in place on the part of the hearer or reader in order to make sense of the message. Although language is not the only medium through which this work is done, language plays an important ideological role in many communicative contexts.

OVERVIEW OF CHAPTERS

Texts in the book, as I noted above, were chosen because they were interesting and not too outlandish, but also because they represent a spread of different situations, modes (spoken or written), and interesting linguistic characteristics.

Chapter 2 deals with the language of written news reporting, concentrating on the story of Tracey Andrews, whose lover was stabbed to death in an apparent 'road rage' murder of which Tracey herself was subsequently found guilty. Apart from the inherent interest of the story, it provides the opportunity to examine the changing attitudes in the press to Tracey herself throughout the case, from a position of sympathy to one of suspicion. The chapter also sets out in some detail the conventions of constructing written news narrative, and presents a framework for describing the difference between how events happen in the world and how they are reported in the news. The chapter also looks at conventions for attributing views and speeches to news actors, and at how people are named, and blamed, through the use of certain linguistic constructions.

Chapter 3 examines a spoken form of language: the language of sports commentary. Using transcripts from football and racing, the chapter describes the distinctive sound and pace of the commentary, including the kinds of errors that are often made in such fast speech. We look at the kinds of functions commentary serves, and at how two commentators signal to one another how turn-taking should happen between them, smoothly and usually without error. The chapter also examines the distinctive syntactic constructions that arise out of the need to locate sports protagonists, particularly in football, by verbal means before identifying who they are – often because it takes a while for the commentator to work out their identity, and needs a way of playing for time.

Chapter 4 looks at the language of instructions in two contexts: written instructions and spoken instructions. In the first case, we look in detail at the instruction leaflet for some home hair colour and, in the second, at the language used by an instructor during a step aerobics workout. The chapter first examines in some detail the myriad choices available in English grammar for telling or asking someone else to do something, and the choice between these is presented as a flow chart that takes into account issues such as social distance and the perceived benefit to the hearer of doing the action. However, it is also noticeable that instructions do not just consist of being told what to do: there are a lot of other language functions, such as describing, warning, narrating, identifying, and teaching, that also take place. We look at the rhetorical structure of both the written and spoken instructions to ascertain how the text is segmented into these different functions, and at the grammar and vocabulary to see how readers or hearers manage to work out which is which.

Chapter 5 focuses on the language of interviews, looking at three different interviewing situations: a police interview with a suspect, an interview between lawyers and a client who is interested in taking someone else to court, and an interview for an academic post in a University. Using techniques from conversation analysis, the chapter sets out how interview language differs from casual conversation, and what it is that makes the participants feel that the situation is 'formal' in some way. The chapter presents a framework for arranging the many kinds of interview on a grid of perceived threat or benefit to the interviewee, and of degree of compulsion to attend the interview, and relates this to the kinds of behaviour that can be expected from the participants. The chapter shows in some detail the way in which power is constructed and allocated in formal face-to-face interactions, and how this is linked to language use. It is also shown what interviewers are not expected to do, such as tell stories about themselves, or appear impressed with interviewees' answers.

Chapter 6 looks at magazine features, concentrating first of all on the kinds of characteristics that enable features to be identified as such. The discussion then focuses on 'in-depth' features, looking at an example from the *Guardian* newspaper's magazine section on the 'chicken flu' virus in Hong Kong which resulted in the slaughter of millions of chickens. We look in detail at the rhetorical structure of the feature, showing how the aims of the feature – to give evidence for a position, to elaborate arguments, and to give a point of view – are met by the use of text segments with particular goals, and with particular relationships between them. The chapter discusses how point of view is also supported by vocabulary choice, as the point of a feature is not to remain neutral on a topic, but to give an interpretation of events. There is also a discussion of how magazines appeal to certain audiences, and how they 'position' or 'place' readers ideologically by their choice of content and language.

Chapter 7 is devoted to the discussion of advertising language. After a look at how advertisers get to know who is buying their products, we look at the available media for advertising and the kinds of advertising strategies that producers can adopt. The chapter looks at printed advertisement structure, outlining some common rhetorical organizations for print ads and looking at characteristics of advertising syntax. We then look at how ideology works in advertising, following a framework in which consumers, products, and the relationships between them are all seen as being 'built' by successful adverts. Linguistically, the chapter focuses on the kinds of construction and vocabulary choices that are used to convey, imply, or even elicit certain knowledge and beliefs in readers and hearers, encouraging complicity with the advertising message and a certain amount of voluntary positioning of the part of the consumer.

Chapter 8 describes how to go about planning and carrying out a linguistic project that involves getting hold of your own data, written or spoken. It provides a means of working out an interesting project idea, and practical guidelines for taking the project through from the planning stage, through recording and transcribing conversation, to presenting the finished product.

There is an extensive glossary, which includes additional references, giving further explanation of many terms and concepts used in the text. The glossary was designed in part to be scanned in its own right, and not merely used for look-up. It may be a particularly useful aid in planning projects, since it provides a comprehensive list of the linguistic phenomena discussed in the book.

CONVENTIONS USED IN THE BOOK

The following conventions are adopted in the book:

Bold type	Bold type, when it appears in running text, refers from this point on to an entry in the glossary.
Italics	Italics are used in running text to quote words or phrases of linguistic data, and for emphasis.

A simple set of conventions is also used for the presentation of tape-recorded and transcribed speech:

A:	indicates who is speaking
15	lines are numbered in long extracts of data for ease of reference
(.)	indicates a pause of less than a second
(3)	indicates a pause of a counted number of seconds
[yeah	utterances that are bracketed together indicate speakers talking at
[to buy some	once, and where this begins and/or ends
to::	colons or double colons indicate a drawn-out syllable; number of colons give an impression of length
hhhh	audible breath
(2 sylls)	a number of syllables inaudible on the tape
it's NOT	capitals indicate special volume or emphasis on the capitalized element

Some additional transcription conventions, not used in the book, are given in Chapter 8, for potential use in a personal project. There is no universal agreement on the 'right' conventions to use, although those given here are relatively common.

One thing that may strike the reader on a first encounter with transcribed speech is how messy, disfluent, and disorganized it looks. We filter out a great deal of this when listening, and are not so aware of it. On the relatively conservative medium of the page, where we are used to seeing planned, edited, and revised material, the contrast with transcribed speech can be particularly striking. This surprise is often alleviated by attempting to transcribe a close friend's, or even your own, speech, even for a couple of minutes. This can be a very revealing exercise. This, and the tools and concepts presented in the book, will show that speech is not only quite messy, it is also highly organized.

RECOMMENDATIONS FOR ADDITIONAL READING

Many references on the specific kinds of language dealt with in subsequent chapters are given throughout the book. There are many good general source books, however, that are relevant background and will prove a considerable help in taking your study further.

A handy reference on the kinds of grammatical ideas used in this book is Crystal (1996), which explains concepts such as the parts of speech, clause structure, and how clauses are combined into sentences very accessibly. Hurford (1994) provides a thorough reference-style treatment of grammatical terms. A more exotic, but delightfully readable, grammar reference book is Gordon (1993). An extremely comprehensive, not to say definitive, grammar of the English language is Quirk et al. (1985), which, although out of reach of most purses, is an excellent reference source if you can find it in a library. A reduced and less expensive version of the same grammatical framework is Quirk and Greenbaum (1993). Also recommended is Biber et al. (1999), a study of the grammar of spoken and written English based on a 40-million word computer corpus composed of different registers of text.

A very good reference on conversation analysis, an approach to describing conversation in great detail that stems from sociology, is Eggins and Slade (1997). This book describes in detail the nature of casual conversation and the tools and concepts proposed in conversation analysis for understanding how it is achieved. A briefer overview of the CA approach is given in Schiffrin (1994, Chapter 7): this book also provides a useful overview of other approaches to language, including discourse analysis and pragmatics. There is also useful advice on collecting your own data.

Carter (1987) is a useful reference on vocabulary, while Carter and Nash (1990) is an engaging and enlightening approach to a range of different text types. Fairclough's books, which are referred to in many places throughout this book because of the many very fruitful insights he has into the relationships between language, society, power, and ideology, are in my view somewhat indigestible because of the intricacy of theory that builds up throughout. However, they are well worth the effort, and I would particularly recommend Fairclough (1989) as an introduction to the general framework of what is now termed 'critical discourse analysis'. Bolinger (1980), although now somewhat dated, is still a very readable, if somewhat eccentrically organized, overview of the political and persuasive functions of language.

2 The Language of Written News Reporting

News reporting is important to us because it is a key source of access to events that affect our lives culturally, politically, economically, and often emotionally. News is necessarily selective and partial, both in what is selected as worth reporting, and in how it is presented. This chapter describes some important elements of the language found in news reports, looking in particular at some of the frameworks that have enabled researchers to reveal how news writing achieves its social and informative purpose. Pointers for further reading in this thriving field of research should enable you to follow up specific areas for further study.

WHAT IS NEWS REPORTING?

A look at any newspaper will reveal a range of different kinds of texts with different aims, presentation, and content. Bell (1991: 14) divides written news coverage into the following categories:

1 Hard news.
2 Soft news, such as feature articles.
3 'Special topic' news, such as sports or arts.
4 Headlines, subheadings, photo captions, etc.

In this chapter, we will concentrate on just one of these text types: hard news, and, in particular, 'spot news' (cf. Bell, 1994: 100), stories of crime, disasters, fires and so on. However, as Bell notes, the category of headlines, captions, and other such devices cuts across the others, since all news writing will feature some or all of these.

The chapter will draw on the reporting, over a period lasting from December 1996 to April 1997, of an alleged 'road rage' killing. Lee Harvey had, according to his fiancée, Tracey Andrews, been drawn into a 'cat and mouse' car chase and had been stabbed in a remote country lane by the passenger in the other car, a dark blue Ford Sierra. The other car was never found, and Tracey herself was subsequently charged and later found guilty of Lee Harvey's murder. Apart from allowing us to explore some of the typical characteristics of news reporting, it is also interesting to observe the change in sympathy that is present in the reports as, day by day, Tracey's treatment in the press changed from that of a defenceless victim to that of a possible murderer. It is therefore possible to see from these reports how language reflects these changing beliefs about her role, and how it communicates them to readers.

SELECTING THE NEWS

Work by Galtung and Ruge (1965) and Bell (1991: 156ff.) gives a useful overview of the elements that make a story 'newsworthy' – factors that are termed **news values**. While some of these relate to the way news is collected and aspects of its presentation, the most central news values are arguably those that determine the choice of news content or which elements of the story are chosen for particular emphasis. The most basic of these is *negativity*: newsworthiness often depends on something bad happening, such as a crime or disaster. News is also expected to be *novel* and unusual, rather than routine, and it must be *recent*, ideally fitting into a 24-hour span: punctual events are therefore more likely to be reported than drawn-out ones. In addition, news should wherever possible be *attributable* to respected sources, and should give as many supporting *facts* as possible.

A large group of the values that Bell suggests can be summarized in terms of the readers' desire for familiar elements even within the most unexpected and novel situations, invoking interest and self-identification with the story. Events that are *geographically close* are therefore more newsworthy than distant ones, and situations or participants that are *culturally close*[1] and familiar, even if geographically distant, will be found more meaningful. Despite the need for novelty, newsworthiness in a story may also depend on the compatibility of the kinds of people involved or the typical pattern of the type of event being reported with what readers expect of that social group or that kind of event: Bell terms this *consonance*. This results in dominant frameworks and metaphors often being applied to news stories in order to render them more familiar and predictable. Events that can be presented in more *personal* terms are more newsworthy than those that are relevant to large impersonal groups, which explains why news reporting often focuses in on the experiences of individuals involved in great events to personalize the story. Finally, reference to 'élite persons' already well known to readers always makes for newsworthiness.

In order to see how a specific report reflects these values of newsworthiness, we can turn to our collection of articles concerning the Tracey Andrews case. The first reporting of Lee Harvey's killing occurred on 3rd December 1996. The following news report is taken from the *Guardian* on that date:

Road rage victim stabbed to death
SARAH BOSELEY
A DRIVER bled to death in front of his girlfriend after being stabbed in the face, neck and body in a frenzied attack of road rage, apparently by a passenger in a car he overtook.

West Mercia police are hunting for the attacker who killed Lee Harvey, aged 25, and injured his girlfriend Tracie[2] Andrews, aged 27, in a frenzied knife attack on a lonely country road on Sunday night.

'As far as we are concerned, it is a murder,' said Carl Baldaccino, spokesman for West Mercia police. 'It seems to have arisen out of a motoring incident – a normal overtaking manoeuvre. There is no suggestion that they had known or met the occupants of the other car before.'

The couple, who lived together in the village of Alvechurch and each had a young daughter by a previous partner, had gone out for a drink with friends at a quiet country pub called the Marlbrook, near Bromsgrove.

As they drove home on the A38, they overtook a dark F-registration Ford Sierra hatchback, in poor condition, near junction 1 of the M42. Police said they did not know what Mr Harvey had done to anger the other motorist. 'The only witness was Tracie. She was leaning down taking a tape out of the glove compartment. She was only aware of the car swerving.'

The couple crossed the motorway and turned left on to the small roads and lanes that would lead them back to Alvechurch, with the car following them. It pursued them for three miles, close to their rear bumper, with headlights flashing. 'Gestures were exchanged,' said Mr Baldaccino.

The Sierra is believed to have overtaken Mr Harvey and Ms Andrews in their white G-registered Ford RS Turbo and the two cars came to a stop. Mr Harvey and the driver of the other car got out. 'There were verbal exchanges and there might have been a bit of a push,' said Mr Baldaccino.

The other driver got back into his car.

'Then the front passenger, a fat man, got out and approached Mr Harvey and stabbed him. It was a sustained attack taking place over several minutes. He was stabbed at least 15 times in the face, neck and body. The attack continued as he fell to the ground. His girlfriend tried to intervene and she was struck and cut and punched to the ground as well. She required a few stitches just above her eye.'

The cars had stopped outside an isolated house. Those inside heard nothing, but one of them happened to be leaving just after the incident, and saw Ms Andrews on the road, cradling her boyfriend in her arms. They called the police.

Det Supt Ian Johnston, in charge of the investigation, said: 'We are treating this as murder, a murder that stems from a road-rage-type incident. This was a vicious crime, one of the most vicious I've seen in 30 years.'

The attacker is described as white, aged 25–26, about 5ft 9in to 6ft tall and very overweight. He was wearing a thigh-length, donkey-type jacket and would have been very heavily bloodstained, said police. The driver of the car was white, 18–19 years old, and slim with very short dark hair.

The story certainly reflects the important news value of negativity, since it concerns a murder. It is also recent: 3rd December was a Tuesday, with the incident having taken place on Sunday night, too late for the news to have emerged in time for the Monday edition. In fulfilment of the news values of familiarity and unexpectedness, a tension between the ordinariness of the circumstances and the unpredictability of the event is carefully maintained in the report, and this serves to heighten the sense of shock at the killing. Background information which establishes familiarity includes details of the couple's small village lifestyle, the pub visit on a Sunday night, and the very ordinary cars involved, all of which establish the closeness to reader experience that Bell (1991: 157) describes as *relevance*. The ordinariness of the background events leading up to the killing, and hence their relationship to everyday experience, is heightened by the reporting of the fact that the apparent cause of the killing was a 'normal overtaking manoeuvre', and Tracey's leaning down to take a tape from the glove compartment. Personalization is given by the portrayal of the couple's relationship, promoting identification with Tracey and Lee: the mention of their children, the fact that Tracey is referred to three times as Lee's girlfriend, and the tragic picture of her 'cradling her boyfriend in her arms'. Against this background of normality and relationships, which encourages readers to self-identify, the most unexpected 'frenzied knife attack' occurred. Parts of the story are attributed to a named West Mercia police spokesman and the named Detective Superintendent in charge of the investigation. Facts, too, are emphasized: the ages of everyone involved, the exact road location where the attack took place and the route the couple took, the precise details of both cars, and the appearance of the attacker. Finally, in this brief analysis, the description of the event as a 'road rage' killing (which persists in subsequent news reports even after Tracey herself has been charged), connects the story to a much wider preoccupation in the media with 'road rage' as a phenomenon with its own logic and way of proceeding. The 'road rage' attribution is given both by the copy-editor writing the headline, and by the police officer in charge, who goes so far as to describe it as a 'road-rage-*type* incident', thereby connecting it explicitly with a class of similar crimes. This clearly reflects the news value of consonance: in this case, assumptions about how particular kinds of events unfold. 'Road rage' attacks are popularly understood, largely through media reporting, as consisting of savage verbal or physical assaults on other drivers, arising through minor motoring irritations or simply through having spent too long at the wheel. It is highly likely that, given the cultural prominence of this idea at the time – the judge of a case in May of the same year had described road rage as an 'epidemic' (the *Guardian*, 20th May 1996) – anyone witnessing such an event would have seen 'road rage' as a putative explanation. More sinisterly, since she herself was in fact the perpetrator, Tracey Andrews would have understood that 'road rage' would strike her audience as a plausible scenario that 'explained' the murder, and may even have modelled her evidence on similar cases previously reported in the press.

THE STRUCTURE OF THE NEWS STORY

Having seen something of the way news content is selected and created, we can turn now to look at the way the story is structured. In comparison with the ordering people choose for relating stories in conversation, news stories have some interestingly different characteristics. Labov and Waletsky (1967) and Labov (1972) have analyzed the structure of spoken narrative, finding that such stories often follow a set pattern, as follows:

1   Abstract: a summary of the main point of the story and its central action;
2   Orientation: scene-setting information about participants, location, initial situation;

3 Complicating Action: central part of the story;
4 Evaluation: teller's justification of the point of the story, demonstrating that it is worth telling;
5 Resolution: end of the sequence of events;
6 Coda: a statement that ends the story, returning the speaker to the present and offering the floor to other speakers.

Of these elements, only the complicating action and some element of evaluation are obligatory: the other elements may or may not be included.

Bell (1994) performs a comparison between the narrative structure found by Labov and the structure of news stories, and finds a range of important differences. *Evaluation* is as vital to news stories as it is to personal narrative: in both cases, it serves to justify telling the story and demanding attention for it. While in personal narrative evaluation typically occurs throughout the story, Bell (1994: 104) finds that evaluation is concentrated in the lead and headline of the news story: it serves to pinpoint how the story relates to the important news values described above. *Resolution* is often provided for personal narrative in a way that it cannot be for news stories, which often relate a further stage in unfolding events. Neither do news reports typically feature a *coda*, since this seems more appropriate for spoken face-to-face contexts as a way of returning the floor to other speakers and signalling the end of the story. The most striking difference, however, that Bell finds between personal narratives and news stories concerns their sequential organization. Labov found that action descriptions in personal narrative are invariably told in chronological order: that is, in the order in which the events occurred. Van Dijk (1988a: 15) suggested that events in news reporting do not follow this order, occurring instead in an 'installment-type, discontinuous way'. Bell, too, finds that events in news reports are almost never related in real-life order. Often, events are described in reverse, and results of events are frequently placed before the event descriptions themselves. Bell points out that, while chronological coherence is a central aim of the personal narrative, 'perceived news value overturns temporal sequence and imposes an order completely at odds with the linear narrative point. It moves backwards and forwards, picking out different actions in each cycle' (1994: 106). This backwards-and-forwards cyclical movement may be due in large part to practical concerns: the cycles of information reflect, according to Bell, content of decreasing importance towards the end of the article, and editorial cutting takes place from the bottom up. A writer therefore does not know how much of the article will survive on the printed page, and must be sure to get the main points placed early on (Bell, 1994: 106), and readers know that they can find the most important information at the top of the story (van Dijk, 1988a: 15).

Analyzing Story Structure

As we saw above, there is a tension between the way events happen in real life, and the way they are described in news reporting. The extent to which news reports deviate from real-life ordering can be seen from a close analysis of newspaper texts that makes a clear contrast between the two: what happened, or **event structure**, on the one hand, and how it is presented, or discourse structure, on the other. In this section, we will present a method for comparing the two. Both van Dijk (1988a) and Bell (1991, 1994, 1998) present detailed strategies for dissecting news stories into their component parts: what is given below represents a considerably simplified method that still exposes some of the important elements of structure. To introduce the analysis, we will first of all examine a shorter report on the Andrews case from the News In Brief section of the *Guardian* of 7th December 1996:

> News In Brief: Road rage fiancée in hospital
> Tracey Andrews, fiancée of the road rage victim Lee Harvey, has been taken to hospital after a suspected overdose.
> Mr Harvey, aged 25, was knifed to death in a savage attack after he and Tracey were pursued by another car in a 'cat and mouse' chase near Alvechurch, Worcestershire.
> West Mercia police said Miss Andrews, aged 27, had collapsed on Wednesday, but her family had initially wanted this kept secret.

The method involves looking first at the facts that are reported and working out as far as possible what happened in real life, and secondly at the way in which these facts are woven into the story of the newspaper report.

Step 1: What happened? The first step of the process is to capture the events that occurred that are reported in the story, and number them as far as possible in the order in which they occurred in real life. It will be helpful at this stage to make an approximate distinction between two different kinds of things that can take place: **events** and **states**. Events can best be understood as things that happen (*the ice melted, the car crashed*) or things that are done (*Sally played the violin, Peter coughed, the cat washed itself*). States, on the other hand, don't have clear protagonists or agents: rather than someone *doing* a state, it is more accurate to say that a state is *true of* someone or something. Bach (1986: 6) gives the following examples of events and states:

(a) Events: build something, walk to Boston, recognize, notice, flash once, die, reach the top.
(b) States: sit, stand, lie in bed, be drunk, be in New York, own something, love someone, resemble someone.

Events may occur quickly and/or within a clearly bounded time. Moens and Steedman (1988) distinguish two kinds of events: atomic events, which happen 'at once' (*Harry left early, John arrived*), and extended events, which take time (*Sue built a sandcastle, the ice melted completely*). They also note that some events have consequences, such as building a sandcastle or leaving, while others don't: *Sandra hiccupped*, to use Moens and Steedman's example, does not really make any difference in the world. In contrast, though, Moens and Steedman argue that what is different about states is that they can't be differentiated into atomic or extended states, and they don't have any necessary results. They may often hold *at the same time* as other events are going on. It is not always easy to say when states begin or end, what caused them, or what the concrete results are.

In the analysis of the newspaper text, it is helpful to list states and events separately. For clarity, in what follows, I will term both states and events **eventualities**. Although we know when *in the text* states are first mentioned, we are attempting here to work out their relationship *in the world*, and should not therefore be too influenced by the order of their introduction in the report. In the summary below, events are labelled 'e', and states 's'. States and events that are reported within another event, usually that of someone making a statement, are repeated in square brackets:

e1   LH and TA pursued by another car
e2   LH knifed to death
e3   TA takes overdose/collapses
e4   TA taken to hospital
e5   WMP make statement [e3, s1]
s1   Family want TA's situation kept secret

Note that someone saying something – in this case, the police making a statement – constitutes an event in itself. However, because the police are saying something *about* other states and events, it makes things clearer to add the identity of these into the statement: here, the police statement, e5, refers to Tracey's collapse (equivalent to the suspected overdose of e3) and the fact that the family wanted secrecy (s1).

To clarify the relationships between the eventualities in the story content further, a timeline can be drawn that shows the order of events and where any simultaneous states begin and end. Where states begin and end is, in practice, often left up to a reader or hearer to guess. Here, the only state is that of the family's wanting secrecy, or s1, and we can infer that it begins just after e3, where TA takes an overdose (or is taken ill, since this is a *suspected* overdose), and ends just before e5, the point at which West Mercia Police make a statement, presumably permitted by the family, that reveals the state of affairs. The timeline is therefore as indicated in Figure 2.1. Events are indicated as occurring in a sequence along the timeline, while states, which overlap some events and precede or succeed others, are each given a separate line to make their extent clear.

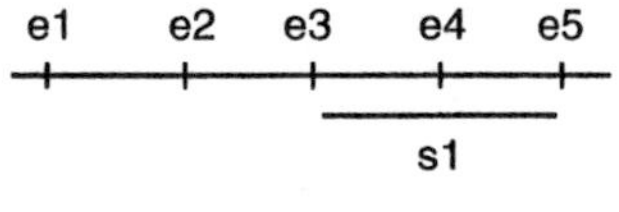

FIGURE 2.1   Timeline for 'News in Brief' Story

Step 2: How is it presented? Discourse structure   The next step is to look at how these eventualities are reported. Here we can introduce some of the basic components of the written news story. Three major components are identified by both Bell and van Dijk: the *headline, lead paragraph*, and *story*.

e4	*Headline*	[Road rage fiancée in hospital
e4	*Lead*	Tracey Andrews, fiancée of the road rage victim Lee Harvey, has been taken to hospital]
e3		[after a suspected overdose.]
e2	*Story*	[Mr Harvey, aged 25, was knifed to death in a savage attack]
e1		[after he and Tracey were pursued by another car in a 'cat and mouse' chase near Alvechurch, Worcestershire.]
e5		[West Mercia police said]
[e3]		[Miss Andrews, aged 27, had collapsed on Wednesday,]
[s1]		[but her family had initially wanted this kept secret.]

Bell (1998) describes the headline and lead as equivalent to the *abstract* of the story in Labov's narrative terms. The lead is the most important paragraph, compressing the important elements of the story and representing most fully what are seen to be the most important elements for news value. Here, then, the most important elements are e4 and e3: Tracey's being taken to hospital, and her possibly taking an overdose. The hospital stay, e4, is taken as the 'hook' for the headline. It is this that is most recent, negative, and unexpected, rather than, for example, the car pursuit and the knifing (which are by now 'old news'), the police statement, or the family's preferences. Note, too, that within the lead paragraph, Tracey's relationship with Lee is emphasized. We will say more about this in the discussion of reference and naming of *news actors* – the people involved in the story – that is to follow. What is important, for the moment, is what the example already shows about the ordering of reporting of events: something that is often described as the **inverted pyramid** of information. That is, the opening, composed of headline and lead, singles out the crucial events, while the subsequent story represents a series of 'takes' presenting different perspectives, comment, and background, as well as a repetition of the events themselves. This is a preferred strategy for news reporting that is explicitly taught to trainee journalists: as Friedlander and Lee state in their training manual, 'In the typical inverted pyramid structure used in a news story, the information at the top of the pyramid – the lead – is the most important . . . as the reader goes deeper into the story, the value of the information decreases . . .' (Friedlander and Lee, cited in White, 1997: 7). In the News in Brief story, we can see this disruption of the temporal (time) sequence of events immediately: e4 is referred to twice, and e3 is introduced as the cause of e4, thereby elaborating on it. Straight away, then, the report has departed from the chronology of events: the presentation of 'results first' to get the material with the most impact to the top of the story. The body of the report after the lead, the 'story' proper, now fills in background information on previous events, and adds a comment from an official source. This comment, the event e5, recapitulates on the previously introduced event of the collapse (e3) but also introduces the new state, s1, which is that of the family wishing to keep the situation secret. Information about the news actors – their ages, for example, and where they lived – is distributed throughout the story, to avoid diluting the initial impact of the lead. As Bell summarizes:

> The story cycles round the action, returning for more detail on each circuit, and interspersing background and other events. The technique moves like a downward spiral through the available information. This is in fact described by journalists as the 'inverted pyramid' style – gathering all the main points at the beginning and progressing through decreasingly important information. (1991: 168)

This departure from chronology is perhaps the most commented-upon feature of the structure of news reporting: see also van Dijk (1988a: 15) and Bell (1998: 96). Bell (1998: 99) gives a useful discussion of the cognitive implications of this cyclical and often reverse-order presentation of events; see also van Dijk (1988b) and Bell (1991, Chapter 11).

A More Complex Example

Having looked at a short and relatively straightforward example, we will now examine the longer story from 3rd December, reproduced above. This time, we will refine the analysis by distinguishing between different segments of the story, since it falls into separate parts, and introducing some further categories that make the functions of different textual elements clearer.

In this report, there are no fewer than 24 distinguishable events, and nine states, to organize. The eventualities reported in the text are as follows. Because, as is often the case, there are different sources being co-ordinated in this report, it is helpful where possible to place in brackets the initials of the various sources next to the eventuality descriptions attributed to them. The news actors involved are:

LH   Lee Harvey
TA   Tracey Andrews
FM   Fat Man

We might also want to add the Ford Sierra to this list: even though it is not a person, it is certainly, as we shall see later, an **agent** in the action described. The sources involved are:

CB   Carl Baldaccino, spokesman for West Mercia Police
P   Unspecified 'Police', presumably from this constabulary
?   Unspecified source, but given with verb of perception such as *understood* or *believed* or a verb of saying such as *described* that suggests a human source
DSIJ Detective Superintendent Ian Johnston

In the case of Carl Baldaccino, there are some cases where what is said is given in quotations but not clearly attributed to him: these eventualities are marked [?CB]. Finally, some of this information must have come from TA (the 'only witness'), but this is not stated, so no reference to her as a source can be included. Any unattributed eventualities like this are taken to be what is being presented as 'fact' in the report.

e1	LH and TA go for drink in pub	
e2	LH and TA drive home (details of route)	
e3	LH and TA overtake Sierra	[CB]
e4	Sierra pursues	
e5	Sierra flashes headlights	
e6	Drivers exchange gestures	[CB]
e7	TA gets tape from glovebox	[P]
e8	Sierra overtakes	[?]
e9	Two cars stop in front of lonely house	
e10	Drivers get out	
e11	Verbal exchanges and a push	[CB]
e12	Sierra driver goes back to car	
e13	FM gets out	[?CB]
e14	FM attacks and stabs LH	[?CB]
e15	LH falls to ground	[?CB]
e16	TA tries to intervene	[?CB]
e17	TA is injured	[?CB]
e18	LH dies	
e19	TA cradles LH on the road	
e20	Person leaves lonely house, sees TA and LH	
e21	Person calls police	
e22	Police hunt attacker	
e23	TA has stitches	[?CB]
e24	Police make comments	
s1	LH and TA live in Alvechurch	
s2	LH and TA each have a young daughter	
s3	TA is only witness	[P]
s4	LH does not know occupants of other car	
s5	Police do not know what LH did to anger FM	[P]
s6	TA is aware of car swerving	[P]
s7	People in lonely house heard nothing	
s8	The attacker has a certain age and appearance	[?]
s9	Police treat the incident as murder	[CB, DSIJ]

Clearly, for a text as complex as the 3rd December text, a timeline will be correspondingly more complicated, but this step of the analysis is still instructive. The timeline appears in Figure 2.2. Again, the extent of the states involved has been deduced simply from world knowledge.

The 3rd December text contains a proportionally higher number of state descriptions than the News in Brief text, but there are still many fewer states than events. To explain this, we can refer back to the news values described earlier: events are simply better news than states, since they are more likely to provide a close fit to news values. They have agents or 'doers' (which are often people, heightening interest at once), many of them have consequences or results, and some of them are punctual and brief and their location on a

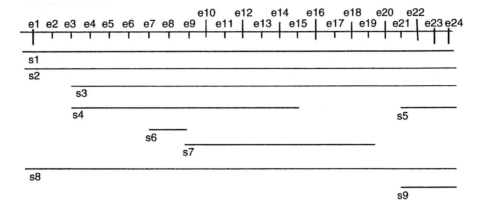

FIGURE 2.2   Timeline for 3rd December Text

timeline can be specified easily (which is never the case for states). For states, too, it is not so easy to answer the question 'when did it happen?', and so states do not so clearly satisfy the news value of recency. States can be very drawn out, and they may either have no results or their results are hard to ascertain. For these reasons, states appear more plausibly to contain background information than information that is crucial to the development of the story.

Looking more closely at the states reported in the 3rd December text, we can see that three in particular, s1, s2, and s8, have a duration that plausibly outlasts the events of the story. These three states are apparently in force before the events of the story take place, as well as throughout those events. State 1 (the fact that the couple live in Alvechurch) and state 2 (that each has a young daughter) are clearly background information. State 8, the fact that the attacker has a certain appearance, is arguably also in force before the events take place, but since this person only becomes an 'attacker' because of the events of the story, his age and appearance only become relevant around e13 when he gets out of the car. It is not possible to reflect this change of identity within the scope of the timeline framework, so we will address this further later in the chapter. Apart from these three states, all the other states are generated or at least made salient by the events in the story: the state of TA being the only witness, for example, is only made relevant once there is something to witness, namely the chain of events set off by the overtaking event e3. Similarly, LH's state of ignorance about the occupants of the other car (s4) is only relevant at the same point, since this is when the other car first comes into view. States s5 and s9, which both refer to the police's beliefs and attitudes, could only come into force relatively late on, once the police have been called and are therefore in a position to know about the events. While still being more 'background' than the events, we can say that states that came into force during the critical timeframe set by story events e1 to e24 are arguably more newsworthy from the point of view of 'spot news' than those that were in force prior to the story taking place. However, these very background states such as a person's age, family circumstances, and home address may be more important for establishing the human element of the story that satisfies the news values of cultural or geographical closeness, consonance, and relevance described earlier.

Having looked in some detail at the relationships between the eventualities reported of the text, we can now turn to the structure of the text itself. Once again, we can divide the text into headline, lead, and body. The order of reporting of the eventualities is as follows:

e14	*Headline*	Road rage victim stabbed to death
e18	*Lead*	A driver bled to death in front of his
e14		[girlfriend after being stabbed in
e3		[the face, neck and body in a frenzied attack of road rage, apparently by a passenger in a car he overtook.
e24	*Body*	West Mercia police are hunting for the
e14		[attacker who killed Lee Harvey,
e18		[aged 25, and injured his girlfriend Tracie
e17		[Andrews, aged 27, in a frenzied knife attack on a lonely country road on Sunday night.
e23		'As far as we are concerned, it is a
[s9]		murder,' said Carl Baldaccino,
[e3, e8]		spokesman for West Mercia police. 'It
[s4]		seems to have arisen out of a motoring incident – a normal overtaking manoeuvre. There is no suggestion that they had known or met the occupants of the other car before.'
s1		The couple, who lived together in the
s2		[village of Alvechurch and each had a
e1		[young daughter by a previous partner, had gone out for a drink with friends at a quiet country pub called the Marlbrook, near Bromsgrove.
e2		As they drove home on the A38, they
e3		overtook a dark F-registration Ford Sierra hatchback, in poor condition, near junction 1 of the M42.
e23		Police said they did not know what Mr
[s5]		Harvey had done to anger the other
[s3]		motorist. 'The only witness was Tracie.
[e7]		She was leaning down taking a
[s6]		tape out of the glove compartment. She was only aware of the car swerving.'
e2		The couple crossed the motorway and
e4		turned left on to the small roads and
e5		lanes that would lead them back to Alvechurch, with the car following them. It pursued them for three miles, close to their rear bumper, with headlights flashing.
e23		'Gestures were exchanged,' said Mr
[e6]		Baldaccino.
e8		The Sierra is believed to have overtaken
e9		Mr Harvey and Ms Andrews in their

e10	white G-registered Ford RS Turbo and the two cars came to a stop. Mr Harvey and the driver of the other car got out.
e23 [e11]	'There were verbal exchanges and there might have been a bit of a push,' said Mr Baldaccino.
e12	The other driver got back into his car.
e23 [e13] [e14] [e15] [e16] [e17] [e22]	'Then the front passenger, a fat man, got out and approached Mr Harvey and stabbed him. It was a sustained attack taking place over several minutes. He was stabbed at least 15 times in the face, neck and body. The attack continued as he fell to the ground. His girlfriend tried to intervene and she was struck and cut and punched to the ground as well. She required a few stitches just above her eye.'
e9 s7 e20 e19 e21	The cars had stopped outside an isolated house. Those inside heard nothing, but one of them happened to be leaving just after the incident, and saw Ms Andrews on the road, cradling her boyfriend in her arms. They called the police.
e23 [s9] [e3–e17]	Det Supt Ian Johnston, in charge of the investigation, said: 'We are treating this as murder, a murder that stems from a road-rage-type incident. This was a vicious crime, one of the most vicious I've seen in 30 years.'
e23 [s8]	The attacker is described as white, aged [25–26, about 5ft 9in to 6ft tall and very overweight. He was wearing a thigh-length, donkey-type jacket and would have been very heavily bloodstained, said police. The driver of the car was white, 18–19 years old, and slim with very short dark hair.

Once again, where an event is one of reporting or describing, as in the case of e23, what events or states are reported or described are given in brackets. In the case of Detective Superintendent Ian Johnston's statement near the end of the report, the whole chain of events from e3 to e17 is summarized by the phrase 'a road-rage-type incident', where a **noun phrase** is used to describe an entire sequence. Trew (1979) focuses particularly on the progression from event descriptions to nominal (noun phrase) constructions, arguing that this is a means of moving away from an event with an explicit doer and a done-to to something that has more vaguely 'taken place'.

From the discourse structure stage of the analysis it is possible to see that e14, the stabbing event, has been selected for presentation as the most newsworthy: it appears alone in the headline, is repeated with elaboration in the lead paragraph, and is given once again in the first paragraph of the body of the story. We can therefore assume that e14 is the central event of the story from the point of view of representation as news. What is clear once again from this exercise is the cyclical nature of news reporting: the central event of the stabbing is not placed in a sequence of events until the third paragraph of the story body, where e1, the couple going out for a drink, is mentioned for the first time. This is interrupted, however, with the police statement about how the incident came about, after which details of their route, e2, are restated to place the story 'back on track' in terms of its narrative sequence. Throughout the report, however, it is possible to see how events have been arranged to reflect not temporal sequence but newsworthiness. In the second paragraph of the body of the story, for example, there is an indication of the importance of news *sources*: rather than going directly into a narration of the sequence of events, the report presents a police spokesman's summary of the West Mercia police perspective on the central event and its probable cause. In this second body paragraph, the first state descriptions are introduced: the police treatment of the incident of murder, s9, and Tracey Andrews and Lee Harvey's lack of knowledge of the occupants of the other car, s4. Note, however, that these state descriptions are introduced *within* an event, namely event e23, the police commenting *about* those states. This is a pattern that is repeated throughout the report: states s3, s5, and s7, for example, are introduced within a police statement; likewise, states s9 and s8 are given as part of another description of the police statement at the end of the report. Only states s1 and s2, describing the couple, and state s7, the state of the people inside the house not hearing anything, appear outside the scope of police statements. These three states are important in establishing human interest in the case of s1 and s2, and in explaining why nobody else came to Lee Harvey's aid in the case of s7. For the most part, however, we can see that states do not in their own right make good 'news', but are instead presented as events of other people describing them.

Frequent reference to police statements, too, establishes the credibility of the details of the story, satisfying the news value that news should be attributable to respected sources. Much of the action of the story, as well as the police attitudes towards it, is presented in the scattered references to e23, the police statements from Carl Baldaccino and Detective Superintendent Ian Johnston. Other descriptions of events such as e12, e9, and e19–21 are not attributed to police sources. It can be assumed that these are the views of the reporter and the newspaper, although the fact that these event descriptions are tucked in between two explicit quotations from the police gives the impression that they are from the same source. While there is not the space here for a complete analysis of the use of sources, the attribution of facts to individuals is particularly crucial in the Tracey Andrews case, as it became clear subsequently that many of the events reported as fact both by the police and by the newspaper turned out to be fictitious. For the moment, however, it is sufficient to note the way in which the factual claims of the story are represented. There are three basic ways in which this can be done:

1 **Statement:** Unattributed, and therefore taken to be the opinion currently held by the reporter and the newspaper. Example: *The other driver got back into his car.*

2 **Direct Speech:** Direct quotation, usually in inverted commas, and usually attributed to a named speaker or the more vague 'spokesperson' or 'source'.

Example: '*There were verbal exchanges and there may have been a bit of a push*', said Mr. Baldaccino.

3 **Indirect Speech:** Paraphrases a statement by someone else, who may or may not be named.

Example: *Police said they did not know what Mr Harvey had done to anger the other motorist.*

Any of these categories may contain phrases that **mitigate** or 'hedge' the strength of the claim. For example, a statement in the lead of the report is hedged by an adverb, *apparently*, that indicates some doubt as to the identity of the attacker:

A driver bled to death in front of his girlfriend after being stabbed in the face, neck and body in a frenzied attack of road rage, *apparently* by a passenger in a car he overtook.

The use of a verb that specifies a state of mind may also act as a hedge, weakening the strength of a claim, as does the use of *believe* in a statement later in the report:

The Sierra is *believed* to have overtaken Mr Harvey and Ms Andrews . . .

Although this is a statement, the use of such a verb prompts the question, who is doing the believing? The reader is left to infer whether it is the newspaper, the reporter, the police, or all three, and so the source of this belief is left unclear.

Hedges may appear within direct speech, as in the use of *seems* in the first quotation from Carl Baldaccino:

'It *seems* to have arisen out of a motoring incident . . .'

Modal verbs such as *may*, *might*, and *could* also act as hedges, weakening the strength of a claim, as in the use of *might* in this direct speech from Carl Baldaccino:

'There were verbal exchanges and there *might* have been a bit of a push,' said Mr. Baldaccino.

Another way in which the report indicates strength of belief lies in the use of what is termed **presupposition**. What is particularly noticeable in this report is the use of expressions that presuppose the existence of people or things, often termed **existential presupposition**. Such presupposition is typically achieved by certain types of noun phrases which, by referring to things as if they exist, make it clear that the reader or hearer should share the belief of existence. The following examples demonstrate what aspects of noun phrases are sufficient to trigger an existential presupposition:

(a) **Proper names:** Lee Harvey, Tracey Andrews, Bromsgrove.
(b) **The definite article:** *the* attacker, *the* other motorist, *the* Sierra, *the* cars, *the* attack.
(c) **Possessive adjectives:** *his* girlfriend, *her* boyfriend, *his* car.

This presuppositional effect is not shared by some other kinds of noun phrase: for example, the use of an **indefinite article** as in *a bit of a push*, and other indefinites such as *some* or *any*, do not appear to suggest that any community of people believes in the existence of the thing referred to. Presupposition, however, is presented as non-negotiable, as already believed by certain speakers, as *known fact* – and, as such, as something readers are expected to accept as the truth. Once again, this is particularly poignant in the context of this story: police subsequently came to believe that there was no Sierra, no other car at all, and no attacker apart from Tracey herself, which meant that the presuppositions contained within the 3rd December text and many following it turned out to be false. In analyzing the expressions that denote strength of belief such as presupposition, therefore, it is also important to relate them to the sources that the presuppositions are to be attributed to. In this case, the police speakers appear to have subscribed wholly to the existence of another car and an attacker who was a passenger in it, since presuppositional expressions such as *the occupants of the other car*, *the other motorist*, and *the front passenger* appear in direct speech attributed to them. Presuppositions of similar kinds also appear in statements made by the newspaper: *the Sierra, the other driver, his car, the attacker*, and *the driver of the car*. On 3rd December, then, it seems clear that both the police and the *Guardian* subscribe to a version of events which could only have been given to them by Tracey Andrews, although she is not mentioned as a source anywhere in the report. Whatever the police *appeared* to believe by their statements at press conferences, however, need not be taken as an indication of their *actual* beliefs regarding who was responsible for Lee Harvey's killing. Each stage of the presentation of information, from taking witness statements to giving press briefings, or from hearing press briefings to presenting written news reports, is subject to its own processes of ideology-laden transformation dependent on a particular agenda, political or practical (see, for example, Kress 1983 for a comparison of two newspaper reports on a single event and a discussion of 'truth' in this regard).

NEWS ACTORS AND NEWS EVENTS

Turning from the grand structure of the news report and its relationship to news values, we will now look in more detail at a second area which has given rise to a great deal of research in news reporting: the relationships between news actors and the events they take part in, and how this is reported in the press. Central to this research has been the concept of **transitivity** as developed by the functional linguist Michael Halliday and his followers within the framework of Systemic Functional Grammar (see, for example, Halliday, 1985: 101ff.). In this section, we will examine the notion of transitivity in detail and see how it applies to written news reporting. In addition, we will look briefly at the role of the different kinds of expressions that can be used to refer to news actors in the construction of the 'angle' a report takes on events.

Taking Part in the Action of the Clause

The notion of transitivity captures the basic facts about how clauses create an impression of what took place, linking together three main elements for creating meaning:

(a) predicate: the nucleus of the description of what happened, usually contained within a verb, sometimes also termed the 'process';

(b) **participants:**   the people or things involved in the action of the predicate, both doers and done-tos; and

(c) **circumstances:**   where, when, how, why, etc. the eventuality happened or is happening.

Together, these three elements combine to create meaning in the form of a clause. For Hallidayans, 'process' is a general term covering what is at the core of all types of clauses. 'Process' is therefore closer to what we have so far called 'eventuality'. Both terms are attempts to capture how clauses describe something occurring. Halliday (1985: 106ff.) classifies eventuality descriptions into several different kinds. The following are the most common:

Material Processes: Processes of doing. Example: *The mouse ran up the clock.*

Mental Processes: Processes of sensing. Example: *Mary liked the gift.*

Relational Processes: Processes of being. Examples: *Sarah is wise; Peter has a piano.*

Behavioural Processes: Processes of psychological or physical behaviour. Examples: *Martin coughed; the Mock Turtle sighed deeply; Marianne breathes.*

Verbal Processes: Processes of saying. Examples: *I said it's noisy in here; John said 'I'm hungry'; John said that he was hungry.*

We might expect all of the above kinds of processes to occur in news reporting. For example, in the News in Brief story discussed earlier in the chapter, we find material, verbal, behavioural, and mental processes, as follows:

Tracey Andrews, fiancée of the road rage victim Lee Harvey, has been taken to hospital after a suspected overdose.	material: *being taken to hospital*
Mr Harvey, aged 25, was knifed to death in a savage attack	material: *knifing to death*
after he and Tracey were pursued by another car in a 'cat and mouse' chase near Alvechurch, Worcestershire.	material: *being pursued by another car*
West Mercia Police said [. . . .]	verbal: *saying*
Miss Andrews, aged 27, had collapsed on Wednesday	behavioural: *collapsing*
but her family had initially wanted this kept secret	mental: *wanting*

It is important to note that some sentences may have more than one process described within them, as the report above shows. There is not the space here to go into further detail regarding process types of all these different kinds: readers are referred to Halliday's own description (see in particular Halliday, 1985: 101ff.). However, it is interesting to look more closely at one kind of process, the material process, since this is one about which useful work has been done in relation to news reporting.

Material Process Clauses

As we saw above, clauses are composed of processes, participants, and circumstances. In the material process clause, participants can be of two kinds: doers, which are referred to as **actors, and done-tos, which are referred to as goals.** Halliday's own example of a basic material process clause showing all its components is shown in Table 2.1 (adapted from Halliday, 1985: 102).

TABLE 2.1 Clause Components

The lion	chased	the tourist	lazily	through the bush
Participant: actor	Process	Participant: goal	Circumstance	Circumstance

A similar structure from the collection of Tracey Andrews reports used for this chapter appears in Table 2.2, taken from a headline.

TABLE 2.2 Headline Clause Structure

Police	quiz	woman
Participant: actor	Process	Participant: goal

In material process clauses such as these, the role of an actor is always assumed in the process, whether or not they are explicitly named. For example, in some clauses, the actor is not specified. This is particularly relevant in the case of clauses describing the stabbing or attack, since the whole purpose of the investigation will be to identify the missing actor. The clause analyzed in Table 2.3 contains no actor, although it does give three separate sets of information about circumstances.

TABLE 2.3 Clause with No Actor

He	was stabbed	nearly 40 times	as they drove along a quiet country lane	near Alvechurch, Worcestershire
Goal	Process	Circumstance	Circumstance	Circumstance

Although no actor is named, one is clearly involved in the stabbing.

The example in Table 2.3 also serves to point out another important element of clause classification, namely the distinction between active and passive **clauses**. Arguably, the 'ordinary' expectation about clause ordering in material process clauses is that the actor will be presented first, with the goal presented after the process. This would be the case in a clause such as that shown in Table 2.4, the constructed example 'Killer stabs road rage victim', where the killer is named as explicit actor.

TABLE 2.4   Constructed Example with Actor

Killer	stabs	road rage victim
Actor	Process	Goal

This clause organization is known as an active clause. In the previous example, however, the clause arrangement is different: the *goal* of the process (he, or Lee Harvey) is presented first. This kind of clause is termed passive. In passive clauses, there is a choice whether or not to name the actor at all: in the example above, no actor is named. Because actors, as we have said, are always assumed to be involved in material process clauses – that is, someone has to have done the action – the omission of an explicit reference to the actor nevertheless still allows for a reader or hearer to infer or guess who the actor might be. However, if the actor is named in a passive clause, it appears after the process (and sometimes, after circumstances, if any are present) in a 'by' phrase, as in the constructed example in Table 2.5.

TABLE 2.5   Constructed Passive Clause with Actor Named

He	was stabbed	nearly 40 times	by road rage killer
Goal	Process	Circumstance	Actor

But what can this transitivity analysis tell us about news reporting? Trew (1979) identifies active and passive description of events as crucial to the 'sanitization' of news over the course of time, as unpleasant events are digested and rendered less unpalatable during successive reports. Clark (1992) suggests that the lack of an explicit agent in the reporting of violent crimes enables the reporter to direct blame towards or away from the attacker. For example, in the headline 'Fiend rapes woman in Big Mac bar' (Clark's own example, reproduced from the *Sun* newspaper of 27th November 1986), the actor, the 'fiend', is placed first in an active clause, the process is 'rapes', the goal is 'woman', and the circumstance is the place in which it occurred. However, in Clark's example from the following month's *Sun* coverage of a different violent attack, the headline 'Girl 7 murdered while mum drank at pub' does not name the attacker explicitly. This passive clause has 'Girl 7' placed first as goal, 'murdered' as process, and no actor; however, 'Mum' is named in a circumstance description. This circumstance appears in the position where one might expect an actor in a 'by' phrase. Clark argues (1992:

213) that the murderer is removed from the scene by this passive deletion, but that the repetition of the mother's presence at the pub in a circumstance clause that occurs throughout the news report serves to establish a causal relation between the mother's absence and the girl's murder. Despite the missing actor, therefore, it is still possible to establish blame through particular clause structures.

This is perhaps our first mention in this book of linguistic processes that are directly influenced by **ideology**: a set of ideas or beliefs through which the world is viewed. Many linguists are interested in how ideology is manifested in language, especially in situations where that language is presented as 'neutral' in some way. Trew (1979) makes this argument in reference to the use of active and passive clauses in news reports of the killing of Black South Africans by police: he suggests that 'Using the passive form put the (syntactic) agents of the killings . . . in less focal position' (1979: 98), noting that, next day, agents are deleted in the news coverage, and other transformations take place in reporting on subsequent days that serve to lessen the impact of, and even suggest justification for, the killings. He compares the treatment of a shooting event in two different newspapers, and also examines the description of events in headlines, comparing these with the body of the newspaper reports. For example, the *Guardian* from the relevant day uses an active clause in the headline, with 'police' placed first as actor: 'Police shoot 11 dead in Salisbury riot'. Trew does note, however, that the use of the term 'riot' is a loaded one, since it prompts the assumption that police intervention was required and justified. *The Times* report of the same incident contained: '11 Africans were shot dead when police opened fire . . .'. Here, the construction is a passive one with the actors, the police, relegated to a circumstance clause describing a time at which the event took place. In subsequent days' reporting of events following the shootings, *The Times* had the headline: 'Split threatens ANC after Salisbury's riots'. The news has moved on, and now the actors and the goals – the police and the victims of the shooting – are not specified at all. Instead, the whole event has been described by a **nominal**, 'Salisbury's riots'. This phrase is used as the circumstance component of another clause, describing the process of 'threatening'. The actors, goals, and the process of the killing are no longer part of the message.

The strategy of examining process types can therefore be used to good effect in the description of news reporting. In particular, close attention to verbal processes (who is saying what) and material processes (who is doing what) can be revealing: as Trew shows, an event can be described as 'Blacks rioting' or 'Police shooting', depending on the ideological slant of the newspaper. In addition, the use of passive constructions is often indicative of a need or wish to take the focus away from the agent of an action. For example, to return to the Tracey Andrews story, the News in Brief story previously analyzed contained, as we saw, three material process descriptions. All of these are passive: Tracey Andrews being taken to hospital (by whom?); Lee Harvey being knifed (by whom?), and their car being pursued (by whom?). What is important here is not so much who the perpetrators were, but the fact that Lee and Tracey are portrayed as passive victims (goals) of material processes.

In later newspaper reports about this case, however, suspicion begins to fall on Tracey herself, and she is eventually charged on 19th December with the murder of Lee Harvey. As suspicion about her version of events grows, Tracey's role in the newspaper reports begins to change. Two specific changes are noticeable. First, in the early report we examined from 3rd December, Tracey herself was silent: no version of events was heard from her, and we were instead told the chain of events by police sources and, as we saw, by the newspaper report itself. Looking in particular at processes of saying, we find in that article that we have three key 'sayers', to use Halliday's term: Carl Baldaccino, Detective Superintendent Ian Johnston, and the source described as 'police'. We can see that the facts of the case as they are understood at that point are 'owned' by police sources, therefore, and, through statements simply reporting unattributed fact, by the newspaper itself. By 20th December, however, when Tracey has been charged, the sources of the facts change: in the report for 20th December, there are two principal sayers: Tracey and her solicitor. This has the effect of highlighting how the detail of Tracey's story has come from herself alone, and it portrays her as isolated.

The 20th December report is as follows:

'Rage victim' charged with murder
VIVEK CHAUDHARY
Tracie Andrews, who claimed her fiancé, Lee Harvey, was stabbed to death in a road rage incident on an isolated country lane, was last night charged with his murder.

Ms Andrews, aged 27, was due to appear at Redditch magistrates court this morning.

She faced the media two weeks ago, giving details of the death of Mr Harvey, aged 25. Shortly afterwards she was arrested but detectives were unable to interview her because she was admitted to hospital immediately after her arrest.

Speaking outside Redditch police station, in Worcestershire, last night, where Ms Andrews was questioned throughout yesterday, her solicitor, Tim Robinson, said: 'There were four lengthy interviews . . . but I'm not at liberty to reveal their content. She continues to vehemently deny any involvement in the murder.'

Mr Robinson added that he did not believe police were looking for anyone else in connection with the death. 'That is the case they are putting to Ms Andrews. It is a theory that is full of holes and not substantiated.'

Two days after Mr Harvey's death, Ms Andrews made an emotional appeal to catch his killer. She claimed they had been returning home on Sunday night nearly three weeks ago after going out for a drink. She said they were driving along Coopers Hill, a country lane just outside Alvechurch, where they lived together, when another vehicle began following them.

The other car, an F registration Ford Sierra hatchback, had pursued them for three miles, bumper to bumper, after they had passed it near junction 1 of the M42. The two cars had stopped outside an isolated house. Those inside said they heard nothing.

Mr Harvey and the other car's passenger, whom she described as a fat man with staring eyes, had confronted each other and a fight had started. Mr Harvey was stabbed at least 15 times in the face, neck and body, including a slash from ear to ear. Ms Andrews, who was the only witness to the attack, claimed his death was a road rage murder.

The couple, each with a daughter by a previous partner, had lived together for two years. Ms Andrews described Mr Harvey soon after his death as 'a lovely, kind, generous, funny man'.

Of 32 processes contained in the 20th December report, there are 13 processes of saying. Of these, 8 are given to Tracey as sayer: Tracey *claimed* (3 times), *gave details, made an appeal, said, described,* and *continued to deny.* Her solicitor was the sayer in three cases: he *said, was not at liberty to reveal,* and *added.* Two other sayers are used in the report: the people inside the isolated house, who *said* (1 occasion), and one clause, *Tracey Andrews was questioned . . .* , which, being a passive clause with no explicit sayer, leaves the sayers (the questioners) implicit and places Tracey in a prominent position in the clause. The information of the case is now 'owned' by Tracey and her solicitor, while the police have largely disappeared.

A side-effect of this move to verbal processes in the description of the events is that Tracey herself is increasingly portrayed not as a victim (the goal) of a process but as a key protagonist: as sayer, she is more frequently the 'agent' of the events reported, rather than someone suffering them. In fact, the 20th December headline refers to *Tracey* as a 'victim', but in inverted commas, showing a move in sympathy from Tracey as victim of a third party to Lee as *her* victim. Tracey, however, is still a victim in one respect: in processes relating to the police and the law reported in the 20th December article, such as being charged and arrested. Tracey is still the goal of these material processes, which places her now as subordinate to the authority of the police.

NAMING IN THE NEWS REPORT

As well as looking at how clauses are constructed, much can be learned about the ideological slant of a news report by examining the vocabulary that is used, particularly to describe the key news actors. Trew (1979), for example, in his discussion of violence in Africa, found that, where the *Tanzanian Daily News* had described a shooting event as 'Racists murder Zimbabweans', *The Times* had referred to 'police', 'shootings' or 'killings', and 'Africans'. There is clearly a contrast between 'racists' and 'police' as descriptions of the same group of people. Selection of vocabulary, then, carries ideological content. In a similar vein, Clark (1992) analyzes how tabloid newspapers apportion blame in violent male-on-female crime. She argues that tabloid newspapers in particular, in reporting such crimes, decide to blame one party or the other, and convey this view through their choice of vocabulary. For example, male attackers to whom the newspaper wishes to apportion blame are referred to as 'monster', 'fiend', 'maniac', or 'beast', suggesting subhumanity and therefore blame. Men who were taken to be provoked or otherwise not to blame for a violent attack were called by their own name or some neutral term. For female victims, there was a similar distinction between the blamed and the blameless: blamed victims, argues Clark, are referred to by such terms as 'blonde', 'unmarried mum', 'Lolita', 'blonde divorcee', 'blonde mum', 'woman', or 'victim', many of which are terms which carry some taint of sexual availability or exclusion from 'safe' society. Interestingly, the women referred to in this way were not attacked in general by 'fiends', but by men given a more neutral or even exonerating description. Where attackers were 'fiends', however, the blameless women were referred to in other ways: often by positive emotive terms such as 'bride', 'schoolgirl', 'daughter', and many other terms emphasizing either innocence or a secure position within the family and therefore within society (Clark, 1992: 211ff.).

Both the negative words (fiend, divorcee, Lolita) and positive words (hubby, bride) have what can be termed **affective meaning**, in that they indicate something of the writer's attitude, positive or negative, towards the person referred to. This notion is described in more detail in Leech (1990), and we return to it in more detail in our discussion of advertising in Chapter 7 of this book. In addition, terms such as 'bride' have positive **connotations**, in that, beyond simply indicating that the writer intends a positive interpretation, there are positive mental pictures and associations that go with 'brides': youth, good looks, and sexual naivety, perhaps. Likewise, 'monster' and 'beast' carry negative connotations: sexual rapacity, extreme ugliness, and even having big teeth.

A brief comparison of news reporting in the *Guardian* newspaper during the course of the Tracey Andrews case exposes an interesting slant in the naming of Tracey. In the first report of the killing of Lee Harvey (the article of 3rd December, analyzed earlier in the chapter), Tracey is portrayed as a grieving girlfriend, and many references to her are to her as half of a couple: she is described as *his* (LH's) *girlfriend* three times, and LH is called *her boyfriend* once. The connection between LH and TA is reinforced by references to *they, them* or *their* (5), *the couple* (1), *each* (1), and *Mr Harvey and Ms Andrews* (1). It is also the newspaper's assertion that she was *cradling her boyfriend in her arms*. TA is referred to as an individual in the words of the police spokesman as *Tracie* (1) and *she* (3), while the news reporter describes Tracey as *Ms Andrews* (1) and *she* (1). The *Guardian* on 20th December reports Tracey's arrest and her being charged with LH's murder. In this report, the focus changes: Tracey is no longer part of a couple, and a much greater focus is placed on her descriptions of events, rather than on her being part of a scenario described and apparently adopted by other agencies such as the police. She is described as *Tracie Andrews* (1), *Ms Andrews* (6), and *she/her* (7), and there is one reference to *her arrest*. If Clark's suggestion is correct, Tracey as part of a couple is blameless, since her engagement to Lee gives her a respectable position in society. In this report, though, Tracey is on her own: there is only one reference to *the couple*. Tracey as a singular entity now moves into the focus of attention, and even the relationship with LH is described from Tracey's rather than Lee's perspective. Lee is referred to as *her fiancé* (compare with the earlier report in which she was three times *his girlfriend*), and the article finishes with Tracey's own description of Lee: Ms Andrews described Mr Harvey soon after his death as '*a lovely, kind, generous, funny man*'. We can see, then, that the changing pattern of naming tracks a change in perspective: Tracey and Lee begin as a pair, joint victims of crime as observed by third parties (the attacker, the police, the public). In the later report, Tracey is recast as alone, an independent observer of events. She is moving from the position of 'done-to' to that of 'doer', as the High Court subsequently found.

SUMMARY

There is a rich volume of research on news reporting, and this chapter has attempted to pick out particularly significant linguistic frameworks that have been applied to such texts. The chapter first of all described the role of **news values** in selecting what is to be reported, and then went on to look at the influence of news values and reporting conventions on the structure of the text. The structure of news reports was shown to be different from that of oral narrative, following instead a cyclical or '**inverted pyramid**' structure. A method was introduced for comparing **eventuality structure** (what happened) with **discourse structure** (the structure of the report), making the distinction between **events** as key news components of the story and **states** as 'background'. The chapter then described a way of looking at clauses as descriptions of **processes** with particular **participants**, showing through the analysis of **transitivity** how changing roles in relation to **process types**, in particular **material** and **verbal** processes, could expose different **ideological** perspectives on events. Finally, work on naming of news actors was described, showing how terms of reference could also carry ideological content.

TOPICS FOR STUDY AND DISCUSSION

1. Examine a news report using the framework for describing eventuality structure and discourse structure given in this chapter. Do you find a similar discrepancy between the two structures? Based on the news values described, can you say why the news report has been organized the way it has?
2. Look at a range of headlines, or headlines and lead paragraphs, examining how many of the key eventualities described in them are events, and how many are processes. For example, a headline might have said either *State of emergency renewed* (event) or *State of emergency still holds* (state). Is there a difference in the frequency with which states and events are involved in headlines? If there is, why? Does it accord with expectations based on this chapter?
3. Look at some short news reports comparing the type of story involved and how sources are used. When do reports use direct speech, indirect speech, or straight statements? In what ways are 'hedges' or mitigating devices used to distance speakers or the paper itself from the story content?

4. Take a short news report and try to find the most important process descriptions within it. What kinds of processes are the most prominent? Look at the use of active and passive clause structures. Why have passives been used in your story?
5. Look at how news actors are described in a longer news report, or in several reports on a similar topic or on the same event across time. What kinds of referring expressions are used for naming the news actors? Why? What processes does each actor get associated with? Can you suggest any pattern to the association between people named in certain ways, and the kinds of things you find them doing in news stories?

FURTHER READING

For immediate further reading beyond this chapter, van Dijk (1998) gives a very readable discussion of how ideology is presented in the press. Bell (1998) in the same volume describes a method for describing the structure of news stories. For a very useful book-length study of all aspects of news production, see Bell (1991).

Several interesting areas in the description of news reports fall outside the scope of this chapter. Page organization, headings, and other elements of the physical layout of the text are an important component in the creation of meaning. In particular, headlines can play a key role in determining how the accompanying text will be read, or at least in indicating the slant that the paper has taken on a given story. A useful overview of layout in newspaper front pages appears in Kress and van Leeuwen (1998). It has also been noted that newspaper reports differ in their grammatical structure from 'ordinary' spoken language. Bell (1994: 107), for example, suggests that newspaper reporting language is 'more complex' than that of the Labov-style personal narratives with which he compares it; see also van Dijk (1988a: 111ff.) for a discussion of grammatical complexity in the news. Halliday (1994) compares speech and writing very accessibly, and this may be of use in comparing written news reporting with other genres, such as spoken news.

For insights into how stories are collected and some of the processes that result in their final appearance on the page, see Manoff (1987) and Bell (1991). Bell (1991, Chapter 1) also gives a very useful overview of the different aspects of the nature and function of news media language that have been studied throughout the 1980s. Kress (1983: 121ff.) also briefly discusses the role of different agencies in the writing and rewriting of a story, stressing the difficulty of assessing any one version's relationship to any 'truth' given the fact that all of the processes of reporting constitute a kind of mediation.

Van Dijk (1988a: 31ff.) gives a very comprehensive account of news treatment of different international stories, looking at very high level considerations such as which stories get reported at all, to lower-level considerations such as who is reported as speaking, or who is reported as the agent or cause of particular events. A particular focus on the creation and reproduction of racism in the press is pursued through a development of these analytical techniques in van Dijk (1987).

For more on the use of modal verbs in how reporters indicate the strength of their belief in a claim, see Fowler (1991: 85ff.). Sanders and Redeker (1993) give a more detailed description, supported by psychological experiments, of how different linguistic devices indicate the perspective of speakers and writers, or of news actors themselves, on the events reported in a short news story. Short (1988) gives a useful description of the use of different devices to report others' speech with greater or lesser faithfulness, comparing news reporting with fictional narrative.

Carter (1988) describes the use of basic ('core') and unusual ('non-core') vocabulary in creating the meaning of news reports. For more on different types of meaning beyond 'basic' word meaning, see Leech (1990), see also Bolinger (1980) for a general discussion of ideologically loaded uses of terminology. This is discussed later in this book in relation to magazine features (Chapter 6) and advertising (Chapter 7).

While much work has been done in describing the language and appearance of newspaper reports, less is understood about why certain forms are chosen and not others. In the literature in general, explanations of expressive choices, particularly linguistic ones, rest on quite vague assumptions. For example, Kress (1983: 126) in describing the relationship between a verb and its adjectival complement (the explanation of the difference between structures such as *are certain* vs *seem likely*), suggests that 'the complement probably has the greater impact', and that 'as readers we are more interested in the quality of the object'. Crystal and Davy (1969), in their earlier description of newspaper language, invoke the need for clarity, the need to catch the eye and spark interest, and the need to be readable as putative explanations for linguistic choices, as well as design choices such as the use of particular typefaces and styles. Writers such as Trew (1979) and Clark (1992) *inter alia*, in their analysis of transitivity, make the assumption that actors are more salient, and active processes in some way more straightforward, than the use of passive processes and participant roles such as 'affected' and 'circumstance'. Suggestions regarding what is salient and what is less so, what will catch the eye and therefore affect processes such as reading order, and what are the effects of linguistic choices such as actors position and passive voice are in fact statements about cognitive information processing, and as such are testable through psychological experimentation. Van Dijk and his school (see, for example, van Dijk, 1985) are notable for taking the psychological causes and effects of different linguistic choices seriously in their research, establishing the field of cognitive linguistics as an important approach towards the analysis of newspapers and other types of text. For example, Zwaan (1991) has shown that memory for linguistic structures is greater when reading a text billed as a 'novel' than for 'newspaper' texts, while texts understood to be fiction are read on average more slowly than newspapers. Sanders and Redeker (1993), in the same tradition, show how readers react to the use of different means of filtering the description of events through a writer's or character's perspective, comparing levels of acceptability of different devices for doing this in fiction and news reports.

NOTES

1 See Chapter 7 for a discussion of the creation of 'ordinariness' in advertising.
2 The *Guardian* used this spelling of Ms Andrews' name interchangeably with 'Tracey'.

3 The Language of Sports Commentary

In this chapter, we look in detail at commentary in football and racing. What is offered below is an approach to the close linguistic analysis of commentary which identifies its characteristics, and which can be applied subsequently to different kinds of sporting texts, with the help of the recommended additional reading given at the end of the chapter.

RACING COMMENTARY: AN EXAMPLE

The text below is transcribed from television racing commentary. The transcription conventions used in this book are described in Chapter 1. The commentary lasts from the moment the starting gun fires to the end of the race. The figures in italics in the left-hand margin refer to seconds elapsed:

	and they kick away over seven furlongs
	and Rock Falcon a little bit slow er
	and that's a surprise he normally eh (.)
	wants to make the running (.)
8	Nigrasine (.)
	a horse that's sweated up gave Carl Lowther such eh (.)
	an unfortunate fall at Nottingham (.)
	fitted with a breast girth today (.)
15	
	but it's er Rock Falcon despite that slow go
	has er come to (1 sec)
	share the lead and just be ahead (.)
	Dazzlin Lady in the check sleeves (.)
	n the check jacket (.)
	the purple cap (.)
	on the far side (.)
20	is Ho Leng there (.)
	one two and three (.)
	then Late Night Out and Nigrasine followed by Sensori (2 secs)
	as they go through the first quarter mile and (.)
	Hornbeam who's a soft ground performer as the divots really fly
	here (.)

32   there's nothing the ground staff dislike more than torrential rain
during the meeting (1 sec) because these horses do imprint
very heavily and (.) they will be er filling up with water

45   As Rock Falcon under Dean McKeown blazes the trail here (1 sec)
in this seven-furlong race Dazzlin Lady (.)
coming second (.)
Nigrasine on the left in the er horse with a big white face (1 sec)
is er sharing third with (.)
Ho Leng (.)
as they come down past the two they tart to start to turn the screw
(.)
It's Rock Falcon the leader (.)

60   made virtually (.)
all the running (.) to eh (.)
Dazzlin Lady then Hornbeam (.)
look at the top of the picture (.)
on the right (.)
he's started to make ground now (1 sec)

68   also Sensori is on the left with (.)
er {chuckle} what should be (.)
white sleeves (.)

72   but they come down to the final furlong (.)
and the pink cap stand side

75   it's Sensori under Darryl Holland who goes on now and with
Dazzlin Lady in second (.)
Rock Falcon Nigrasine Ho Leng Hornbeam all beaten (.)
so too is Late Night Out (.) but it's Sensori (.) who's coming
storming three or four lengths clear to win comfortably (.)

83   to in second place Dazzlin Lady Nigrasine and third Rock Falcon (.)
then Hornbeam (.) then Late Night Out (.) Ho Leng (1 sec)
trailed in last of all (.)

95   and so the result (1 sec) of this (1 sec) Racing Post Condition
Stakes (.) and they are {chuckle} pretty terrible conditions (.)
weather wise here (.)

102   Sensori has won in the colours of Khaled Abdullah (.) Lambourne
trainer Barry Hill has called in the services of Darryl Holland to
help his Selkirk home and he came stand side (.)
content to bide his time early on (.)
and really picked up well (.)

115   second horse home is Dazzlin Lady (.)
who was er placed again (.)
ran a brave race (.) but not quite good enough (.)

125   eh George Duffield in the check sleeves there (.)
had no answer to (.)
the pink capped Darryl Holland who's in the Abdullah jacket (.)
on this home-bred Selkirk (.)

132   who was really stretched in the prevailing conditions and the ability to
handle the ground (.)
is er paramount today (.)

135   (1 syll) had won one before that was on fast ground at Leicester (2 secs)
but the stride (1 sec)

carried him home well (1 sec)
in testing (1 sec)
testing (.)
conditions

150

Any attempt at describing the language of sports commentary should perhaps first mention the kind of vocabulary that is used. Any vocabulary that immediately suggests to us some field of activity is termed in linguistics **field specific**, a term that derives from the study of **register**, discussed in Chapter 1. Special vocabulary associated with horse-racing is present here:

furlongs
make the running
breast girth
cap
soft/fast ground
divots

A further characteristic of commentary is the way in which **clauses** are linked together. A very small number of **conjunctive** elements are used to link clauses together, often rather loosely. In this commentary, *and*, *but* and *as* are by far the most popular conjunctions, suggesting two main kinds of relationship between clauses. *And* and *but* are known as **co-ordinating conjunctions**, which link elements of similar grammatical status, as in:

socks *and* shoes, knife *and* fork (co-ordinated nouns)
he went in *and* he picked up a paper (co-ordinated clauses)

Note that *and they kick away over seven furlongs* is the first utterance of the race commentary proper, which is itself stereotypical. *And* is not conjunctive with anything that has gone before, but the use of *and* to start a new commentary is frequently heard in racing.

And and *but*, as we noted above, serve to co-ordinate elements with one another. *As* is somewhat different, since it serves to introduce a grammatical **adjunct** to a clause. This often indicates, in this data, a point in time in the race:

as they go through the first quarter mile . . .
as they come down past the two . . .

These *as* clauses are **subordinate** to main clauses, since they provide the context in which an action, to be described by a main clause, is to take place. The sense is: *as they go through the first quarter mile, something* *happens*, where the 'something happens' is to be reported in a main clause, as in:

as they come down past the two *they tart to start to turn the screw*[1]

The clause introduced by *as* therefore acts as an adjunct in the structure of the complex clause as a whole. Sometimes, the *as* clauses are not grammatically complete:

as they go through the first quarter mile and Hornbeam
who's a soft ground performer as the divots really fly here

Here, although the *as* clause leads us to expect it, there is no following full clause: instead, the commentator begins another structure with the co-ordinating conjunction *and*. *And* does not in the end introduce a full clause, either: there is a reference to Hornbeam, itself made complex by a further subordinate structure introduced by *who*, followed by another *as* clause. The various clauses, then, are loosely linked, and the complex clause structures that we would expect on the basis of the conjunctions used do not material-ize. This is a characteristic of **unplanned**, stream-of-consciousness language: an appearance of connectedness is maintained, but the more considered planning required for grammatically complete complex constructions is not possible.

There are some cases, however, when complex structures are managed completely, and these can be used to identify two different phases in the commentary. After 32 seconds, for example, the commentator uses a gram-matically complex construction involving a *because* clause, introducing a reason for the content of the main clause. The main clause is italicized:

there's nothing the ground staff dislike more than torrential rain during the meeting because these horses do imprint very heavily

Here, a more complicated clause structure is possible because the com-mentator has stepped away from the moment-by-moment narration of the race, in which he judges nothing critical is currently happening, to talk about the soft going and the ground staff's views about it. These interludes often correspond with a slower speed of speech and lower pitch of voice. Complete and complex clause structures can be seen as characteristic of background or summary information, while looser concatenations of clauses refer to the ongoing action. Kroll (1977, cited in Ochs, 1979) reports a study of planned and unplanned narratives, in which it was found that planned narratives contained over 20% of subordinate clause constructions. In unplanned narratives that figure dropped dramatically to just over 7%. During the commentary, we can expect the proportion of subordinate clauses to rise and fall, depending on whether the commentator is engaged in fast commentary, or providing more leisurely background information.

These facts about clause linking show that unplanned speech is often loosely connected and syntactically incomplete. Ochs (1979: 55) provides some further characteristics of unplanned discourse, which she characterizes as 'discourse that lacks forethought and organizational preparation', contrasting it with planned discourse: 'discourse that has been thought out and planned (designed) prior to its expression'. In fact, as she goes on to note, most discourse is at neither of these extremes, but somewhere in between. Furthermore, discourse may be relatively planned at one level of organization, but unplanned in another: it may be relatively unplanned, for example, in terms of the words and phrases that are used, and in what order units of meaning (propositions) are expressed, but highly planned with respect to what it is the language is intended to accomplish. Sports commentary is clearly planned in the latter sense: the event it describes is formally scheduled, a speaker or speakers are chosen far in advance, and the nature of the sporting event, also known in advance, determines to a great extent both speakers' and hearers' expectations about what *kinds* of language, and language structures, are to be expected. Moreover, the broadcasting event of which the commentary forms a part is also highly planned. We will look further at these 'norms' for sports commentary shortly. Despite planning at these levels, however, the discourse is relatively unplanned at the local level, dealing with choice, organization, and production of words, phrases, and clauses. Sports commentary therefore shares with other kinds of unplanned speech (casual conversation, for example) some of the same characteristics. Moreover, the speed of the commentary accentuates some of these features, further than would perhaps be the case in relaxed conversation.

Ochs (1979) points out that unplanned discourse uses structures which first identify a **referent** (a concept to talk about) and then predicate some action, property, or quality that is true of that referent. The semantic relationship between the **subject** element and what is said about it, or the predication, is left quite loose. So, instead of *Rock Falcon is a little bit slow*, which would be a full clause, the sports commentator says *and Rock Falcon . . . a little bit slow*. Here, Rock Falcon is identified as the referent, and the next thing that is said is some property (slowness) predicated of Rock Falcon. This habit of leaving things out that would normally be expected in the clause structure is called **ellipsis**. In particular, we see ellipsis of the verb *to be*. Here are some other examples – in each case, the likely elided element is given in brackets:

Dazzlin Lady [] in the check sleeves   [is]
Rock Falcon Nigrasine . . . Hornbeam [] all beaten   [are]

In each of these cases, a referent is identified (in each case here, a horse) and a predication (wearing check sleeves, being beaten) are predicated of them, although the exact link is left inexplicit.

Ochs' point is that such communication, although inexplicit, saves time for the speaker, and requires the hearer to make the links through inference. Properties are linked to subjects simply by 'nextness'.

Speed

Another well-known characteristic of sports commentary is its speed. Over the whole horse race, the commentator produced 471 words, an average of just over 188 words per minute. The average speed, however, hides the fact that there is a variation in speed throughout, and this indicates something of the relationship between language and the action it reports upon: the nearer the race comes to its deciding point, the faster the speech becomes. For example, between seconds 75 and 83, the average speed of the commentary went up to over 322 words per minute. As a rough comparison of how fast this is, I produced 191 words per minute in fluent non-stop reading from a book: you may like to make your own timed comparison with other kinds of speech, such as lectures or conversation. While the different text types are not of course comparable, it is interesting to note that, at his fastest, the commentator is producing spontaneous *unplanned* speech at speeds far in excess of my reading words from the page. Moreover, Beard (1998: 77) notes that radio commentary is faster still than television, since it does not rely on the visual availability of information to supplement the message.

FOOTBALL COMMENTARY

Before continuing, we can enrich our pool of examples by adding in another kind of data to supplement that from horse-racing. Football (soccer) commentary shares many characteristics with racing, as we shall see, but there are also some important differences. The extract below is taken from the second half of the 1998 World Cup match between England and Romania. Numbers in italics in the left-hand margin refer to minutes and seconds elapsed in the game. Two commentators appear in this extract, as is common with football commentary. One takes the role of commentator (Brian), who narrates the match play-by-play. An 'expert', Kevin, provides comments and opinions when required:

54.55
Brian: Ciobotariu (3 secs)
dummy (.) by Hagi but er Gary Neville refused to buy
that was a nice turn there by Scholes (2 secs)
Beckham couldn't quite pick it up
but he might pick this up (2 secs)
and he's played a ball inside the full back (.)
but eh Petrescu was there (.)
ahead of Le Saux (.)
who's making a lot of great forward runs
it's with (.) Sheringham now (.)
Anderton's gone into the middle (2 secs)

it's with Beckham (3 secs)
it's with Scholes a little flick by him but Beckham
couldn't get on the end of it (5 secs)
it's David Batty (7 secs)
finding Beckham (5 secs)
he's got his Manchester United team mate available Gary
Neville but there was just a little bit too ambitious and it's
(1 sec) Hagi challenged by (2 secs) Darren Anderton (.)
a throw to Romania (13 secs)
Neville (3 secs)
up to Shearer (4 secs)
it longed there towards Sheringham but he was very well
marked and there's Le Saux (2 secs)
scored only once for England b'd it was a (.)
pretty spectacular goal from that sort of range actually
against Brazil at Wembley I remember (4 secs)

56:25
Kevin: I think there's also something that could give England a bit
          of a 'ope in the game against Colombia (.)
          they visibly tired in the last half hour and the coach said (.)
          we were very tired but we had (.)
          we were clever enough to get a victory (.)
          I mean there's a lot of players o over thirty in this side so (.)
          if we get the tempo (.) up a little bit maybe (.) just maybe (.)
          they'll start to tire again
          the Colombians did it in the last twenty minutes and we're
          good enough to do it
          We've just just got to believe and we've got to push forward
          and we can we can cause them problems (1 sec)
Brian: Le Saux (.) from Campbell (.) but it was difficult to take and
          there were too many Romanians around him (.)
          and it's Popescu on the break (2 secs)
          Ilie (2 secs)
57:00
          and Hagi (.) on to the left foot (.) real troubles now but (.) er
          his first touch deserted him (2 secs)
          and eh in any case (.)
          Seaman was swooping out there (.)
          but just at that moment there you could suddenly see
          another disaster for England but Seaman was out quickly (.)
          Hagi had lost his way a little bit (1 sec)
          unlike him (3 secs)
          Batty (2 secs)
          to Sheringham (5 secs)
          Batty again (1 sec)
          here's Beckham (3 secs)
          if you've just joined us Beckham (.)
          in that central mid-field role (.)
          Paul Ince went off injured (.)
          during the first half (3 secs)
          Beckham again (2 secs)

                playing it in for Sheringham (1 sec)
                looking towards (2 secs)

57:46

                Gary Neville (1 sec) ohh (.)
                and in the end it's (.) Ilie the forward who's back there (.)
                I thought (.)
                Neville was in for a shot there (2 secs)

Kevin: well (.) he hasn't scored many goals Brian (.)
                maybe that's why cos he lacked the confidence (.)
                he's tried to roll it for Scholes but surely (2 secs)
                he had a better chance than (.) than Scholes could
                ever have had (.)
                to just have a crack and (.)
                maybe Scholes could have picked up a rebound (2 secs)

Brian: but they are playing well (.) Romania (1 sec)
                they're playing they're playing passing well (.)
                they are keeping (.) as we were saying earlier on (.)
                they're keeping the ball together so well (.)
                some great work there from Munteanu (2 secs)
                and a goal kick for England (12 secs)

Kevin: very ambitious shot (.) was   [n't it   [Brian but they (.)
Brian: [it was [wasn't it
Kevin: they have tried a few long range shots you know (.)
                thank goodness none of them (.)
                have been on target really (3 secs)

58:52

Brian: Batty (.)
                to Shearer (3 secs)
                  Beckham (11 secs)
                defeat here would put an enormous pressure on England
                to win their next game which (.) comes up on Friday against
                er (.) Colombia (2 secs)
                it's still over half an hour of this game remaining (4 secs)
                Batty to Beckham (9 secs)
                just look at the way he's being tracked there by Hagi
                and Petrescu (2 secs)
                no but he's (.) he's done well (.)
                and he's found Campbell (.)
                this is a good run by the big defender (3 secs)
                Moldovan playing it inside (5 secs)
                Munteanu to (.) Ilie (.)

59:30

                look at Hagi again (.)
                into that channel and Adams coming across quickly there (.)
                did really well (2 secs)
                that's a couple of times that Hagi's been made to look very
                dangerous and er finding some space in that particular area (.)
                Shearer again being outnumbered
                and still battling on manfully
                he's given away a free kick there (.)

Kevin: nothing much going right for Alan Shearer tonight but the
                one thing you can be guaranteed of (.) he'll keep going (1 sec)

               he'll he'll be going in the ninety-first ninety-second or
               whatever (.) the (.) referee decides to play on (.)
               you can be assured of that

Brian: Hagi (.) playing it in and then giving it away (.)
               Beckham (3 secs)
               Munteanu (2 secs)
               Ilie (2 secs)
               left Beckham be (.) oh it must be offside (2 secs)
               Moldovan (.) by a yard or so (4 secs)
               yeah just ooh (.) just about (.) I would say (.)
               but the certainly eh (.) the linesman on the far side
               had the flag up at once (2 secs)
               it's Gary Neville (.) for England (.) a goal down (4 secs)
               Batty's made a run for it (.)
               Beckham's available in this central midfield area (7 secs)

60:43

               Teddy Sheringham (2 secs)

In this extract, we can distinguish utterances with several different functions:

1 **Narrating**: Describing what is happening play-by-play;
2 **Evaluating**: Giving opinions about play, players, teams, referee decisions, etc.;
3 **Elaborating**: Giving background information about team and player records, the ground, the crowd; speculating on motives and thoughts of the players;
4 Summarizing: Giving an overview of play so far.

We can split these utterance functions into two broad types, both of which relate to different phases of the commentary. Narration is composed of **time-critical utterances**, which occur at the time of play and serve to describe it. These form the main structure of the commentary and are central to describing what is going on, a function most viewers and listeners would agree to be the primary purpose of live commentary. The other kinds of utterance tend to occur in less frenetic parts of the game, and consist of more subjective content: evaluating, elaborating, and summarizing are of this nature. Utterances with these functions tend to be more syntactically complete and complex, and are regularly cut short when play starts up and time-critical commentary is again required. The switch between the two utterance types is often marked by speaker change: football coverage often has two commentators, one of whom is only called upon to evaluate and give background in slower parts of the game. In addition, change of **tense** often occurs: evaluation and summary are more frequently given in the past tense, while time-critical commentary is given in the present.

    One form of narrating consists of describing who is controlling the ball. In football, one important function of utterances is therefore to describe possession. Narration of this kind is bounded by time: the utterance, and its accompanying pause, mark how long each player has possession:

and looking now as Shearer came to that one and eh Petrescu (.)
with a little nod over (.) his Chelsea team-mate (2 secs)
Graham Le Saux (2 secs)
Scholes (2 secs)
having it back (2 secs)
Batty (.) to Le Saux
David Batty again (2 secs)
Sol Campbell's handy (2 secs)
Le Saux again (.)

Two points to note about the language of narratives of this sort are, firstly,
the minimal use of verbs: clause structures here are not syntactically complete,
consisting mainly of **nominals** (noun-like constructions) such as names, or
descriptions of moves such as *a little nod over*. Second, the verbs that do
appear are not finite **verbs** that carry tense (*he looks over now, he has it back*)
but present participle forms (*looking now, having it back*).

This kind of narration forms the backbone of the whole commentary, and
it is possible to see other kinds of utterance as temporary diversions from it.
For example, around 19 minutes into the England–Romania match, the
expert, Kevin, offers an evaluation of the play on one side of the pitch.
Instead of answering his evaluative move, Brian returns directly to the
business of play-by-play narration:

Kevin: it's a real eh (.) tussle down this side
         because Petrescu and Le Saux of course (.)
         both play for the same club so
         (.) they can't sort of <u>hide</u> behind the fact (.) that they
         both get surprised by each other (2 secs)
Brian: Galcu (2 secs) Popescu (6 secs)

A second type of narrative specifies 'set pieces' in the game, acting as
punctuation marks that introduce new episodes of play. Examples are 'free
kicks' and 'corners', commentated as follows:

well kick to Romania

and eh a free kick to England

but it's England's corner which Anderton will take

Utterances of this narrative type, being closely linked to the action of the
game, will always take precedence over, and may cut across, all the other
categories of utterance. Above, we saw Brian's narrative interrupting an
evaluation from Kevin. Narrative is never provided by experts, only by
commentators. In the next example, Kevin is elaborating on the characteristics of Alan Shearer. While he does finish his utterance, syntactically and
in terms of its meaning, there is no gap before Brian comes in with further
narrative:

> Kevin: nothing much going right for Alan Shearer tonight but the
> one thing you can be guaranteed of (.) he'll keep going (1 sec)
> he'll he'll be going in the ninety-first ninety-second or
> whatever (.) the (.) referee decides to play on (.)
> you can be assured of that
>
> Brian: Hagi (.) playing it in and then giving it away (.)

Much has been written about the ways in which successful **turn taking** is achieved in conversation. The way in which speakers know how to take turns in conversation is also discussed in this book in relation to interviews (Chapter 5) and advertising (Chapter 7); for an overview, see also Graddol et al. (1994: 162). Below are some of the ways in which speakers know they can take a turn in conversation. It is most likely that more than one of these cues occurs at a time:

(a) Explicit nomination: speaker 1 can name speaker 2 explicitly;
(b) Pause: a gap allowing speaker 2 to speak;
(c) Syntactic completion: the grammatical unit speaker 1 is embarked on has clearly finished;
(d) **Gaze**: speaker 1 may look at speaker 2;
(e) **Intonation**: falling intonation, or rising for a question, may indicate turn completion.

During the commentary on the match, we cannot see how the expert and the commentator are interacting with one another directly. We cannot therefore speculate on gazes and gestures that are used (although it would be possible to analyze the non-verbal cues that take place in the 'panel-style' discussions at half-time, for example). In the football data, though, we can examine some linguistic cues for turn taking. When Brian is involved in narrating the game, a long pause is required before Kevin will contribute, since narrating is not one of the moves to which he has access. Here, there is a very long pause in the narrative before Kevin speaks.

> Brian: and a goal kick for England (12 secs)
> Kevin: very ambitious shot (.) was [n't it   [Brian but they (.)
> Brian: [it was [wasn't it

In this example, Kevin nominates Brian specifically for a reaction to his opinion.

If Brian moves away from narration into one of the other move types, the floor is open to Kevin to contribute without such a long pause. In the example below, Brian is elaborating: the combination of a speculative *I remember* and a gap of four seconds may give Kevin his cue to speak:

> Brian: pretty spectacular goal from that sort of range actually against Brazil at
> Wembley I remember (4 secs)

56:25
Kevin: I think there's also something that could give England a bit
          of a 'ope in the game against Colombia (.)

Similarly, Brian speculates on Neville's failure to shoot with *I thought* . . . ,
which allows Kevin to collaborate. Note, though, how he once again nominates Brian as if for approval of his contribution. The fact that Brian does not
name Kevin to bring him in may indicate the unequal power relations between
them in the joint construction of the commentary. Kevin's contributions must
be opportunistic, as Brian does not apparently accord him pre-established
rights to speak.

Brian: I thought (.)
          Neville was in for a shot there (2 secs)
Kevin: well (.) he hasn't scored many goals Brian (.)

Likewise, Kevin can contribute after a summary of Hagi's role in the game.
There may also act as an indicator that the turn is complete:

Brian: that's a couple of times that Hagi's been made to look very
          dangerous and er finding some space in that particular area (.)
          Shearer again being outnumbered
          and still battling on manfully
          he's given away a free kick there (.)
Kevin: nothing much going right for Alan Shearer

Here, then, we can see how the collaborative element of football commentary
is constructed. The turn-taking principles at work in this match illustrate
something of a mismatch in power, but also that, as Sacks et al. (1974)
suggest, speakers' ability to identify turn types may influence how turn taking
is managed. In this case, we have seen that a knowledge of the kinds of things
one can do in commentary – elaborating, evaluating, and narrating, for
example – influences when Kevin, as the less privileged speaker, makes a bid
for a turn.

Speech Errors

A feature that is familiar in conversation in general, but certainly in fast
speech, is that speakers make mistakes or 'slips of the tongue' (see, for
example, Fromkin and Rodman, 1997: 459ff.). These **speech errors** are of
interest particularly to psycholinguists investigating how language is processed
in the brain: a confusion between two sounds, one earlier in the planned
sentence and one later, for example, demonstrates at least that the units in
which sentences are planned are bigger than single words. Speech errors can
also show the relationship between meaning and sound in the planning of

speech — if, for example, a sound is produced accidentally that belongs to another word that is related in meaning. Linguists and psychologists have classified speech errors into a range of different types (see, for example, Fromkin and Rodman, 1997: 459ff.). For example, an **anticipation** is an error in which a sound is replaced by one that is due to appear later in the sentence, as in *tart to turn* rather than *start to turn*: here, the *t* of turn is anticipated at the beginning of *start*. **False starts** often appear in fast speech, and in these cases the speaker almost invariably goes back to the beginning of a phrase and repeats it, observing the coherence of the phrase as a grammatical unit. For example, in the football commentary data, we have the sentence *they are keeping as we were saying earlier on they are keeping the ball together so well*, where the speaker returns to the beginning of a clause to repeat it rather than simply resuming, as in *they are keeping as we were saying earlier on the ball together so well*. Another example is *he'll he'll be going in the ninety-first*.

Replanning of clauses occurs in many instances in the sports commentary data studied in this chapter. In these examples, the speaker embarks on a particular structure, abandons it halfway through, and replaces it with another. In this racing example, Nigrasine was to have been identified by the rider's colours (*in the . . .*) but the commentator replans (*er...*) and identifies him by his white face instead:

Nigrasine on the left in the er horse with a big white face (1 sec)

Kevin, in the football commentary, doesn't complete his original thought about the Colombian team, which he voices from their coach's perspective. He replans the clause beginning with *we had* to *we were clever enough*:

we were very tired but we had (.)
we were clever enough to get a victory (.)

Replanning, or planning pauses in general, are often filled: instead of a pause, the speaker articulates *um* or *er*. These filled pauses may occur when time is needed to identify a player, for example:

dummy (.) by Hagi but er Gary Neville refused to buy

Pauses are often used for player identification:

Munteanu to (.) Ilie (.)

and it's
(1 sec) Hagi challenged by (2 secs) Darren Anderton (.)

Of course, the most famous errors often identified in sports commentary are those referred to as 'Colemanballs' after the commentator David Coleman. These are not normally performance errors in speech, but errors in the semantic sense — meanings that are just plain daft, rather than slips of the tongue. Beard (1998: 71) provides a list of these errors, and more can be found in the relevant column of the British magazine *Private Eye*.

All of these **non-fluency phenomena** – false starts, hestitations, replanning, and all kinds of speech errors – occur regularly in everyday conversation. We return briefly to this topic in the discussion of advertising (Chapter 7), in relation to the use of natural-sounding speech in television advertising.

Intonation

Sports commentary can usually be identified by its **intonation**. Even when the words themselves cannot be heard, the fact that the speech is sports commentary: it is discernible even through a closed door. Intonation, or the prosodic 'tune' of language that is perceived by hearers, has a range of components, of which **pitch** and volume are two. All speakers have a natural pitch range, over which the voice rises and falls. If we are angry or excited we may use a higher section of our natural pitch range than we would use when we are calm. Similarly, as the event and the accompanying commentary picks up speed, the commentator both reflects and communicates this excitement by using a higher segment of his natural pitch range, with a marked drop down into the the lower reaches of his pitch range as the race ends and things return to normal. Without even hearing the words, it would be possible to distinguish this characteristic pattern of a sporting event, and even what part of the event was currently taking place, by hearing the 'tune' of the commentary resulting from this pitch range compression into the higher part of the range followed by the re-expansion into the full normal range.

A second notable element of sports commentary 'tune' is the way in which pitch differences in a speaker's voice are used to create pitch contours which give utterances different meanings. These contours operate over what have been termed intonation units, which are units of information that are often roughly equivalent to clauses in length but that could be longer or shorter depending on factors such as speed of speech or position of pauses. While linguists do not always agree on the number of distinctive pitch contours, or **tones**, that exist in English, a sensible system is suggested by Roach (1991), who distinguishes five, described below. I adopt Roach's (1991: 138) notation to indicate each tone:

Fall \no	The 'final' sounding tone, used for making statements or ending a neutral (for example, non-question) utterance. Could answer a friend's question: 'Do you mind if I just use your phone?' 'No.'
Rise /no	Incomplete: an invitation to another speaker to continue. Used for sounding interested. Could answer: 'Did I tell you what happened last night?' 'No.'
Fall-Rise Vno	Roach describes this as 'limited agreement'. Used to indicate uncertainty or concession. Could answer: 'Are you annoyed with me?' 'No' (when there's a sense of 'no, but . . .').

Rise-Fall	Conveys surprise, vehemence, or disapproval.
Λno	Could answer: 'Are those your bacon rinds in the sink?' 'No!'
Level	This can indicate boredom or resignation. Level
-no	tone is also used for 'list-like' utterances: going along a rack looking at unsuitable clothes, for example, and repeating 'no'.

The following short extract of racing commentary features examples of three of these tones: falling, rising, and level. Boundaries of intonation units are indicated by vertical bars; underlining indicates special emphasis:

Itsanothergirl staying on in -<u>four</u> (.)| as they race up towards the \line | it's Boogie Woogie and Tough Guy in a head to \<u>head</u> | and it's time to boogie -<u>woogie</u> | \<u>who</u> goes on to /<u>win</u> | Boogie Woogie   \<u>takes</u> it | Tough Guy is \<u>second</u> (.) Zmile is \<u>third</u> (.) Itsanother girl (.) coming home \<u>fourth</u>

Falling tones appear at the ends of intonation units to mark ends of statements, while a rise on *win* indicates that a continuation is to take place immediately. A sense of climax is provided as the race finishes with the level tone on the name of the winning horse (Boogie Woogie). Tench (1997) identifies level tone as typical of sports commentary: the flat, list-like intonation that people informally identify as synonymous with fast commentary such as that of horse-racing. Tench suggests that in fast, unplanned, and hastily delivered utterances, the commentator has less time to decide on the kind of intonational signalling that needs to be done, leaving level tone as the 'neutral' option. This is perhaps also its function on *four*, at the beginning of the extract. The dramatic fall on *who* indicates the end of the race; after the race is over, falling tones appear at the end of the subsequent intonation units, and the speech slows down.

CLAUSE STRUCTURE

Above, we looked at clauses that feature ellipsis of items, and at some basic ways that sports commentary links clauses together. In this section, we look more closely at some of the features internal to the make-up of clauses. Sports commentary frequently contains clauses that do not contain the basic English structure of subject, verb, and object, adjunct, or complement. Sports commentary uses these non-canonical (i.e. re-ordered) clauses for a range of reasons:

(a)   to achieve particular prominence for some elements, perhaps by placing them at the end of the clause;

(b)   to enable certain types of elements, such as references to actions and locations on the course or pitch, to be placed early on in the clause to allow the viewer to locate them visually;

(c) to give the speaker extra time to identify sports protagonists correctly by name.

Once such clause structure is known as **inversion**. Green (1989: 584) notes that commentary is 'one of the few situations where inversions are used in speech with any appreciable frequency'. In clauses of this kind, the subject **noun phrase** element appears after the verb, rather than in its more usual position before the verb. Of the clauses given below, those on the left are the inversions that appeared in the football and horse-racing commentaries, while those on the right are constructed equivalents that are not inversions. In each case, the subject of the sentence is underlined:

up goes Sheringham	Sheringham goes up
in the middle of the field is Munteanu	Munteanu is in the middle of the field
picking up very well indeed is Boogie Woogie	Boogie Woogie is picking up very well indeed
on the far side is Ho Leng	Ho Leng is on the far side
second horse home is Dazzlin Lady	Dazzlin Lady is [the] second horse home
in the grey colours [is] Diamond Geezer	Diamond Geezer [is] in the grey colours

Ferguson (1983: 161) notes that the verbs which most frequently occur in sports commentary inversions are the verb *to be* and verbs of motion such as *come* and *go*. This is because one of the most obvious functions of inversion in this context is to identify players, riders, or horses by naming their current action (e.g. Boogie Woogie), position (Munteanu, Ho Leng, Dazzlin Lady), direction of motion (Sheringham), or sometimes appearance (Diamond Geezer). Green suggests that one reason for its frequency in commentary is that it allows the commentator time to identify the player, or, in this case, the horse: for example, the commentator may be able to see the horse on the far side gaining ground, and can only subsequently identify it as Ho Leng. While the inversion does have this advantage, another reason for its use may be that it allows the key information – names of players and horses – to be mentioned in the prominent position at the end of the clause: a position that is often reserved for what linguists term new information: information that is intended to be presented as unknown, or perhaps known but prominent in some other way. In this case, there is a fixed number of players and horses, and these are mentioned repeatedly. The commentary regularly switches between them as control of the ball, or position in the race, changes. While the protagonists therefore are not strictly 'new' once they have been mentioned, they are prominent in that they contrast with one another, frequent switching making first one, and then another, salient in the hearer's mind.

In addition to placing names and identities in this focal or prominent position at the clause end, inversion may equally be motivated by the need to place certain elements *first*. First position in the clause is argued by linguists, especially Halliday (e.g. 1985), to contain the **theme** of the clause: the 'starting point' of the clause 'message'. The standard case is when the theme of the clause is its subject, and this is termed **unmarked theme**, as in the example in Table 3.1.

TABLE 3.1   Theme-Rheme Distinction

Adams	came across quickly there
Theme	Rheme

More remarkable, because it requires more processing effort on the part of both the producer and the consumer of the text, is when the theme is something other than the subject. This is termed **marked theme** and is exemplified in Table 3.2.

TABLE 3.2   Marked Theme

on the far side	is Ho Leng there
Theme	Rheme

Textually, these 'starting points', in the case of 3.2 an **adjunct**, are understood to link up with one another to create a strong sense of what the text is really about. In the racing commentary, the presence of many visual themes involving appearance and position, and movement themes describing actions, create a strong sense of the values and starting points of sport: what is thematized is visual action, and it is this that is then used as a basis for identifying protagonists.

Another clause organization that occurs in sports commentary is the *it*-**cleft construction**. This is the first time this construction is mentioned in this book, but it reappears in the discussion of magazine discourse in Chapter 6. *It*-clefts are so called because they seem to 'cleave' in two the information that is presented in the clause. The following are examples from racing and football respectively:

it's Sensori under Darryl Holland who goes on now

and in the end it's (.) Ilie the forward who's back there

Constructed non-cleft alternatives for these are:

Sensori under Darryl Holland goes on now

[In the end] Ilie the forward is back there

What *it*-clefts do is to take a single element in the clause and preface it with *it* plus the verb *to be*, thereby forming an **equative** construction. This construction serves to make the reader or hearer dwell on the first element briefly before further information is attached to it by means of a **relative clause**. In the case above, the *it*-cleft serves to separate out the name of the horse or player (Sensori, Ilie) for the purposes of contrast with others, before saying what it is about them that is remarkable (that he *goes on now*, meaning pulls

ahead in the race, or that he is *back there* where the ball is). Additionally, the
it-cleft presents the information in the relative clause in a special way, as
presupposed: information that is either known by the recipient, or which the
recipient is intended to interpret as knowable. In this case, *[some horse] goes
on now* and *[someone] is back there* is the presupposed information –
information that is arguably knowable from the fact that this is a horse race,
or that the viewers can see some player now has the ball. For more on the
known or knowable element in cleft presuppositions, see Prince (1978) and
Delin (1992). Presupposition is discussed extensively elsewhere in this book,
most thoroughly in relation to magazine features.

Both *it*-clefts and inversions serve to postpone the identification of protagonists. In each case, the name of the player or horse is located on the right-
hand side of the verb. Two similar constructions also begin with *it*, but do not
share the semantics of the *it*-cleft and do not have the following relative-
clause-like element that appears in these constructions. The first type is as
follows:

> and it's Tough Guy (.) pressed by Boogie Woogie
>
> it's Gary Neville (.) for England (.)

Here, the *it* is used as a dummy subject, perhaps to postpone and thereby
draw attention to the name of the player or horse. *It* does not, in this instance,
refer to anything in particular. A second *it* construction, however, does use *it*
as a referring expression (to identify a referent, as described earlier in this
chapter). Here, *it* refers properly to the ball. In the example below, the ball is
referred to by *it* on three occasions:

> it's with (.) Sheringham now (.)
> Anderton's gone into the middle (2 secs)
> it's with Beckham (3 secs)
> it's with Scholes

Beard (1998: 75) suggests another construction that is used to gain time for
the commentator: the **passive** construction, introduced in the discussion of
news reporting in Chapter 2. Here, the reason for its use appears practical,
rather than ideological. The distinction between passive and the corresponding 'ordinary' active clause structure depends on a change in order. The object
of the active clause becomes the subject of the passive, while the subject of the
active clause appears in a 'by' phrase at the end of the clause. The following is
an example of an active/passive pair:

Active:	Hagi and Petrescu	are tracking	him
	Subject	Verb	Object
Passive:	He	is being tracked	by Hagi and Petrescu
	Subject	Verb	Adjunct

The former subject is still the agent (doer) of the action being described, but
not the subject of the clause. The reference to Hagi and Petrescu as doing the

tracking is therefore postponed, and the English player is made to act as theme, the 'starting point' of the clause. Interestingly, passive is one of the constructions singled out by Ochs (1979) as a clause type that does not appear in unplanned speech, since it does require a level of planning and is therefore costly for the speaker to process. However, it may be so well established in sports commentary that speakers in this register have it closer to hand, so to speak, than might be the case in unplanned casual conversation.

SUMMARY

In this chapter, we identified a range of linguistic characteristics that are of interest in sports commentary, both single-speaker and collaborative. Both horse-racing and football commentary contain utterances with a range of different functions, but the backbone of both consists of utterances which narrate the action. **Turn taking** was found to operate on the basis of an unequal distribution of utterance types open to each speaker in a two-party commentary. Some characteristics of the language of commentary have their basis in the fact that sports commentary is fast, spontaneous and **unplanned**, such as **ellipsis** and the use of loose connective links between clauses, and between referents and what is predicated about them. Clause structuring and the use of **non-canonical syntax** suggest that more planning is possible than may meet the eye, and arise out of the need to **thematize** some elements, **presuppose** certain knowledge, and place some elements in focal positions. The special **intonation** of sports commentary arises out of the desire to create excitement, and may exaggerate the systems already in place in the tones available for casual speech.

TOPICS FOR STUDY AND DISCUSSION

1. Make a simple transcription of the commentary of another sport: motor-racing, cricket or ice-skating, for example. What do you notice in common with the kinds of data examined in this chapter? What is different?
2. It was suggested in this chapter that sports commentary, particularly in its narrative parts, uses a very small number of conjunctions (*and, but,* and *as* being the most popular) and little **subordination**. Compare transcribed sports commentary such as the football extract above with a written report on the same match. What co-ordinating and subordinating conjunctions do you find? Further subordinating conjunctions to look for could be *although, because, since, before, though, until, whereas,* and *while*. What differences do you find between the written and spoken language? What can you conclude about the grammatical complexity of each?
3. Using the five kinds of intonational tone described in this chapter, compare an extract of sports commentary with an extract of casual conversation.

You may find it difficult to hear the tones correctly to begin with, and may find it useful for more than one person to code the same piece of transcript independently and then compare answers. Once you have a transcript you agree upon, what features do you find it has in common with the sports commentary? What is different? Are there other aspects of the sound of either, such as speed, rhythm, and so on, that strike you as interesting?

4. Make a comparison between television sports commentary and that on the radio. For this, you may find it particularly useful to consult the analysis of the two **modes** of commentary presented in Beard (1998).
5. Find out what other kinds of speech errors occur in unplanned speech (see, for example, Fromkin, 1973; Garnham, 1985: 207). In your own study of sports commentary, how many of them do you find, and what kinds?
6. Take an example of spoken commentary and identify the themes that are used. Theme is normally the first element of the clause, and what is thematized says a great deal about how the text is organized. What are the predominant themes of motor-racing commentary, for example, or of skating? Do these contrast with those types of commentary presented in this chapter?

FURTHER READING

Whannel (1992) gives a fascinating and seminal account of what happens to sporting events when they are televized, and how events, players, and audiences are transformed in the process. Whannel argues that the two central values of sporting television – realism and entertainment – are always in conflict, and that the overall aim of TV sport is to convey 'maximum action in minimum time'. The extent to which the sport naturally satisfies this aim determines how much 'transformation work' needs to be done by the resources offered by television. Whannel (1992: 26) identifies commentary as the basis for broadcast sport, among the first offerings on BBC radio when it began in 1926. His account of the developing principles for commentary, beginning with early radio through to the television of the present day, is recommended reading.

There is not a great deal written about sports commentary *per se*: much of what is available addresses written texts such as newspaper sports pages. However, Beard (1998) provides a useful basic overview of sports commentary, looking in particular at how commentary differs between radio and TV sports coverage. The book covers a range of linguistic phenomena, with clear descriptions and useful exercises. Ferguson (1983) is a detailed and more linguistically sophisticated description of sports commentary, looking at what features distinguish this kind of talk as a specific and unique register of discourse.

If you are interested in sports language in general, from the representation of sport and its players in speech and writing to sport advertising, written reporting, and pre- and post-event discussion, Beard (1998) is a useful reference, as it ranges from how sporting figures are described to how language is used in both written and spoken sports coverage.

Notions of stereotyping in sports media are addressed in a collection of papers edited by Wenner (1998), which additionally contains papers addressing a wide range of issues such as sexuality, masculinity, national identity, and the creation of heroes through sport on TV and other media. The relationship between sport, nationhood, and representation of sportsmen and women is also addressed by Boyle and Blain (1998). Looking at representation of players based on ethnic group and gender, Messner et al. (1993) compare reporting of men's and women's sports, and the description of black and white players.

Useful references on intonation are Roach (1991) and Cruttenden (1986). A simple summary of the same five-tone system used by Roach and described in this chapter is provided by Jeffries (1998). For a discussion of non-canonical syntactic constructions, see Green (1989) and Halliday (1985). For more on co-ordination and subordination, see Crystal (1996) for a simple introduction, and Quirk et al. (1985) or Hurford (1994) for a thorough description.

NOTE

1 Note the speech error, an anticipation of the 't' sound in *turn: tart to*. Speech errors are dealt with in more detail later in the chapter.

4 The Language of Instructions

Whenever we learn to use a new product or appliance, we are given a set of instructions describing the sometimes complex sequences of actions we need to undertake in order to use and maintain our coffee machine, bicycle, toaster, or computer, or to use the hair colourant, soup mix, paint, or even toothpaste in the correct way. These instructional texts can range from single sentences – 'Make sure all nuts and bolts are tightened after every adjustment'; 'Use a small pea-sized amount for supervized brushing' – through to whole texts contained in leaflets or manuals. For written language, then, there seems to be a fairly intuitive way of deciding what texts count as instructions: we might say that instructions are those texts conventionally accompanying a product or appliance that inform the user how to use, construct, or operate it.

In addition to the conventional definition of instructions as part of the material that falls out of the box when we buy something, there are also expectations about the relationship between instructions and the world. Instructional texts can be distinguished from other texts through the nature of the relationship they have with activities. Instructional texts are primarily concerned with making actions happen, and these take place in the outside world that forms the context in which the text is intended to be read. The text, the product or appliance, and its user (the reader) are involved in a complex and varied interaction: the user looks at the appliance or product for information about its nature and likely function, consults the instructions, and carries out activities in a series of consultative steps, using signals from the product or appliance (did it act as the instructions predicted?) as well as applying their own background knowledge (how do coffee machines usually work? Which kinds of vessels are likely to be good receptacles for water?) throughout the process to ensure it is going smoothly. This close involvement with action, which has clear implications for the way the text is consumed, differentiates instructions from texts that are, say, narrative or simply informative. These may have an effect on the reader's knowledge and understanding, but they do not routinely predict activities and events, and, while reading descriptive or informative text may involve breaks for thinking or doing other things, the context for consumption of the text is not assumed to be one of any specific activity beyond reading and remembering. Instructions, then, are task- or action-orientated.

A third expectation about instructions follows from this, and that is a linguistic one: instructions contain *language* that is conventionally interpreted as requiring action from the reader. Utterances[1] that presuppose or require action can be termed **directives**. In order to see some of the range and nature of directives, consider the following extract from an instruction leaflet accompanying a wok:

> **Preparing and Seasoning Your Wok**
> Before attempting to use the wok, it is important that you clean off the protective coating from inside the bowl. This coating will cause you no harm, but might taint food if not fully removed. Place the wok on a hob and heat gently to soften the coating. Scrub the bowl (a scouring pad is ideal) until all the coating is removed and you have reached bare metal.
>   The bowl should then be washed well and dried. The final drying can be done by placing the wok back on the hob to heat for a minute or two. Now the wok is ready for seasoning.

In this extract, we can see a range of syntactic constructions that convey directive intent more or less strongly. The clearest cases are **imperatives**, repeated below in italics:

> *Place* the wok on the hob . . .
> . . . *heat* gently . . .
> *Scrub* the bowl . . .

These appear to leave the user with little choice about whether to act. However, the overall idea that the wok should be cleaned before use – a goal that needs to be accepted as a good idea before any of the others are attempted — is stated not as an imperative command but as a recommendation, as in the following example:

> Before attempting to use the wok, it is important that you clean off the protective coating from inside the bowl.

To help the reader see why she should adopt this goal, an informative state-ment is used in support of the directive:

> This coating will cause you no harm, but might taint food if not fully removed.

Another directive involves washing and drying the wok afterwards, and is again couched in indirect terms as a statement:

> The bowl should then be washed well and dried.

Note that the indirectness of this statement arises at least partly out of its **passive** form: it does not name who should do the washing and drying as would its **active** counterpart *you should then wash and dry the bowl.* (For a full description of the active-passive distinction, see Chapter 2). Finally, the idea that the wok should be placed back on the hob to dry is stated indirectly as a matter of choice, the use of *can* invoking possibility – that is, that this is one good way of drying the wok, while the user might be able to think of others:

The final drying can be done by placing the wok back on the hob to heat for a minute or two.

Here, not only is the passive form used (*the final drying can be done* rather than *you can do the final drying*), but the necessary action that the user would need to perform is tucked away in a *by* phrase ('by placing . . .'). In this way, the directive is doubly indirect: the goal of drying is presented first, but the action that the user might perform is given in a phrase expressing a means of achieving the goal should it be adopted.

Finally, some directives are designed to prevent or avoid an undesirable action. For example, the following admonitions appear in an instruction leaflet for a telephone:

Do not install your telephone in hot or humid conditions. Do not place your telephone in direct sunlight. Do not spray with aerosol polishes as they may enter the holes in your telephone and cause damage.

Several conclusions regarding instructional text follow from this brief analysis of the written instruction leaflet. First of all, directive utterances may be more or less indirect, ranging from recommendations to commands. Second, not all directive utterances result in action in every case. Some instructions refer to something that should be done only every so often, or in a certain case: note that the whole sequence of actions described in the extract above should only be performed 'before attempting to use the wok', and so would be irrelevant if the wok had already been in use for some time. The recommendation about placing the wok on the hob to dry, moreover, is optional: it could be done another way, should the user prefer. We do not have to insist, therefore, that every utterance we think of as directive *has* to result in an action. Looking at the utterances themselves, it is often impossible to predict which directives will result in compliance on any given reading and which will not. It is more straightforward, then, to characterize directives as having a potential to result in action.

DIRECTIVES IN WRITING

The directives that are used in speech, and those used in writing, tend to be rather different in form. In this section, we will look briefly at the forms that are found in writing, some of which were exemplified in the discussion of the wok leaflet. In a study of more than a thousand directive utterances in written instructions, Murcia-Bielsa (1999) found four main forms of directive. Nearly 80% of examples were imperatives, such as those exemplified earlier. The next most popular forms were **modal verbs**: statements with *should* and *must*, as in the following examples:

The bowl should be washed and dried after use and before storage.
This instruction book must be kept handy for reference.

These formed around 15% of examples. Another 5% were what Murcia-Bielsa terms 'appeals to the reader', which present the benefits of the action to encourage the reader to comply. These are forms such as *we recommend that* and *it is a good idea to*, as in the example below:

It is a good idea to clean the inside of your fridge after defrosting.

A minority of examples, finally, were other kinds of statements, such as the use of the future tense:

The minimum height of the cooker *will be set* at 900mm to the top of the hob.

Present tense and the passive may also be used:[2]

. . . optimum performance *is achieved* by pre-heating the grill for about one minute.

In written instructions, then, imperative forms are in the vast majority. It is worth noting, however, that the remainder, although only around 20% of the cases in Murcia-Bielsa's study, are statements of a range of different kinds. Murcia-Bielsa attributes the choice of the various expressions at least partly to the degree of necessity of the action involved. Directives that are intended as advice or suggestions for best practice, such as *we suggest, we advise, we recommend* (and forms that don't name the agent of the recommendation, such as *it's recommended/advisable*) relate to less necessary actions, while imperatives and expressions with *should, must, have to,* and *need*, for example, specify more necessary actions.

SPOKEN DIRECTIVES

Ervin-Tripp (1976) has looked at directives in conversation, and found forms rather different from those in writing, although the two sets of forms overlap. Ervin-Tripp (1976: 29) suggests the following set of directive types, based on a range of spoken contexts (from family conversations to interactions in shops, classrooms, and, most extremely, a US Marine Corps recruiting depot). Her categories are named below on the left, with her examples on the right:

Need statements	*I need a match.*
Imperatives	*Gimme a match.*
Embedded imperatives	*Could you gimme a match?*[3]
Permission directives	*May I have a match?*
Question directives	*Gotta match?*
Hints	*The matches are all gone.*

It is interesting to note, first of all, that the range of forms identified by Ervin-Tripp contain many more question forms than are found in the written instructions examined by Murcia-Bielsa. However, Tsui (1994) points out that Ervin-Tripp's spoken directives do not include a range of other forms, such as threats (by which the speaker threatens, either explicitly, or implicitly, to do something to the detriment of the hearer if he or she does not comply) and warnings (by which the speaker indicates some other undesirable consequence). These negative directives are not explicitly catered for in Ervin-Tripp's framework, but many of them can be included within her grammatical descriptions: warnings and threats, for example, could be accomplished by the use of an imperative (*don't touch that, it's hot* as a warning; *pick up your coat or I'll spank you* as a threat, to use Tsui's own examples) or a hint (*that kettle's close to the edge*, as a warning; *noisy boys don't get ice-cream*, as a threat).

DIRECTIVES, AUTHORITY, AND SOCIAL RELATIONS

So far, we have looked at directive utterances with a range of grammatical forms used, from imperatives to simple statements. How is it decided which form to use when? First of all, it is easy to assume a simple link between 'straightforward' forms, such as imperatives, and greater politeness. We can see straightaway, though, that such an association is not reliable.

In spoken discourse, we might expect imperatives to appear in cases where directness or even rudeness is desired, such as in the discourse of sergeants to drill recruits in the mid-1970s[4] (as in the first example below); we can also expect to find it in the language of intimates, as in the second:

Now get out, get out. Bring me more coffee cups.

A: [to friend B, after lending her a book]
Just put it back on my desk when you've finished with it.

We cannot straightforwardly say, then, that imperatives are necessarily 'rude'. Being indirect, too, has a range of functions. It can be used to assert authority while maintaining the appearance of politeness, as in the following example:

It would be preferable if you were to hand in your work on time.

Indirectness can also be used to offer the recipient more options: the utterance given below, for example, can be interpreted either as a directive, or as a genuine request for information about workload:

Do you think you can get that finished by five?

Indirect forms of expression, because they weaken the relationship between the speaker and the content of the request, and allow (at least on the surface) more options for the addressee, can be described as **mitigated**. Mitigation was referred to earlier in this book in relation to news reporting. Using mitigated directives, the intention of getting another person to act is achieved implicitly, leaving the hearer to infer the relationship between the directive utterance and what is actually intended. These forms include questions, which often focus on the possibility or necessity of doing something and can therefore be interpreted as requests for information rather than for action:

[To hotel receptionist]
Do you have a double room available for this coming Saturday?

[To secretary]
Are the essay questions out yet?

[To partner]
Is there any more of that cake left?

Questions like these fall into Ervin-Tripp's (1976) category of *question directive*. Ervin-Tripp's category of *hints* is another indirect form. This category consists of directives which are presented as statements. These are, she argues, easy for hearers to ignore and therefore the most 'open' form of directive in terms of giving options to the hearer (Ervin-Tripp, 1976: 42). Further examples of such hints are as follows:

[Student to tutor, asking for help]
Example C2 was the most difficult.

[To friend, standing in the way of TV]
You make a better door than a window.

[Secretary to other staff members]
There seem to be a lot of bodies in this office.

The form of expression, then, can leave the hearer's options more, or less, open, and are therefore perceived as more or less polite.

Two further factors are central to the choice of directive expression: *authority* and *perceived benefit* in doing the action. To take **authority** first, if a speaker has authority over a hearer, choice of expression can be less mitigated: even the most indirect forms from a superior to an inferior may be interpreted as commands. Direct forms may be chosen by the superior when time pressure exists, for example, or if he or she decides that it is worthwhile to draw attention to the authority relation. If no authority relation exists, however, such as between friends, the choice of a direct form may be interpreted as impolite. However, Ross (1968) and Tsui (1994) among others distinguish a second factor that is relevant here: that of who is perceived to benefit if the action is performed. Ross suggests that personal directives (i.e. those with a clearly defined recipient and producer) can be either **speaker-interested** or **hearer-interested**, depending on who benefits by the hearer performing the action. If the benefit lies with the hearer, a more direct form will not be interpreted as impolite, regardless of authority relations: the hearer will know they are doing something in their own interests. If the benefit lies with the speaker, however, authoritative speakers may choose to invoke their authority by using a direct form. In cases where either no

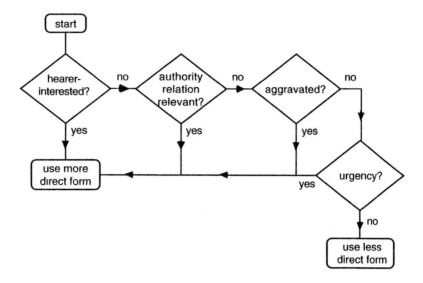

FIGURE 4.1   Factors in Choosing More or Less Mitigated Directives

authority relation exists, or if an authoritative speaker has decided for some reason not to invoke or even to play down the authority mismatch between speaker and hearer, a more persuasive or explanatory approach will need to be adopted, perhaps eliciting the hearer's sympathy ('I can't reach those; can you get them down for me?') or explaining why the action should be performed. Finally, any speaker may choose to use a direct form if they wish to aggravate (it need not always be assumed that a speaker intends to be polite), or if there is some urgency involved in the directive, such as lack of time, or the presence of danger.

The speaker options relating to speaker/hearer interest, authority, aggravation, time constraint, and use of more or less direct forms are summarized in the flowchart in Figure 4.1.

The issues touched on so far have much in common with the broader issue of politeness and how we gauge certain forms as more or less polite. Basic to the notion of politeness as it has been studied in linguistics and anthropology is the idea that humans routinely perform speech acts that threaten one another's **face**. According to Brown and Levinson (1987: 61), who have done pioneering work on politeness, there are two kinds of **face wants** that need to be attended to in conversation:

1   **positive face**: the positive consistent self-image or 'personality' (crucially including the desire that this self-image be appreciated and approved of) claimed by interactants; and
2   **negative face**:   the basic claim to territories, personal preserves, right to non-distraction – i.e. to freedom of action and freedom from imposition.

In other words, speakers want to feel that they are valued, and that they will not be imposed upon. Preserving this positive and negative face is something they expect other speakers to help them to do, and something they assume that they will do for others. It is easy to see how a directive speech act – i.e. one that requires someone to do something – is a potential threat to negative face. The choice of indirect forms goes some way towards redressing this face threat, since indirect forms appear to allow the addressee some choice. The speaker may choose not to redress the threat, however, either because they are in authority, or because of urgency, or because they actively wish to aggravate the hearer. The possibility that aggravation could be a part of the speaker's wishes has been built into the general framework describing politeness by Turner (1996); readers are referred to that paper for a succinct and very thorough overview and critique of the theory of politeness.

The points made so far about choice of directive and the social relations that are presupposed by these choices can be used in an examination of what Fairclough (1989: 39) terms **subject positioning**: the placing of the reader or hearer in a particular relationship with the text and its producer through the implicit assumptions about his or her beliefs and wishes that the text communicates. This idea relates to research on the ideological function of language referred to in relation to news reporting in Chapter 2. For example, we know that more direct forms are often used if the action is to the benefit of the reader or hearer. Direct forms can then be used to *create the suggestion* that the action is hearer-interested, as is frequently done in advertising, or in the fashion, home, diet, or make-up features in women's magazines:

(19) Reveal your hair's true potential.
      [Shampoo advert]
(20) Simply file all your nails to the same length and apply one coat of a pale shade with a little shine.
      [Beauty tips feature]

Since direct forms also convey authority, there is an interesting ambiguity here that perhaps serves advertisers' purposes well. In the case of instructions, these factors are also relevant: it is worth considering in any given case what kind of relationship is being created and reinforced by the use of particular directive forms, using the flowchart presented in Figure 4.1. The creating and reinforcing of personal relationships can be referred to in general as the **tenor** of the text or discourse, and this may change as the discourse or text progresses. Tenor is one element of the three-part description of register introduced by the linguist Michael Halliday described in more detail in Chapter 1.

Although the presence of directive utterances is an important feature of instructions, not all the utterances in instructional discourse are directive. Many discourses which we intuitively think of as instructional contain utterances that serve a range of other purposes, from supplying information that may or may not be in direct support of a directive, to congratulating you on your purchase, or describing the legal situation relating to guarantee and your and the manufacturing company's rights if something goes wrong. For example, in an instructional context such as an aerobics class, the instructor will not only issue clear directives (*Up. Now four singles.*), but will also teach the class to perform new sequences of actions without requiring the actions at the time of utterance (*Okay, we're going to do four of these, and then four single leg lifts*), chat to them (*Are we warmed up yet?*) and praise them on their progress (*Great, you've worked really hard*). These different utterance functions are often referred to as speech act types, capturing the fact that language is used to perform certain acts in the world. To accommodate this range of speech acts within the intuitive notion of what is 'instructional', we cannot simply expect the discourse to be composed purely of directives: indeed, it is hard to find such texts.

Let us turn now to two examples of instructions at work: one written, one spoken, illustrating the application and use of the concepts introduced so far in these two different contexts, and examining some other aspects of written and spoken instructions.

A WRITTEN EXAMPLE: THE INSTRUCTION LEAFLET

In this section, we will look closely at the language and general organization of a written set of instructions for a home hair colourant: Clairol's 'Natural Instincts'. The instructions cover the equivalent of two sides of A4 paper, with a pair of plastic gloves attached to the reverse side. The fact that the instructions come tucked inside the box indicates that they are for use by someone who is committed to using the product, rather than serving as a means of attracting a purchase.

As with most sets of written instructions, the Clairol leaflet is not a homogeneous, unbroken block of text. Not only does it include pictures, diagrams, and graphical devices such as variations in typeface, lines, and boxes, but the segments of text themselves are set off from one another by white space, bulleted displays, and headings. For example, at the top of the page there is an illustration of the colourant box and contents, and some text that advertises the product, emphasizing its naturalness and speed of use. The page heading is reproduced in Figure 4.2.

This part of the instruction leaflet, then, is not devoted to telling the reader how to use the product. Instead, it overlaps substantially in form and content with the language of advertising. It identifies the product by means of a distinctive logo, introducing the leaf motif that appears throughout the instructions to reinforce the message that the product is *natural* – one of the most popular current advertising themes. In fact, the header contains the word *natural* no less than six times. It also stresses the innovative nature of the product – *the first conditioning colourant with natural ingredients* – its 'unique' nature, and its speed of use, novelty and speed being highly valued by modern consumers. In going into detail about the ingredients, it uses scientific-sounding terms (*Botanicolour complexes, plant-derived conditioners*) to imply a scientific basis for its formulation – another important cultural value frequently invoked in advertising. The function of the heading, then, is what Fairclough (1989: 202ff.), in his discussion of advertising discourse, terms building the image of the product: building up the product in the esteem of the reader. In addition, however, this piece of text also serves to build relations

Clairol Natural Instincts is the first conditioning colourant with natural ingredients.

Conditioning colour with natural ingredients - Unique Botanicolor Complexes with Aloe, Jojoba, Ginseng and plant derived conditioners A hair colour that is so gentle it actually leaves your hair better conditioned than before you coloured it.

So gentle and works in 10 minutes - Natural Instincts works in just 10 minutes.
To ensure you get the best results with Natural Instincts, please read the instructions carefully.

FIGURE 4.2   Clairol Natural Instincts: Header

between the product and its consumer, mentioning *your hair* and *you* in its description of its gentleness and conditioning ability. An alternative phrasing of the text of this section, *actually leaves hair better conditioned than before it was coloured*, would have been less effective, since it fails to specify the relationship between the user as a person and the product. We will discuss the building of products, consumers, and the relations between them further in Chapter 7, where advertising is dealt with in detail.

Beneath this heading are four blocks of text, each set off from one another by a heading and the small graphic of leaves, and each containing a bulleted display. One of these, 'Important information', appears in Figure 4.3.

'Important information' consists primarily of directives, predominantly negative. Many of these could be characterized as warnings, since it is either explicit or implicit that failure to comply could result in injury to the user or wasting the product. Most are direct imperatives, but two are indirect: *Natural Instincts is not recommended . . .* and *Natural Instincts should not be used for . . .* (rather than *do not use for . . .*). A second box, 'Helpful Hints' (Figure 4.4), contains positive directives: it is understood that compliance here will result in success, but that non-compliance will not result in injury.

As we noted above, it is quite possible to phrase positive directives negatively (for example, *always protect clothes . . .* could equally be phrased *do not allow the mixture to come into contact with clothes*) and vice versa. The preponderance of negative directives in one section, and positive directives in the other, however, highlights the difference between important warnings and positive advice for good results.

The piece of text that forms the focal point for the reader — how to actually apply the product in full use — appears in the centre of the page, and is boxed (Figure 4.5). This is picked out using colour, headings, and a box, and contains pictures summarizing the activities to be carried out step-by-step. 'Full head application' and 'Re-touch application' represent alternative plans, although it is clear that full head application is expected to be the norm. In contrast with the text elsewhere in the instructions, the language in this section tends towards the **telegraphic**: for example, omitted articles such as *the* in *work evenly through hair* (rather than *the hair*), *pull up tab to remove tip* (not *the tab, the tip*). This is presumably done in the interests of

IMPORTANT INFORMATION

- Never use on eyelashes and eyebrows. Rinse eyes immediately with water if product comes into contact with them. If any irritation persists seek medical advice.
- Never use hair colourant if scalp is irritated, sore or has any cuts, abrasions etc.
- Use the colourant mixture immediately after mixing.
- Natural Instincts is not recommended for **darkening** bleached, highlighted or hair tinted to pale blonde. Natural Instincts should not be used on hair treated with colour restorers or henna
- If you select a shade darker than your natural colour, the colour will not wash out in 24 shampoos.
- KEEP OUT OF REACH OF CHILDREN

FIGURE 4.3   Important Information

HELPFUL HINTS

BEFORE YOU BEGIN

- Always protect clothes, fabric and furnishings during the colour process.
- Wear the plastic gloves throughout the entire application.
- Natural Instincts is applied to damp hair so if your hair has a build-up of styling aids, shampoo and towel off excess water before colouring.
- Natural Instincts can be applied the same day as a perm.

FIGURE 4.4   Helpful Hints

succinctness: it is likely that the user will refer to this section while actually using the product, and will not have time, with her hair covered in colourant and while timing the application, to scan through very much text to find what she needs. Care is taken in the 'Re-touch application' section to refer the reader visually as well as textually to the appropriate parts of the 'Full head application' text, where information is shared between the two: 'Prepare' and 'Rinse & Condition' are rendered in the same distinctive coloured type, achieving visual cohesion (linking) between the sections and guiding the reader to the right information.

We can see, then, that the text falls into different functional sections: the ones reproduced here are (broadly) an advertising statement/praise of the product, warnings, additional advice, and step-by-step instructions for use. But how general are these categories for instructional leaflets and manuals? Are they exhaustive of the content of instructions?

While noting that different sets of instructions may be very different from one another, Ciliberti (1990: 300) suggests that an organizing framework for instructions (she is talking about appliances, but the ideas are still applicable here) would include at least four elements:

1   Identification of the machine;
2   Description of the parts and/or functions;

EASY APPLICATION

FULL HEAD APPLICATION

Ideal for first time users of hair colour or if there is no colour remaining from a previous application.

1. PREPARE

Dampen hair thoroughly and gently towel dry. Put on plastic gloves. Empty contents of hair colourant into the developing lotion and replace nozzle. Shake well. Pull tab to remove tip. **Apply colour mixture straight away.**

2. APPLY

Apply mixture to damp hair. Work thoroughly through hair to ensure even distribution.
Pile hair loosely on top of head. If any colour gets onto your skin, simply wipe it off with a damp tissue.

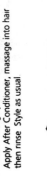

3. TIME

Leave colour on for 10 minutes or the time indicated by strand test. For porous or recently permed hair wait only 7–8 minutes. For increased coverage of resistant grey leave colour on longer. **Discard any unused mixture immediately.**

4. RINSE & CONDITION

Add a little warm water to hair and work into a lather gently massaging hairline and scalp. Rinse thoroughly until water runs clear. Apply After Conditioner, massage into hair then rinse. Style as usual.

RE-TOUCH APPLICATION

Application for coloured hair where your hair still retains colour from a previous application.

- PREPARE product as noted in section 1 above. Part hair into 4 sections. Starting with one section, use applicator tip to make 1 cm partings and apply colour only to new growth at the roots. Continue section by section until all root hair has been covered with colour mixture and leave colour on for 5 minutes or time indicated by strand test. Then work remaining colour through ends of hair. Leave for a further 5 minutes, for porous or permed hair leave for 3 minutes.

- For resistant grey hair leave colour on new growth for 10 minutes and then work through to ends for a further 5 minutes. **Discard any unused mixture immediately.**

- For RINSE & CONDITION instructions, please see Section 4.

FIGURE 4.5   Instructions for Application

3 Instructions for use; and
4 Technical characteristics.

She notes, however, that these different functions would not necessarily be fulfilled by separate sections of text: much instructional text combines and mixes the various functions. Even if we were to apply the textual sub-functions suggested, with suitable alterations to deal with the fact that we are analyzing the instructions for a product rather than a machine, we find that not all of the elements are present in the Clairol leaflet. In fact, some categories appear in need of further sub-division to capture the different kinds of language present within them.

Identification of product	Elements of the page header, and repeated references to the product throughout the text, serve to identify it.
Description of parts and/ or functions	The picture at the top of the page shows the product's box, the two bottles, and the sachet, but no text exists with the sole purpose of informing the user what will be in the box. The first mention of the different items occurs in the instructions for use (Figure 4.5), in the sentence *Empty contents of hair colourant into the developing lotion and replace nozzle.*
Instructing the user	Apart from the main 'instructions for use' reproduced in Figure 4.5, other parts of the instructions contain information requiring actions on the part of the user: we can also include 'important information' (Figure 4.3) in this category. In addition, the user is advised to do both a *sensitivity test* and a *strand test* 48 hours before using the product, to test for allergic reaction and for the timing required to get the right colour respectively. Each test has a separate instructional section. There is also an instructional section headed 'helpful hints before you begin', and a guide to selecting hair colourants from the whole range of Clairol products. Finally, a box gives details of how to contact the makers for advice.

There is no identifiable text describing 'technical characteristics', which are perhaps more frequently present in machine rather than product instructions.

A framework for describing instructions in general will require several additional categories for textual function beyond Ciliberti's suggested four. Not all of these will appear in every instructional text:

• Warnings and hints (as in 'Important Information')
• Advertising description (as in the Clairol page header)
• Product range information
• Trademark/legal information

- Manufacturer contact information/advice line number
- Tutorial element
- Care, cleaning, and repair

I have differentiated 'warnings and hints' from 'instructions for use' because the former are frequently composed of single statements or directives, and are not textually or sequentially related to one another. The main 'instructions for use' sections are almost invariably organized step-by-step, uniting the whole text into a time sequence. For items that are to be used more than once (equipment rather than products) we would also expect to find advice on maintaining the equipment in good order. Finally, some complex items – software, for example – require a tutorial element in the instructions that enables the user to try a practice run to become familiar with the product before proper use. These tutorial elements constitute a recognizably different 'sub-text' of instructions, and will not be considered further in this chapter.

As Ciliberti points out, it is not always possible to predict from a particular section of the instructional manual or leaflet what kind of language will occur within it. Indeed, there is significant overlap between the forms we expect to find, say, in a 'warnings' section and in an 'instructions for use' section. For example, the Clairol leaflet's 'Important Information' in Figure 4.3 could be categorized as a warnings section. Many of the warnings consist of negative directives phrased in imperative form, but some are positive directives (*Keep out of reach of children*; *Rinse eyes immediately* . . . and so on). Positive directives are, of course, a common feature of the 'instructions for use' section: *Dampen hair thoroughly and gently towel dry*; *Pile hair loosely on top of head*; *Style as usual*. In fact, there is often little to choose between a positive and a negative phrasing of essentially the same directive intention: *Keep out of reach of children*, for example, could be rendered as *Do not allow children to tamper or play with this product*. Interestingly, nearly all the directives in the Clairol leaflet, in every section, are imperatives, despite the wider range of directive forms available in the written instructions that were discussed above. This may be done for a range of reasons, as we have seen: because the actions are hearer-interested (the user wants to colour her hair correctly, safely, and without mess), and because the interpersonal relationship between instruction-giver and instruction-receiver is assumed at the outset to be one in which the knowledge of the instructor gives him or her authority. Many of them, however, are backed up with informative **purpose expressions**. These are expressions that tell the reader *why* a certain act must be performed – i.e. its purpose. In the following examples, the purpose expressions are italicized:

> *To ensure you get the best results with Natural Instincts*, please read instructions carefully.
>
> Work thoroughly through hair to *ensure even distribution*.
>
> *For Rinse and Condition instructions*, please see section 4.

These expressions are frequently attached to directives, and serve to inform the reader not only why but also sometimes how to do the required action.

With this knowledge, the reader is less likely to miss out the step through not realizing its purpose, or to perform the action incorrectly. Giving the user this information is also respecting her intelligence, acknowledging the possibility of non-compliance and therefore paying attention to the reader's negative face – her right to disobey if she feels like it. In addition, supporting information contained in purpose expressions makes explicit that the action is to the reader's benefit, and therefore retains her goodwill, ensuring that she does not interpret the forms chosen for directives as rude or aggravated.

A SPOKEN EXAMPLE: THE STEP AEROBICS WORKOUT

In this section, we will turn to a spoken set of instructions: the instructions given verbally by an aerobics instructor to a step aerobics class. Step aerobics is a means of improving fitness by moving to music, stepping on and off a low bench in a range of different ways, building up different activities in time to music. This situation fulfils the criteria set out at the beginning for an instructional text or discourse in that it is primarily action- or task-orientated: in conjunction with gestures and music, it determines the activities of the class in an obvious and observable way. Perhaps strangely, the class is not expected to speak or respond except in very constrained circumstances, so the language of the workout is composed almost entirely of the instructor's monologue. As we will see, this monologue serves to position the workout participants, both in the literal sense of moving them around the room, but also in the ideological sense of subject positioning, where beliefs about their behaviour and aspirations are communicated implicitly.

What follows is a transcription of part of a class recorded at a University Sports Centre. It is taken from the very beginning of the class, when the participants are warming up:

i	okay here we go
ii	legs slightly apart
iii	bend on those knees
iv	tuck under
v	and lift the heel
vi	now lift the shoulders
vii	push forward with the arm
viii	another four, three, two
ix	now overhead
x	another four, three, two
xi	forward for four
xii	overhead
xiii	both arms forward
xiv	overhead
xv	single side step
xvi	four, three, two
xvii	now downward row

```
                  4
        _____
        1   2   3   4
           another four


            1           2           3           4
        _____   _____   _____   _____
        1   2   3   4  1  2  3  4  1  2  3  4  1  2  3  4
           for three     for two      last now squeeze
                                      one upward
                                            row

                1
        _____
        1   2   3   4
        up
```

directive

FIGURE 4.6 Workout Transcription Showing Utterances in Relation to Music Beats and Action Repetitions

Once again, directives are central to the activity underway, although, as we shall see, they are not the only kind of utterance produced by the instructor. However many times an action is to be repeated – note, for example, the instructor directs that an action should be done four times in *forward for four* above – the participants will be waiting for a new directive by the time the last repetition of the current activity is nearly finished. Because the activity is performed to beats of music, directives will appear on certain counts. Timing, then, helps them to work out which of the many utterances that the instructor produces is to be interpreted as a directive. In the example above, utterances ii, iii, iv, v, vi, vii, ix, xi, xiii, xv, and xvii are directives: the others fall into different categories of utterance, as will be explained below.

In Figure 4.6 we can see part of the University workout transcribed according to the beat and repetition patterns of the current activity. There are two directives in the short extract, which shows a four-beat activity that has to be performed four times. Note that the directives *another four* and *now upward row*, in bold, occur in the final four before a change of action. It is only when the data is transcribed in this way that the close relationship between beat pattern and interpretation can be appreciated. Placement of utterances is crucial to correct interpretation in this kind of discourse, and only a few other situations share the systematic use of timing as a means of interpreting what utterances actually mean.

The directives used by the instructor in the aerobics workouts examined for this study (reported in Delin, 1998), although spoken, do not look quite like those found in casual conversation. Workout directives are very brief and succinct, consisting of imperatives such as *tap and change* and *now upward row*, for example. Many directives, however, don't even include a verb, referring instead just to the direction of the action (*to the centre, and front*) or its description and count (*side for two*) or just a count (*four more*). Some are just noun phrases that name actions: *single side step*, and *grapevine*. Comparing these to the kinds of directives that Ervin-Tripp finds in casual conversation and in the workplace, we find much less variation in verb forms in the workout: there are no modal verbs (*could, would, will,* for example), and none of the directives is phrased as a question, which is very common in speech. In other words, we find none of the mitigation that we find in indirect directives used in conversation – that is, no real attempt to be polite by providing redress of the negative face threat that inheres in telling people what to do. Workout participants, however, do not appear to be offended by the use of these very direct forms. If we look again at the flowchart for choosing directives given in Figure 4.1, we can see why. First of all, workout participants come to the class expecting that the actions they will be asked to perform will be for their own benefit. The directives issued by the instructor, like those in the written instructions for hair colourant, are assumed to be hearer interested. Second, the participants respect the expertise and the authority of the instructor – and this authority relation is therefore relevant to the situation, leading to the selection of more direct forms. Finally, and this time distinctly from written instructions, directives must be given in a very short time, due to the constraints of the activities, the beats of the music, and the other things that the instructor has to say. Her directives are therefore urgent. There are three reasons, then, to choose more rather than less direct forms, and the participants do not therefore expect the mitigated or polite forms that might be forthcoming in spoken interactions, even between the same people, in another situation.

Although it seems that most of the time the class are simply told what to do, there is some scope for individual choice and optionality in some of the actions (although strong peer pressure to keep going remains). Some directives still feature an imperative, but mitigate it with an *if* clause, detailing circumstances in which participants might want to act:

> don't forget you don't have to do the hop if you don't want
>
> if you're getting tired go back to the basic repeater
>
> take a drink if you need to

A second group uses *can* to indicate optional 'downgrading' of exertion that the participants are permitted:

> now remember, you can stay doing these
> I'm going to add to this with a hop
> you can join in or carry on as you are
> don't feel you have to join in
> keep doing the basic repeater if you'd rather

The opportunities the instructor has to offer options on whether to act are limited, however. Because the directives that carry the most face threat must be brief and cannot be mitigated, this is compensated for elsewhere in the monologue. First, the instructor tries to maintain closeness through positive comments such as those in the examples below:

> this is very good
> well done
> you're really co-ordinated today, s'good

The instructor also uses a marker of elicitation such as 'yes?' to maintain rapport with their class in checking their understanding of teaching points in which new sequences of moves have been taught:

> easy peasy, yes?
>
> remember you go out for three
> then go down, yes?
>
> do we remember our repeaters, yes?
>
> we're gonna do a knee lift hamstring curl side out and over so it's one of each, yes?

In fact, all the examples above can be explained in terms of Brown and Levinson's (1987: 108) politeness theory as strategies for performing **positive face** redress. The specific strategy at work here is that of 'claiming common ground': invoking shared knowledge and experience with the interlocutor. While no real two-way interaction is possible in the context of the workout, the instructor's 'yes?' still serves the purpose that an attentive interlocutor might hope to achieve: that of noticing or 'attending to the hearer' (cf. Brown and Levinson, 1987). The latter two examples above also display evidence of another strategy: Brown and Levinson's strategy to 'include both Speaker and Hearer in the activity'. The use of *we* emphasizes shared activity; another strategy for achieving this is the use of *let's* . . . in directives, as in the following example:

> (31) let's take the arms right through a chest press
>
>   let's hold it for a back stretch in the middle

So, instead of providing redress to negative face by using indirect directives and giving many options regarding compliance, aerobics instructors provide redress to positive face: they praise their classes, tell them that they're doing well, and use methods of making them feel included in the activity.

We have seen some evidence so far that not all the utterances in the aerobics workout are directive. Of the 877 utterances, 43% served other functions. Apart from directives, four other categories of utterance appeared. In the short extract given earlier the utterances *for three*, *for two* serve not to direct participants to what to do next, but instead they **narrate** what should be happening right now. Instead of falling on the beat prior to the action and therefore working as a cue, as directives do, they count down the first beat of each action. They therefore appear too late to work as directives, even though they are similar in form. Another group of utterances serve to signal the exact beat before a change in action is to take place (an example is *squeeze* in the extract above), while still another has the function of teaching participants how to do a new move or how to modify the current one to make it correct (*we're gonna do a basic up tap down tap to the side* is an example of a teaching utterance from elsewhere in the workout, while *too fast, keep with me* acts as a correction). Finally, just over 5% of utterances are comments on other aspects of the class, many of them encouraging: *that's it, that's good, keep it up*, etc. Workout instructions, therefore, just like the written instructions we examined earlier, contain a range of utterances with different functions.

Moving on from the structure and function of specific utterances, we can look at the nature of the workout discourse as a whole. In the discussion of written instructions, we saw that the text of instructional leaflets and documents can be divided into several different textual subtypes. Is this also true of the workout monologues? The answer is yes, although not to the same extent. First of all, the instructor has to begin and end the workout. She opens the class by switching on the music, and saying *Okay, here we go*. 'Okay' is a very common resumptive **discourse marker**, one of a set of elements that serves as a signpost, showing that the speaker is drawing attention to something about the structure of the discourse. The instructor uses 'okay' every time she finishes changing the music, for example, and wants to resume the class. She ends the class by praising the participants:

well done
you've worked really hard this week
we're getting fit

The workout activity is itself divided into several sections: a warm-up, an aerobic stepping section, a section in which the class works on specific muscle groups, and a cool-down stretching section. While these different sections do not give rise to a great deal of difference in the language involved, clear sections can be seen within them, signalled by a change of the positioning of the class, a change in the equipment they are using, and/or a change in music and pace. For example, to end the fast aerobic section of the exercise, the instructor uses the following:

last one
and march
well done

Then, to begin the cooling down section immediately afterwards, she re-orientates them and introduces them to a slower-paced activity by marching on the spot:

come to the end of that step
march on the top for four
march on the floor for four
here we go

In a step aerobics class on video, produced by Reebok for use at home, the opening section is rather different, consisting of a very long teaching interlude in which the basics of step aerobics are explained, and a method of measuring heart-rate is introduced. Throughout the workout, heart-rate measuring occurs several times, each time using an identical stretch of discourse:

OK, now it's time to take your heart rate. Find your pulse, either on your wrist, or the side of your neck. Ready? Count. Stop. Check the chart on your screen.

Find your age, and follow it over to the column where you'll see your target heart rate range. Make sure you fall into that heart rate range before you rejoin the program.

This section is markedly different from the rest of the workout, which consists of the short, timed utterances as described above. In particular, utterances which are not time-critical will be uttered at normal speed, rhythm, and pitch, which is not the case for timed utterances in the main body of the workout.

We can consider the aerobics workout as an interesting context for the study of participant positioning in terms of the assumptions, beliefs, and behaviour that class members are expected to comply with. As aerobics-goers will know, attendance at a class is often confusing in the early stages, and novices stand out from experts in that they are often lost, overtired, or late in performing the exercises. One important skill that must be learnt is to interpret the workout utterances correctly, distinguishing, for example, which utterances are intended as directives and which are narrative. The key to this lies in keeping track of the activities and musical beats, since it is often the positioning of an utterance in relation to the music that determines whether it counts as a directive or simply a comment. A second task is to become familiar with the field-specific vocabulary of the workout: terms such as *side out*, *grapevine*, *chest press*, and *bow and arrow*, for example. As well as these skills, participants are expected to be silent and compliant, and to willingly accept being told how to act for an hour at a time. This dedication rests on the assumption that the participant will benefit from the activity, and that there is a shared belief that the instructor has the skill and authority to ensure this benefit.

SUMMARY

In this chapter, we have looked at some of the important features of written and spoken instructions. After a discussion of which texts and discourses count as instructions, we focused on the importance of one class of speech act, **directives**, as central to accomplishing the **action-orientated** nature of instructional discourse. After an overview of some research on directives in both spoken and written language, the chapter examined some of the range of syntactic forms that directives can take, and presented a flowchart, taking into account **hearer-benefit** in performing the required actions, **authority**, **urgency**, and the possibility of the **intention to aggravate** in choosing a more or less direct form of directive. This framework was also linked to a more general theory of language choice based on Brown and Levinson's politeness theory. In two studies, a written set of instructions for Clairol Hair Colourant and a spoken monologue from a step aerobics workout, we examined not only choice of directives but some other characteristics of written and spoken instructions, including non-directive utterances, the overall structure of the respective discourses and their component parts, and the assumptions about the social positioning of the reader or hearer that are conveyed in each case.

TOPICS FOR STUDY AND DISCUSSION

1. Test out Ciliberti's framework for the description of various sections of instructional text, given above, by collecting some of your own examples. Are her categories easy to apply? Do you need to make alterations? What kinds of language – particularly directives – do you find in the various instruction manuals? Do you note particularly different styles between different companies or products?
2. As we have seen, directives are an important indicator of social and institutional relationships. Many, or perhaps most, conversational language contains directives of some kind. An interesting project would involve examining directives in an institutional context (see Chapter 8 for project ideas). For a short assignment or seminar exercise, you could examine and describe the directives found in a conversation between a couple, a parent–child interaction, in a TV soap, classroom or tutorial interaction. Written contexts in which directives are frequent include magazine advertising. What directives do you find? What patterns do they fall into? What are the social relationships and positioning of the reader/hearer, instructor, and any product involved?
3. Select a context in which instructions are given that are hearer-interested, and then try to find one in which they are not. What is the difference in forms? Suggestions for data likely to include non-hearer-interested directives include television crime drama, some interactions between parents and children, and people speaking to dogs!

FURTHER READING

Very little overview material exists on the description of instructional texts, written or spoken, although several studies specifically about directives exist (see below). However, Ciliberti (1990) is a useful paper that summarizes aspects of instructional language. There is a great deal written about the evaluation of instructions, particularly written ones, and how they should be arranged on the page, phrased, and so on. These studies are not normally linguistic in nature, and attempt to make recommendations about good and bad written instructions. For those interested in this perspective, a good place to start is Hartley (1985). For reading on politeness, readers are referred to the most accessible version of Brown and Levinson's work: Brown and Levinson (1987). Wardhaugh (1998, Chapter 11) provides a useful basic overview of work on politeness. A very useful description and critique of a wide range of politeness research, including an extension of Brown and Levinson's model to include situations in which impoliteness is intended, is given by Turner (1996). Amy Tsui's description of directives in speech, which differs somewhat from the definition used in this chapter, is nevertheless clearly set out and a useful alternative framework to apply to spoken texts:

see Tsui (1994, Chapter 6). Readers are also referred to Ervin-Tripp's (1976) accessible paper, which gives examples of spoken directives in a range of contexts. Finally, Butler (1988) discusses the use of modal verbs in directives.

NOTES

1 Things that people say or write are often referred to in linguistics as utterances: this is because they aren't always a single or complete sentence (so can't be called 'sentences'), and a term is needed that works for both speech and writing (it is strange to think of speech as occurring in sentences, as a glance at the transcription of sports commentary in Chapter 3 will confirm).

2 Murcia-Bielsa's examples.

3 This category is so called because the clause contains an imperative – in this case, *gimme a match* – but this imperative is contained (or embedded) within a surrounding question.

4 This data is taken from Ervin-Tripp (1976: 35).

5 The Language of Interviews

The kinds of interaction that we call 'interviews' occur in a wide range of settings, and have a variety of functions. In a news interview on television or radio, a celebrity, politician, or spokesperson is asked for information or opinions on current events. Clinical interviews, where a client or patient is asked for thoughts or information on his or her background, complaint, or condition, are aimed either to be therapeutic in themselves, or are diagnostic in intent, serving to enable the professional interviewer to make decisions about what course of treatment is appropriate for the interviewee. The employment interview is treated by the interviewee as an opportunity to create the best possible impression with a view to securing the job, and by the interviewers as a means of checking up, screening out, and generally finding out about potential candidates with a view to making the employment decision. In police interviews with suspects, the interviewee may be concerned to create a picture of events with the aim of defending him or herself against a negative outcome. The relationships between interviewees (IEs) and interviewers (IRs) are therefore various, and profoundly affect the attitudes of both IE and IR towards the interview and the language that they use.

Given this variety, what is it that characterizes the interview as a kind of discourse? Labov and Fanshel, in their seminal discussion of therapeutic interaction, suggest that interviews can be defined as follows:

> We may define an interview as a speech event in which one person, A, extracts information from another person, B, which was contained in B's biography. (1977: 30)

A **speech event** is any recognizable cultural event in which language plays a part, and, by 'biography', Labov and Fanshel mean information about IE's life, experiences, and opinions. In the case of political interviews, however, and other situations in which IE is a representative speaking on behalf of an organization such as a company, hospital, pressure group, or political party, we might extend the notion of 'biography' to include information about the actions, constitution, policies and views of the institution itself, decided by the appropriate official processes.

POWER AND EQUALITY IN THE INTERVIEW

Note that we have already made some assumption of inequality between IE and IR, particularly in adopting Labov and Fanshel's view that an interview serves to enable IR to *extract information from* IE. This places IR in the position of controlling the agenda of the interaction, ensuring it serves IR's purposes rather than IE's. However, the situation is not so simple, given the diversity of the kinds of aim that IR and IE may have, and the possibility of those aims coinciding or diverging. Labov and Fanshel also point out two major variables that influence the course of an interview: who initiates the event, and who is presumed to be helped by it. For example, a market research interview is likely to be initiated by IR, and it is IR who is presumed to benefit from it. A therapeutic interview, on the other hand, may be requested by the client or patient (IE) or his or her representative, and the benefit is assumed to lie with IE. Further complications arise from the degree of compulsion that IE is under to attend the interview: a police interview, for example, may be legally enforced. All of these factors influence the form and nature of the interview.

In Table 5.1, I have attempted to set out a range of possibilities representing the interaction of these various factors, and how particular types of interview may be placed on the resulting grid, based on Labov and Fanshel's brief discussion of types of interview. Down the left-hand side of the grid, I have expanded their notion of 'who is to be helped' into four outcomes for IE:

1   a neutral outcome (nothing is changed for IE by the interview having taken place, or the results are negligible);
2   the possibility of IE's gaining the benefit of IR's expertise from the interview;
3   the possibility of IE gaining some promotion of interests, such as employment or favourable publicity; and
4   the possibility of perceived harm coming to IE as a result of the interview, such as bad publicity, an adverse court judgement, a dismissal or reprimand, or a criminal charge.

The second relevant axis, represented along the top of the grid in Table 5.1, is the degree to which compulsion was involved in IE's attending the interview. IE may have sought the interview and therefore volunteered for it, or been advised to attend an interview, or been in some way compelled to attend, either legally or through some fear of sanction. Note that in many cases there may be no clear line between volunteering and being advised to attend: for legal and financial interviews where a professional obtains information about IE's financial standing or legal complaint, for example, IE may approach entirely through their own volition, or be advised to attend by another individual or institution such as a mortgage lender or trade union. Medical and therapeutic interviews cover the complete spectrum from voluntary to compulsory, ranging from voluntary approaches made by patients and clients, to referrals from specialists, through to special orders, such as orders for those convicted of crimes, to undergo a course of treatment.

A grey area in the space represented in Table 5.1 concerns the capability of an interview to promote or damage IE's interests. Political and journalistic interviews that are entered into voluntarily by IE may have the power to help or harm IE's reputation in the public eye, and are consequently placed in a

TABLE 5.1   Parameters of Variation in the Interview

IE's presence is ⟶	voluntary	advised	compulsory
Interview may have ⟶			
Neutral effect on IE	market/other research		police information
Beneficial expertise for IE	legal/financial advice		
	◄ – – – – – – Medical or therapeutic – – – – – – ►		
Power to promote IE's interests	employment – – – – ►		job appraisal
	political		court defence
	journalistic – – – – ►		
Power to damage IE			police interview
			'pursuit' journalism

category that is a borderline between helping and harming. Similarly, several types of compulsory interview may be seen as either good or bad for IE, depending on the specifics of the case and the attitude taken towards the interview by both parties. All four examples of types of interview in the bottom right-hand corner of the grid are of this ambiguous nature. For example, a job appraisal may reveal good points or important shortcomings, and may therefore be seen by IE as having been beneficial or harmful. Court interviews are conducted both to promote and to discredit IE's side of the story. Police interviewing may be conducted with people not suspected of any crime who are merely giving information and who are not to be charged (termed here 'police information'); equally, police interviewing may be undertaken with witnesses who may subsequently be charged, and the interview will therefore be damaging from the perspective of IE. A type of journalism that has been much in debate is what I have termed 'pursuit' journalism, where a celebrity or public figure is compelled through the insistence of potential interviewers to answer questions that may either be to the detriment of their reputation once reported in the press, or which may turn the opinions of readers and hearers in their favour. Interviews that are required for people claiming from funds such as disability, housing or unemployment benefits may be seen either as beneficial if the benefit is awarded, but as detrimental if an existing allowance is to be re-assessed and possibly reduced or withheld.

INTERVIEWS USED FOR THIS CHAPTER

The interviews used for this chapter are taken from different points in the grid given in Table 5.1. First, there is an interview between two lawyers and someone who is thinking of taking a case to court. This IE is therefore volunteering to attend as a potential client of the lawyers, and can benefit from their expertise. It is in IE's interests to state the facts accurately so that good advice can be given to him, but there is no scope for potential harm to him: the worst that can happen is that he will be advised that he would not win his case, and that there would be no point going to court. His grievance is that his car has been wheel-clamped and scratched when parked in a school carpark for a short time, and he is claiming that there was not a sufficiently obvious warning that wheel-clamping might take place. This interview is, in fact, a mock-up: it is a recording of a winning team of student lawyers in a client interviewing competition, talking to an actor. Linguistically, however, it is realistic, and was selected because it was judged by a panel of experts to be an example of 'best practice' in legal interviewing. The video of the competition is used for training law students. The second interview is a job interview between a candidate for a lecturing post in a University and a panel of six established staff members. The candidate is also attending voluntarily, as he has applied for the job, but the interview has the power to promote his interests if it has a positive outcome. He is therefore concerned to present himself in his best light. The third interview is a police interview. There is one officer and one suspect, both male, and the interview may lead to a criminal charge and subsequent trial. Since IE has been arrested for attempted burglary – he has been seen chipping putty out of a house window – the interview is compulsory, but IE has been told that he is within his rights to remain silent. It is very much in IE's interests that he does not appear to have been involved in a crime, and he must weigh up his options carefully: if he admits his involvement quickly, he may be let off lightly, but he does not want to admit guilt unnecessarily.

INTERVIEWING GUIDELINES, TRAINING, AND TECHNOLOGIZATION

Most professional interviews are conducted according to particular principles and expectations. Interviewing technique has come to be regarded as a set of skills that can be described, taught, or learned. In the field of employment selection, for example, there exists a large number of texts whose purpose is to instruct interviewers and interviewees about how to behave in a job interview, and many of these address linguistic issues directly (see, for example, Goodworth 1979, among others). Cohen (1987) describes how to conduct a successful television interview, and this reference itself includes a useful summary of several similar manuals. Interviewing for a range of purposes, including job selection, appraisal, counselling, and disciplinary interviews, are addressed in Hodgson (1987), and a possible structure for each kind of interview is given. Since interviewing is a common research tool in the social sciences, too, much literature exists on how to conduct interviews successfully in fields such as market research and even in linguistics (Wray et al., 1998).

What texts such as these have in common is that they make explicit, for the purposes of learning and reflection, the structure and nature of the speech events they describe. Fairclough (1992) identifies this phenomenon as **technologization**: the development of a set of 'technologies' – explicitly described skills, techniques, and knowledge about particular kinds of speech event. This knowledge can then be taught, learnt, and evaluated, and imposed on to speech events that otherwise might be carried out on an intuitive basis. Fairclough describes these discourse technologies as follows:

> Discourse technologies are coming increasingly to be handled in specific institutional locations by designated social agents. They are coming to have their own specialized technologists: researchers who look into their efficiency, designers who work out refinements in the light of research and changing institutional requirements, and trainers who pass on the techniques. . . . Those who are targeted for training in discourse technologies tend to be teachers, interviewers, advertisers, and other 'gate-keepers' and power-holders, whereas discourse technologies are generally designed to have particular effects upon publics (clients, customers, consumers) who are not trained in them. (1992: 215–16)

Technologization of interview skills is not always merely advisory for the consumption of conscientious professionals wishing to improve their skills and the outcomes of the interviews they conduct. In some cases, the structure, style, and content of the interview is enforced, either by a professional code of conduct or by an actual law. For example, lawyers are highly trained in eliciting information from clients without 'taking sides'. They have extensive explicit tuition in interviewing techniques, and may consult manuals as well as tutors. Legally, they are required to explain their fee system to prospective clients before any agreement is entered into. The police interview is constrained by law to conform to the provisions of the Police and Criminal Evidence Act, which came into effect in the UK in 1986. This requires that the interview be used to collect evidence for a prosecution, rather than to secure a confession, that oppression and inducement must not be used, and that all interviews must be tape-recorded with details of time, place, and participants recorded on the tape. The Act states that the police officer must not indicate to the suspect or threaten him or her with any suggestions about what will happen if he or she answers in a certain way, or chooses not to answer at all. In addition, there are many manuals and training packs available to the police that are commonly used, either nationally or within particular police forces, that set out how and when interviewing should take place. The interview for the lecturing post at the University, by contrast, is largely untechnologized. It is conducted in accordance with the rules of the institution about how an interview panel should be composed (certain people of certain ranks, a certain gender balance, and so on, complying with Equal Opportunities legislation), but is guided largely by the experience of the interviewers, rather than by any explicit technology regarding what should be said, and how.

FORMALITY IN THE INTERVIEW

One key element that we would expect to find in all interview situations is increased formality compared with casual conversation. Formality is a notion that we all feel we understand, but a more detailed definition of it will be helpful. As Atkinson (1982) has shown, interactions that are universally agreed to be 'formal', such as court proceedings, church services, and political interviews, appear to be identified as such precisely *because* they do not share the characteristics of 'ordinary conversation'. Formality is, as Atkinson (1982: 96) suggests, 'a gloss for a myriad [sic] of features that can be heard to be "non-conversational"'. He points out, however, that while many people, both analysts and interactants, complain about excessive formality, the fact that we collaborate in producing formality so frequently suggests that doing things this way serves a valid purpose in allowing us to achieve shared goals. In particular, Atkinson pinpoints a single issue that appears to be common to all interactions that are described as 'formal', namely that they are:

> . . . multi-party gatherings in which a single sequence of interaction is oriented to by all co-present parties (e.g. court hearings, debates, ceremonies, meetings, church services, etc.). (1982: 96)

Formal situations such as these have in common particular aspects of linguistic behaviour that support the orientation of the group towards the goal of the interaction. For example, **taking turns** at conversation by **self-selecting** at appropriate points is too unregulated to allow an orderly sequence of events when many people are involved. A response to this is to control turn taking in advance. Many formal situations, then, will involve what is termed **turn type pre-allocation**: the setting out, either explicitly or implicitly, of what kinds of actions each participant can achieve by their speaking. So, for example, in a TV quiz game, the presenter will tell the participants in advance that they are expected to give a brief description of who they are and where they are from, while the presenter will ask questions, to which participants are expected to respond, and the presenter will provide comments and congratulations throughout to summarize to a studio audience – who are themselves expected to keep quiet, laugh, applaud, or shout suggested answers at particular points – how the game is progressing. The quiz participants are not expected, beyond certain limits, to ask questions themselves, debate, disagree, or remain silent when asked to speak. Similarly, in a court of law, questioning should be done by lawyers and, in some cases, by the judge or sheriff, and not defendants or witnesses. Final summarizing is done by judges, and not by anyone else. In this way, by virtue of their participation, everyone involved is expected to subscribe to a set of principles that constrain the nature of their turns, and in so doing they jointly *constitute* speech events of certain types. Atkinson (1982: 103) also observes that, in these formal situations, turn taking is often **mediated** or controlled by one person, or a small group of people, who have the right to 'police' the turn-taking system and ensure that each participant speaks at the right time. In many formal situations, this person is identified by their position in the room: they may be the only one standing up, they may be seated on a stage or dais, or they may be seated in a special position at the front of the room. In certain cases, they are distinguished by dress: formal attire, a white coat, a badge, a red or black robe, or even, in the case of British high courts of law, a wig.

Some of these characteristics of interactions that people categorize as 'formal' clearly apply to interviews. Heritage and Greatbach (1991), in their study of news interviews, make the observation that conversational turn-taking in these contexts departs from the pattern commonly found in everyday conversation. Turn taking, they argue, is central to maintaining the interview *as* an interview rather than as a discussion or some other type of speech event. There is turn type pre-allocation, then, in that the typical interview consists of sequences of IR questions and IE answers. IEs do not tend to ask questions, indicate greetings, or ask IRs for personal information. For example, IEs are not expected to **initiate** different conversational sequences, open or close the interview, or select themselves to speak at other times, nor may they choose another speaker. Heritage and Greatbach (1991: 93) observe that in the few situations in which IE departs from this expected turn-taking behaviour by doing things like initiating questions themselves, they typically solicit permission from IR first. Even if an interview becomes hostile, they suggest, IE and IR still tend to adhere to the strict structure of pre-allocated speech roles and turns, again testifying to the power of the pre-allocated turn system. Atkinson's observations concerning the agenda-setting role of the professional in formal situations, and the distinguishing marks of this individual, also apply to interviews: throughout the interview, IR will mediate the turn taking that takes place, both in length and type, and IRs are often distinguished from IEs by their position in the room: behind a table, for example. At the very least, IRs will have positioned themselves in the room before IE is asked to enter, and will therefore be perceived as having chosen not only their own position, but IE's also.

We can see an illustration of the way in which IRs control turn taking in our extract from a job interview. As noted above, this interview takes place between a panel of six IRs and one IE. To maintain the formality and structure of the interview, one IR, Beth, is 'Chair' of the panel, and she regulates turn taking explicitly throughout. When the candidate comes through the door, it is Beth who introduces him and begins questioning. The candidate, Peter, has been interviewed the day before for a different post in the same institution, and so is already known to some of the panel members:

```
B:  hello again Peter do sit down
    mmhm [throat clearing]
    I normally go through a (.) business of in (.) introducing us all (.)
    but you met four of us [(.)     in the previous interview
P:                          [yeah
B:  and I think you've met both Claire and (.)    Jenn  [y
P:                                                       [yeah
B:  eh (.)  [since then so we'll (.) dispense with those formalities
P:          [yeah
P:  okay
B:  erm (1 sec) we'd like however to:: start the same way that we
    started last time we saw you which is (.) er really just to ask
    you to talk for a few minutes (.) about (.) what you see as attractive
    in this job and what you think you would bring to it
```

When Peter has finished his answer, the floor again returns to Beth, who explicitly names another IR on the panel, Keith, to pass the role of questioning on to him:

> B: Thankyou very much and we'll probably pick up you know a
> number of of things that you've said as we go through but
> can I turn to Keith now

At this point, Keith asks his question:

> K: Thankyou very much
> yes could I lead off by [mmhm: *throat clearing*]
> following on from what you've just said
> about the teaching (.)
> and you mentioned your flexibility and your experience and
> you clearly are an experienced teacher (1 sec)
> P: mmhm
> K: could you just give us some idea . . .

After Keith has asked a question, and IE has answered, the floor returns to Beth, who nominates the next panel member explicitly. Here, Keith responds to a long answer from Peter (the IE):

> K: thankyou we might come back to that point
> thankyou very much

He then looks at B, the panel chair, who turns to the next panel member, Monica, **nominating** her: that is, prompting her to begin her question by saying her name:

> B: MONica
> M: Erm (1 sec) if you did a different option each semester you
> wouldn't be doing much research . . .

Throughout the interview, Beth controls how turns are allocated, both to IE and to other panel members.

CONVERSATIONAL STRUCTURE IN THE INTERVIEW

In his description of formal interactions, Atkinson (1982) makes some useful generalizations about the structure of conversation and how utterances relate to one another. He notes:

> [Formal] interactions are frequently conducted through pairs of turns that are recognisable as questions and answers, with the professional(s) providing most of the questions and the interviewee or private individual providing most of the answers.

In their discussion of medical interviews, Coulthard and Ashby (1976) adopt a conventional model of conversation structure that it will be useful to apply here. This model, based on the work on classroom interaction in Sinclair and Coulthard (1975), suggests the **exchange** as the basic building block of inter-action. Exchanges are made up of at least two contributions by different people, such as a question and an answer, or a greeting and a greeting. The elements that make up the exchange are usually referred to as **moves**. Sinclair and Coulthard (1975) suggest that moves can be categorized into three different kinds:

Initiating: (I)   A 'beginning' move, which opens up an exchange, and places constraints on what can be said next.

Responding: (R) Moves that link backwards, creating no further expectations about what will be said next.

Follow-up: (F)   Linking backwards, but not obligatory. Commenting and often evaluating on (R) or (I).

Coulthard and Ashby (1976: 75) apply this framework to doctor–patient interviews, as in the following exchange:

Doctor:	Initiating move	You've only had one in all?
Patient:	Responding move	Well as far as I know. There's not been one this severe like.
Doctor:	Follow-up move	Yeah.

As might be expected, question-answer sequences are the most frequent form of exchange in the interview. Sequences of questions and answers are expected to be initiated by the interviewer (IR): as Ten Have (1991: 146) notes, IRs have 'privileged access to first position' in the talk. This notion of 'first position' refers to the structure of the conversation, in that IRs normally provide the first turn in any sequential structure in the interview. In interviews we expect a two-part or a three-part conversational exchange to take place. The following structure summarizes:

First position:	(IR)	Initiation
Second position:	(IE)	Response
Third position:	(IR)	Follow-up

The interview can proceed as a series of two-part exchanges: the third position is less frequently taken up, for reasons that will become clear later. The following example from a police interview shows IR's access to first position in the question-answer exchange:

| Turn 1: | (IR) | Were you there at a quarter to two that afternoon? |
| Turn 2: | (IE) | I wa'nt at the back of eighty-three. I was at the back of er next door to me mum's. |

In what follows, we will look at the moves in the interview exchange one by one with a view to examining its structure more closely.

First Position: Initiating

As we saw above, the first position in the interview exchange is normally occupied by the kind of utterance that is likely to elicit a response from an interviewee – that is, a question. Quirk et al. (1985: 806) distinguish three main kinds of question, as follows:

(a) **Wh-questions**: those that expect a reply from an open range of replies, as in *What is your name?* or *How old are you?*

(b) **Yes-no Questions**: those that expect affirmation or negation, as in *Have you finished the book?*

(c) **Alternative questions**: those that expect a reply from one of two alternatives offered, such as *Would you like to go for a walk or stay at home?*

Wh-questions are so-called because they usually contain a **wh-word** such as *who, what, where, why*, which normally come first in the clause. These questions are also referred to as information questions. An example from the police interview is as follows:

IR: What was he doing?
IE: Trying to break in

Examples of yes-no questions from the police interview are as follows:

IR: Okay?
IE: Yeah
IR: That's the easiest way of doing it isn't it?
IE: Yeah
IR: You were gonna break in weren't you to see what was inside – was it worth anything
IE: Yeah

In the lawyer–client interview, alternative questions are used. In the first case below, IE has the choice of answering *relative* or *friend*; in the second, *morning* or *afternoon*:

FL: and who is he relation or a friend or
JC: er a friend, [friend
FL: [oh right OK
FL: morning or afternoon [was it
JC: [morning

From the point of view of interviewing, manuals on interviewing technique frequently make the distinction between **open** and **closed** questions. Open questions allow for a free answer, while closed questions restrict the possibilities of what can be said in response. Of the types of questions looked at above, *yes-no* questions and alternative questions are clearly closed, since they allow a very limited range of responses. *Wh*-questions, on the other hand, can be used in either an open or a closed way: *what happened?* is open, while *what's your name?* is closed. The open-closed distinction is useful, though, in that it allows us to step beyond the form of the question to look simply at its effect on IE. We can look at the many utterances that are not in grammatical question form at all, but which serve as questions in the interview – that is, which serve to elicit information or other kinds of response from IE. For example, the early stages of an interview may often be made up of closed questions, in order to elicit basic information from IE. The lawyer–client interview begins with a series of closed questions from IR (FL), underlined below:

FL:	your name is
JC:	John David Carpenter
FL: (*writes*)	Carpenter
	and your address Mr Carpenter
JC:	twenty eight (.) nash court,
	N – A – S – H court
FL:	yes where's that
JC:	London North One
FL:	London North One
	can I have your telephone number
JC:	er three five four (.) two eight four one
FL:	two eight four one that's your home number is it
JC:	yeah
FL:	do you have a work number
JC:	yep ehm work number is [*gives number*]

Of the six questions underlined, only the third and fourth are technically in question form. All, however, function as closed questions.

A wide range of kinds of utterance can serve as initations in the interview context. For example, the use of statements acting as questions is very common. In the lawyer–client interview, for example, statements are frequently used to check information, as in the three cases below:

IR: now this is your own company

IR: right so it was last Saturday

IR: right OK so you just went in off the off the road and into the school

These simple statements appear to ask for a yes-no answer, and we might therefore treat them as closed questions. However, a communicative IE can see them as cues for giving further information and therefore appearing helpful. For example, in the police interview, IE provides first a yes-no answer, and then after a pause a longer informative answer, to the questioning statement *Alan Hope was trying to break in?*

IR: Alan Hope was trying to break in?
IE: yeah (1)
       At first ee was goin to the lad who lives next door to me
IR: [yeah

```
IE:    [to buy some draw off im
        that's what I thought ee was doin anyway
        until ee didn't knock on is door an walked round the back (1)
IR:    right
IE:    an walked to the bottom of the garden n bottom of next door's garden an a
        bloke came runnin
        round the gardens  [n
IR:                        [mmm
IE:    I just got back in me mum's garden then I went in
        the [ouse
IR:        [right
IE:    n think nothin of it
```

Statements can also act as obviously open questions. In the job interview, IRs frequently elicit responses by using very indirect statements, such as the well-hidden *we'd like to ask you to talk for a few minutes about . . .* in the following example:

```
B:     erm (1 sec) we'd like however to:: start the same way
        that we started last time we saw you which is (.)
        er really just to ask you to talk for a few minutes (.) about (.)
        what you see as attractive in this job and what you think you
        would bring to it
```

Another popular means of prompting a response is to use an *if* clause. For example, in the lawyer–client interview, IR wants to find out more about the event that IE wants to see the lawyer about. IE uses an *if* clause to invite IR to expand on his description:

```
IR:    right so if you can just outline what happened exactly
IE:    yeah er it was Michael's I'll I'll
        I'll give you the whole story
        Michael got married Saturday
        and I'd been really busy so I'd had to get 'im
        I hadn't had a chance to get him his present
```

Some initiations can be very long indeed. The following is an example from the job interview:

```
IE:    could you just give us some idea of er how you approach (.)
        let's begin with small group teaching could you give us some
        idea of how how you approach (.) taking a class um (.) how
        you set about preparing for it (.) what you expect (.) the
        students to get from it and what signs you are looking for to
        suggest that it's succeeding in its in its aims
```

Some initiations can be made up of several grammatical questions. In the example below, the lawyer IR is attempting to get the client IE to elaborate on the nature of the business that he owns. She tries to do this by linking together three closed questions, with the result that IE only answers the last of the three:

IR: um approximately I mean what's the turnover how long have you been going is it doing well?

IE: yeah we're doing OK

For the purposes of analysis, then, it is often helpful to think of the whole of IR's turn as an initiation, since that is how it is interpreted by IE. IEs are well aware that they are to expect initiations from IR, and, as Heritage and Greatbach (1991) find in their analysis of initiations in news interviews, IEs tend not to speak until IR has produced something that looks like a question, often over the course of several utterances.

Second Position: Responding

Having looked at initiations, which occupy first position in the exchange structure that occurs repeatedly in interviews, we can now turn to look at IEs' responses. Heritage and Greatbach (1991) observe that IE answers are unlike responses in everyday conversation. They found that, in the interview, IEs respond at length, producing what are termed in conversation analysis **multi-unit turns**: turns that consist of several different segments, often quite loosely related, and not all performing the same function. Heritage and Greatbach (1991: 101) provide the following example from a news interview. IR is a man who claims he was jailed for a crime of which he was innocent:

IR: Have you any sort of criminal connections or anything, u: [h]

IE: [No]t at all
I was working for the Gas Board at the time
as a salesman
I had no: (0.2) emphatically no er: associates
that (wo(h)uld had criminal records
or I did not associate with people with criminal
records
.hhhh I I I was living a life o o of
a family man in Stockton on Tees,
.hhh where I was a representative for the Gas
Board
.hhh and it was out the blue to me.

IE's turn here is composed of six segments, each roughly equivalent to a clause. Heritage and Greatbach's point is that, in casual conversation, management of a turn this long requires recipients of the information to 'actively collaborate' in supporting the speaker's possession of the floor, perhaps through using **back-channel** utterances. These are utterances that indicate attentiveness but not desire to take the floor away from the speaker – the *mmhms* and other encouraging noises that oil the wheels of conversation. In news interviews, these are largely absent. Heritage and Greatbach argue that, in news interviewing, there is an expectation that IE's turns will be extended, since the point is to get information from them. Reassurance that a long turn is appropriate is not therefore required. Indeed, gaps between utterances are frequent in news interviews, since IR will not only allow IE to finish without interruption but wait briefly before the next question to see if IE plans to say anything else spontaneously. This behaviour differs from that in casual conversation, in which long turns are taken to be an imposition on other speakers' time and therefore require collaboration from those speakers in support, and which are prone to interruption and overlap.

In the interviews examined for this chapter, we find that long responses from IE are the norm for both the job interview and the lawyer–client interview. In the first case, IE wants to give as much information as possible, and appear intelligent and voluble: lecturers are expected to be highly verbal, and to have individual ideas that they express freely and convincingly. There is, therefore, a strong performance element in this interview, and IE must put on a good show. In this interview, IE may speak for more than five minutes in a turn without being interrupted. In the lawyer–client interview, there is not an emphasis on performance, but the prospective client must describe events clearly and completely. Different factors influence the amount of back-channel that is used by the IRs in each case. In the job interview, there is little if any back-channel, supporting Heritage and Greatbach's observation that in formal interview situations IRs do not collaborate to support the long turns of IE. In the lawyer–client interview, however there is a great deal of back-channel. Here, for example, the lawyer FL gives back-channel both to the other IR, ML, and to the IE, JC:

```
ML:   you didn't see it
FL:                mmm
JC:   it wasn't obvious as far as I'm concerned
FL:                           mmmm
```

We may take absence of back-channel as an indicator of formality, and conclude that the lawyer–client interview is simply less formal and therefore allows it to occur. However, the police officer also provides back-channel while the suspect is speaking: would we not want to say that the police interview is formal? The answer may be found by going back to Atkinson's (1982: 96) exploration of formality, described earlier in this chapter. Atkinson characterizes formal situations as 'multi-party gatherings in which a single sequence of interaction is oriented to by all co-present parties'. It seems that the provision of back-channel is the responsibility of addressees – people who feel that they *in particular* are being spoken to. In formal gatherings involving the co-ordination of a number of people as audience (news interviewing on camera, six-person interview panels), back-channel will not be given unless one particular person perceives themselves as the addressee. (This is why nobody gives back-channel in lectures, and it would be strange to be sitting next to a student who said 'mmhm' and 'uhuh' at everything the lecturer said.)

Client interviewing involving two lawyers as IRs, or police interviewing involving one police officer, does single out the IRs as addressees. They therefore deem it their role to provide back-channel. Although a larger and more systematic study is required to establish the case, it does appear that the co-ordination of large number of co-present parties makes for more formality, while 'one to one' interactions, however serious their potential consequences for IE, are by their nature less formal.

In an examination of IE responses, we can see that the nature of the interview, in terms of benefit or otherwise to IE and degree of compulsion, have quite an effect on willingness to respond. This is most obvious in a comparison of the police interview and the job interview. In the police interview, the officer IR begins questioning with an opening statement. IE does not respond to this at all, without a prompting *Okay?*. He answers this as a yes-no question, leaving IR to wait six seconds for an elaboration. None forthcoming, he elicits again with the closed question *were you there at quarter to two that afternoon?*. Here, IE has the option to answer merely *yes* or *no*, given the form of the question. However, he begins to become more expansive, although still cryptic, especially in response to the open question *well what were you doing there?*:

IR: witnesses have told me that they saw you (1 sec) at the
        rear of eighty-three (1 sec) Sidney Road which is just
        up the road from you
        (2 secs)
IR: okay?
IE: yeah
        (6 secs)
IR: were you there at quarter to two that afternoon?
IE: I wa'nt at the back of eighty-three (2 secs)
        I was at the back of err next door to me mum's
IR: next door to your mum's?
        well what were you doing there?
IE: I was waitin for a lad oo was at the back of eighty-three

It is particularly helpful when reading this data to appreciate fully the true length of the pauses, timing them on a watch. Six seconds or even two seconds' pause in speech seems like a very long time. In contrast, even the simplest statements by IR in the job interview result in prompt and very full responses. In the following example, IR is questioning IE on the possibility of him turning his doctoral dissertation into a book in the near future. IE leaves no gap after IR's elicitation, and not only talks about his planned book but anticipates what he believes IR wants to find out – what his plans are for publications of all kinds:

IR: and presumably cutting it down would be a possibility
IE: yeah (.) sure (.) definitely I mean I'm I'm quite flexible on
        things like that there's things that I mean I'm already kind of
        you know cutting and pasting for articles as well but but being
        careful not to kind of you know er exhaust the material that

> I've got there for a book I mean for example eh Arthur
> Fairley are bringing out er a special edition as well for the
> Stardust anniversary you know and Tina Mellish has asked
> me to send an article about structure which you know I've
> already got[1]

Note that IE here leaves few pauses: when he is planning what to say, he provides no opportunity for IR to break in and cut him short, filling any potential pauses. He uses *you know*, *I mean*, *kind of* and *er* to show that he is still complying with the initiation, proving that he is actively planning and constructing his answer and fully intends to complete his response.

To bring out the contrast in interactional style between the two IEs in response to a statement initiation, I have constructed an example in which the prospective job candidate's utterances mirror those of the police interviewee in timing, duration, and structure:

> IR: and presumably cutting it down would be a possibility
>   (2 secs)
>   okay?
> IE: yeah
>   (6 secs)
> IR: did you plan to publish soon?
> IE: I wasn't planning to publish it this year
>   (2 secs)
>   I was planning to do it next

In the context of a job interview, IE here appears secretive and reluctant. It is clear that, if this style were adopted in a real interview, IE would be unlikely to get the job.

OTHER POSSIBLE EXCHANGE STRUCTURES

So far, the exchange structure we have concentrated on is of a single type, in which IR seeks to get information from IE. Following Coulthard and Ashby (1976), we can term these **eliciting exchanges**. Coulthard and Ashby also found that, in the medical interviews they studied, a further type appeared which they termed an **informing exchange**. In this situation, one participant tells the other something, and this is usually acknowledged. For example, in the police interview, the police officer informs the suspect why he has been arrested:

> IR: I've arrested you on suspicion of attempted burglary that
>   happened last Tuesday about quarter to two in the
>   afternoon (2 secs)
> IE: mmmm

At the beginning of the lawyer–client interview, IR informs IE about the way that the proceedings will unfold:

```
IR:   now don't be alarmed that there are two of us here
      we simply find that at this stage
      you know we can give you a better sort of idea
      of what's going on
      two heads are better than [one
IE:                            [yeah
      no problem there
```

We also expect to find **greeting exchanges** in many interviews. These are composed simply of greeting-greeting (Initiation–Reponse), and do not normally involve a third turn. In the legal interview, one of the two IRs performs the introductions, resulting in a pair of greeting exchanges:

```
Exchange 1   IR:   Hello my name's Simon Hall
             IE:   hello
Exchange 2   IR:   and this is my colleague Joanne Appleby
             IE:   hello Joanne
```

A brief analysis of any transcript of interview talk will reveal the presence, not only of eliciting exchanges, but of these other structures.

CONSTRAINTS ON IR'S CONTRIBUTIONS

We often think of IEs being constrained in interviews: as we have seen, they are expected to comply with the structures set up by IRs, who seem to have control over the interaction. However, there are also constraints operating on IRs that constitute appropriate behaviour when they are followed. There are several utterance types that IRs in formal interview situations are not expected to produce. One kind of constraint on IRs lies in the kinds of things that IRs are expected to say in response to IEs. Several researchers (see, for example, Frankel, 1984; Ten Have, 1991; Atkinson, 1982: 111ff.) have observed that responses by professionals to the utterances of clients or interviewees deviate from what might be expected in casual conversation. Specifically, professionals tend to *avoid* using certain kinds of utterance in responses to clients. One category of utterance that has been observed to be rare or even absent from professional speech in these contexts, although present in the speech of the clients themselves, is the **assessment**. Assessments are utterances which evaluate the content of the speaker's own or another's utterance. Atkinson (1982: 112) gives the following example taken from everyday non-professional conversation, where E provides an assessment of the content of L's utterance:

```
L:   My folks'r coming. They called, 'n they said they're
     [g'nna come.
E:   [Oh that's goo::d. . . .
```

Atkinson's (1982) study of interactions between professionals and lay people in a Small Claims Court found no examples of professionals using assessments, while plaintiffs and defendants regularly used them. A second category largely missing from the speech of professionals are utterances that are termed in conversation analysis **news receipt objects** or **newsmarks**. These are utterances such as 'oh' that are typically used to indicate that the information in another's utterance has not been heard before. Atkinson (1982) and Heritage (1984a; 1984b) both note that these newsmarks are not found in the speech of professionals in work-related interactions with clients. Atkinson (1982: 112) gives the following example of a news receipt utterance in second position in a casual conversation:

A: . . . well anyway, they're opening this place at the Marina
       Airport Hotel.
B: Oh:::wow

B's response here is not one you would expect from an interviewer, but is perfectly in place in a casual conversation such as this.

A third type of utterance rarely found in professionals' speech in interactions with lay people are **second stories**. Typically, in casual conversation, one means of progression open to speakers is for a second speaker to match or 'top' a story given by an interlocutor with a story of his or her own that relates to a similar point or is appropriate in some other way. Storytelling in sequences is a well-known phenomenon in casual conversation (cf. Jefferson, 1978), but stories given as second utterances by professionals were not present in Atkinson's (1982) study. Indeed, as Atkinson notes:

. . . it may even be the case that arbitrators who did second assessments, television interviewers who marked receipt of news with 'oh', or doctors who told second stories about their own ailments, would not be regarded by other participants (or observers) as 'proper professionals'. (1982: 113)

We would expect interviewers' speech, then, to be marked by the absence of utterances of these types. In fact, in the three interviews analyzed for this chapter, only one second story appears, very briefly, in the legal interview. In this short extract, IE is describing what happened to his car. IE asks what kind of car it was, and then shares a brief story that he had owned one of these cars himself:

IE: yes it got clamped (.) and scratched (.) and
IR: [utterance inaudible]
IE: last Saturday
        and it was very distressing
IR: what kind of a sports car was it
IE: five hundred SL Merc
        [utterance inaudible]
IR: I had one of those [years ago
IE: [did you
        yeah years ago
IR: right so it was last Saturday

Although encouraged to continue by IE showing slight interest (*did you?*), IR soon returns to the subject of the interview with 'right'.

A general principle underlying the absence of stories and assessments is the need for interviewers to maintain **neutrality** during the interview. They must not, therefore, participate in language behaviour that reveals too much of their own personal circumstances or attitudes. As Ten Have (1991: 150) reports in his study of doctor–patient interaction, professionals must 'refrain from commentary, utterances displaying alignment, or any indication of their own information processing'. As well as dictating that certain kinds of second turn will be absent, as we saw above, research has shown that *third* turns are also constrained by this principle: for example, when a professional asks a question and receives an answer, an appropriate third turn in casual conversation might be an assessment or news receipt object. Frankel (1984) has found, in a study of doctor–patient interaction, that doctors almost never used these in third position, preferring neutral acknowledgments such as *okay* and *uhuh* almost all of the time.

Despite the research that has found the categories of utterance described above absent from professionals' speech, Ten Have (1991) has found that they do sometimes appear in the less formal parts of professional interactions. In his study of interactions between doctors and patients, he finds that features such as newsmarks and assessments do sometimes appear in doctor's speech in more casual stretches of talk. He found that newsmarks such as *oh* were present in the receipt of information to which patients had privileged access and which the doctor could not have been expected to guess, such as biographical information, private opinions, and feelings. Assessments, too, were used by doctors to indicate that what had been said by the patient was part of 'smalltalk' and of little consequence in the aim of the medical interaction. Ten Have also found assessments present in doctor's speech when they were talking to children, with whom they tended to adopt a more 'conversational' approach. Professionals, then, have access to different styles of interaction, and may use these to signal more and less casual segments of an encounter containing an interview.

SUMMARY

We can summarize the features that have been discussed in this chapter as follows. We expect IRs to have privileged access to 'first position' in the talk, in that they **initiate** most of the **exchanges** that make up the talk, whether they are eliciting exchanges or exchanges of some other type. IRs will maintain **neutrality**, and in doing so will refrain from certain types of utterances, such as stories, **assessments**, and **newsmarks**, which indicate alignment with IEs. Turn taking may be **pre-allocated**, either in sequence, in turn type, or both, and turn-**mediation** may be performed by an IR, controlling the length and position of IE's turns. IEs collaborate in maintaining both their own position in the structure of the interview and IR's **neutrality**. While IR frequently uses questions, he or she may also elicit responses using a range of other utterance types. IEs are primed to expect initiations from IR, particularly **elicitations**, and so will bypass points that might in casual conversations be seen as opportunities to take the floor until they hear an utterance that they can interpret as one requiring a response. Once they have received a question, IEs may take long, **multi-unit turns**. Despite the long turn length, IRs will rarely interrupt IEs, and may not even support them using **back-channelling**. Typically, IR will not take the floor until they are certain IE has finished, leading to gaps between IE and IR utterances. Both IE and IR will orientate towards a single topic during the interview, and it will be assumed that certain types of exchange, such as those opening and closing the interview, will only be initiated by IR. Degree of compulsion set against degree of perceived benefit to IE will influence how talkative they are in their responses, a contrast that is clear on comparing the police interview with the job interview.

TOPICS FOR DISCUSSION AND FURTHER STUDY

1. Manuals on interviewing technique tend to home in on questioning, and types of question, as the linguistic element most worthy of notice. For example, Cohen (1987) summarizes the content of a range of manuals on the proper formation of questions in the television news interview. Among the points he raises are the following:

   (a) Questions should be short;
   (b) Questions should be asked one at a time, without the use of compound questions;
   (c) Yes-no questions (those that only lead to a yes-no answer, often termed close-ended questions) should be avoided.

   Hodgson (1987: 3), in a similar vein, divides questions into three types: open questions, which cannot be answered with a yes or a no and are therefore useful to get an interviewee talking; closed questions, which should be used to elicit further specific detail; and hypothetical questions, used to test out some possibility. Looking at examples of interviews, do you find that interviewers adhere to these advisory guidelines? Do interviewees respond as expected to each type of question? Do closed questions always elicit yes-no answers? Do open questions always elicit free, multi-unit responses?

2. We saw above that a high degree of compulsion coupled with a low degree of perceived benefit in the interview results in an unforthcoming IE, using short and semi-uncooperative responses. Examine a range of interviews and locate them on the grid given at the beginning of the chapter. Apart from *amount* of IE speech, what other elements of the discourse are influenced? Do you notice, for example, any difference in the interpretation of indirect questioning?

3. In what circumstances can IEs initiate?

4. It was suggested above that maintaining neutrality is an important part of IR's role. Do IRs always do this? In less formal interviews, do you find that IRs begin to produce assessments, stories, newsmarks? Can you find other examples of IRs indicating their degree of alignment with IEs?
5. Apply the exchange structure framework described in this chapter to a transcript of casual conversation. Do you find any of the differences between this and interviews predicted in the chapter? What other differences are there?

FURTHER READING

A great deal has been written on interviews of different kinds, with a variety of perspectives on the topic. Greatbach (1998) describes the neutralistic stance that is normally taken by news interviewers, focusing particularly on situations in which IRs seek to challenge IEs' views. Jucker (1986) is a useful book-length study of the pragmatic aspects of news interviews.

The seminal study of therapeutic interviews is Labov and Fanshel (1977), although much has been written since on doctor–patient interaction in general. Labov and Fanshel give a very useful overview of the means by which speakers in therapy perform actions such as representing states of affairs, challenging one another, requesting actions, and narrating events. Other useful references on medical interviews are Hughes (1982), Cicourel (1985), and Fisher and Groce (1990), as well as the work described in this chapter by Ten Have (1991). A useful source on medical interviews, discussing exchange structure in particular, is Coulthard and Ashby (1976).

NOTE

1 Details of names and topics have been changed to protect the identity of the participants.

6 The Language of Magazine Features

In this chapter, we will examine the language of features in a range of magazines. First, we look at how magazines are targeted at particular audiences, and how they in turn help to create or construct those audiences. Looking more specifically at features, we describe some characteristics of feature articles that differentiate them from news on the one hand, and advertising on the other. It is claimed here that features need to show evidentiality (authority through reputable and diverse information sources being used), discursivity (explaining and elaborating, rather than just informing) and point of view (arguing for a particular view, rather than being neutral). We go on to look at the linguistic devices that result from these orientations in features. Moving on from point of view, I argue that features also need to position their readers as consumers, and discuss the linguistic forms and strategies that help them do this.

WHAT IS A FEATURE?

In order to examine the language of features, it is of course important to define what is a feature, and what types there are. As is the case with many of the types of language covered in this book, a body of expertise exists of the 'how to' variety that will help us in defining what a feature is. Expertise on feature-writing is often gained simply by practical experience, but it is also the subject of explicit teaching on courses in journalism and publishing, and in practitioner manuals. One such manual, Hennessy (1989: 61), provides a useful summary of the different kinds of feature that can be found in magazines and newspapers:

- 'how to'
- inspirational
- personal experience
- service pieces
- 'think' pieces
- travel
- review
- interview
- humour
- hobbies and sports
- old age and nostalgia

Of this list, a few require further explanation. The 'how to' feature exists to teach an audience a task, craft, or skill. Examples from a gardening magazine are articles on how to build a compost bin and how to plant up containers. 'Inspirational' pieces, as Hennessy terms them, are either concerned with 'life skills', or with specific situations in which someone has triumphed over illness, misfortune, or heartbreak: an example from *Sugar*, a magazine for teenage girls, is 'Trapped By My Lies', in which a girl describes how she has lied to friends. Personal experience features often deal with a difficult, exciting, dangerous or otherwise newsworthy experience: *Options*, a glossy women's magazine, has a feature on 'Real Lives' in the December 1998 issue, in which women and girls who have won prizes – anything from a cosmetics kit to a cottage in Hampshire – describe their experiences. 'Service' pieces give information that can help readers choose a service or product, often drawing on interviewees' personal views or a survey; fashion tips abound in both men's and women's magazines. These features are often linked to relevant advertising placed close by. What Hennessy terms a 'think' piece is one which explores a topical issue, perhaps a current political or environmental concern. For example, *Elle* magazine, another women's glossy (November 1998), explores what it identifies as a new trend of living, a 'round the clock lifestyle', in which socializing, working, and shopping can take place 24 hours a day, while *Sugar* contains a 'special report' entitled 'Death on the Ice' about the culling of seal pups. The distribution of pieces of each kind will obviously differ between magazines: some magazines, such as *That's Life* (a lower-range women's magazine, featuring a lot of puzzles and recipes), contain a high proportion of inspirational and personal experience pieces, while *Sugar* emphasizes service pieces on fashion and make-up, and how-tos, often about social relationships. *Loaded* (a men's magazine) and *Hello!* (a magazine containing celebrity gossip and photographs) consist largely of interview features, and *Loaded* also contains a complete and distinct section of reviews of food, fashion, books, music and films. The types of feature, and examples of feature titles, are summarized in Table 6.1.

The wide range of text types encompassed by the magazine feature necessarily presupposes a wide variety of linguistic characteristics. In this chapter, we will focus on some of the issues that are raised by particular choices of the content of magazines, and extrapolate some of the general characteristics of feature articles for application across the range of text types. For the purposes of this chapter, however, we will concentrate on what Davis (1995) terms in-depth features: those that go into detail about a topic, rather than the fashion and beauty features that concentrate on pictorial rather than textual content.

THE STRUCTURE OF IN-DEPTH FEATURES

One place to look for general guidance for the structure of features is the feature-writing manuals themselves. Hennessy (1989: 36) suggests that the feature article should have six main elements:

TABLE 6.1   Types of Feature (based on Hennessy, 1989)

Feature type	Examples
how to	*Gardener's World* how to make a compost bin; *Cosmopolitan* 'How to Make it through Everyday Stress'
think piece	*Guardian* 'Chicken Flu'; *Sugar* 'Seal Cull'
review	Film, TV, radio, restaurant reviews; *Loaded*'s review of items sent into the office
interview	*Hello!, OK!* interviews with stars; *Guardian* interview with Neil Hannon (of the band Divine Comedy)
old age/nostalgia	Evacuation in World War II; harvesting pre-mechanization
humour	*Loaded* 'Dr Mick' fake problem page
hobbies and sports	Rallying, football, gardening features
inspirational	*Cosmopolitan* 'The Power of Belief in Healing Illness'
personal experience	*Baby* 'Mother's Talk: How it Feels to Be a First-time Mum
service pieces	Guides to healthy eating; stopping smoking
travel	Single travellers' guide; Thailand feature

1 Introduction
2 Premise or point of view
3 Thesis or theme
4 Body (the core of points/facts/arguments/explanations)
5 Supporting material (anecdotes, quotes, and so on)
6 Conclusion

How a magazine feature is introduced is obviously important in determining whether it will be read. The important elements of the story, as in news reporting, will be encapsulated in the intro, the opening passage of the feature. In addition, instead of a headline, the feature article will have a title and a short piece of text known as a standfirst which is intended to attract the reader's eye and summarize the point of the article. The following example is from *Elle* magazine. It is a feature about successful young women finding meaning in life through a re-discovery of the spiritual values of Christianity, self-awareness, and Buddhism:

Title	'I Swapped Gucci for God'
Standfirst	No matter how good life gets, sometimes we just can't help wanting more. Louise France meets three women who had it all, but gave it up and found just what they were looking for.
Intro	The three women I spoke to have all faced personal what-is-the-point-of-life crises and managed to find a way through. Yet they're not how you might imagine. They're all successful in highly competitive fields and although each has faced moments of intense emptiness, I've rarely met women who are quite this articulate and independent. Certainly all three found their own answers without being influenced by a man or their mum. What struck me most, though, was how happy they were. No one can be cheerful all the time, say the cynics. But I was reminded of that classic line in *When Harry Met Sally* – 'I'll have whatever she's having'.

The title, standfirst, and intro are presented in fonts of the same family, but different sizes, with *Gucci* and *God* in bold. The standfirst appears to the left of a picture of one of the women featured in the article. The rhetorical distinction between these three elements is therefore accentuated graphically. A second example is taken from *Gardener's World* magazine.

Title	'Close Relations'
Standfirst	Ceri Thomas finds how having a designer in the family pays dividends when it comes to designing a garden from scratch
Intro	Far removed from the spacious areas that she usually designs, landscape architect Diana Bell faced a very different challenge when she transformed the tiny backyard of her mother's house. The plot measures just 26.8 square metres (32 square yards) and its triangular shape narrows as it goes away from the house. Unperturbed by these difficulties, she has created a wonderful garden that, according to her mother, 'always has something in flower'.

These two examples are what might be termed, in the categorization of feature types given earlier, inspirational pieces: they refer to transformation, either personal or creative, through life skills or practical skills. However, 'I Swapped Gucci for God' also has strong overtones of the personal experience and interview types of feature: the title in particular suggests personal experience, but the content of the article is not told in the first person.

Despite their difference in content, structurally these features have much in common. The article titles are intriguing rather than descriptive: they do not summarize the content of the article, and are deliberately semantically incomplete: we do not know, for example, the referent of 'I' in the title of the 'Gucci for God' article, nor do we know who the 'Close Relations' are. It is not intended, then, that readers will be able to retrieve a complete message on reading the title, which will lead them to the standfirst for clarification. The standfirst is written in the immediate present tense, introducing not the feature itself, which is a write-up of events in the past, but the event that the feature is based on (*Louise France meets . . .* and *Ceri Thomas finds . . .* rather than *Louise France relates her meeting with . . .* or *Ceri Thomas describes how she visited . . .*). What is foregrounded by the standfirst, then, is part of the process of researching the article presented as a recent happening: a process of doing (meeting, finding), rather than a process of saying (describing, reporting). In the structure of news reporting, the lead paragraph of the report reflects prevailing news values, while feature intros contain elements that set up both the structure of the subsequent argument and the interpersonal relationship that is to hold with the reader.

VALUES OF THE FEATURE

In the discussion of news reporting in Chapter 2, we examined 'news values': the factors that make a story a good news story and which will be emphasized in the writing, particularly prominent elements such as headlines and intro paragraphs. Arguably, a similar set of values exists for feature-writing. Drawing on 'how to' manuals showing how to write good features, such as Hennessy (1989) and Davis (1995), we can separate out three values that feature writers adhere to:

1 Evidentiality: The article will have to give authoritative sources, and be backed up by evidence, and these sources should be diverse;
2 Discursivity: Rather than just informing, the article will be expected to elaborate and explain;
3 Point of View: Feature articles are expected to argue for a point of view, and should introduce and conclude that argument.

Each of these elements will affect language use in the piece. Below, we look at how that happens for each value in turn, using an article from a general interest publication, the *Guardian Weekend* magazine section (appearing in the newspaper on Saturdays), as an example. The article, appearing on 7 August 1999, is about the discovery and spread of the 'chicken flu' virus found in Hong Kong in 1997. This is an article of several thousand words, so we will work with quotations from it and simplifications of its structure, reproduced where necessary.

1 Evidentiality

A key to the content of the feature article, and the kinds of things that language is going to be required to do, is the range of sources of information that go into it. This may be the writer's own opinion, if expert, but is more likely to be based on independent research such as library research, use of previous news cuttings, sources such as books and films, and very often interviews, either with one person or with several. This means that articles must manage their different sources, and make their derivation clear to their readers.

Feature writers will get some of their information from talking to others, or reading what they have written. If the source is a reputable or impressive one, the evidentiality of the feature will be improved. Feature writers therefore need to find ways of introducing other people's words and thoughts into the text. The most obvious expectation is that what is told to a feature writer will appear in direct quotation, or **direct speech**, which we discussed first in connection with news reporting in Chapter 2. The clearest cases of direct speech occur within quotation marks, but with a **reporting clause** – a clause that explains that someone is doing the saying. The following examples are cases of direct speech taken from the *Guardian*'s 'Chicken Flu' feature. Reporting clauses are underlined:

De Jong said: 'It was an H5'.
As de Jong puts it, 'A bird virus should take hundreds of mutations before it can adapt to grow happily in human cells, but this one had infected the child extensively'.

Reporting clauses do not need to be verbs of speaking such as *say*: they may also be verbs of thinking:

I thought, 'That's impossible'.

Apart from *say*, Quirk et al. (1985: 1024) list 40 more popular reporting verbs of speaking or thinking, including *explain*, *insist*, *remark*, *state*, *warn*, *whisper*, and *recall*.

Indirect speech is when the thoughts or sayings of someone are reported without quotation. Reporting clauses are again underlined in the following two examples:

She figured the reagents she had didn't fit this particular strain.

He'd booked a flight, he told her, and was arriving in Hong Kong on Sunday.

Here, the content of the speech or thought does not need to be as accurate: it is mediated now through the writer, who can phrase it and summarize it as he or she wishes.

Direct or indirect speech in which there is no reporting clause is termed **free**. So, free direct speech occurs in the two examples below:

By the end of July, he still had no reaction at all. 'In my whole life, I never saw any virus that didn't react *at all* with *any* antisera. So then I knew we had to hurry very much.'

He remembers it all too clearly. 'All of us were immediately aware of the potential implications.'

Here, the reader is left to infer from preceding context who the speaker is.

Free indirect speech communicates speech or thoughts through paraphrase, as in:

He was beginning to hope that it had been a freak event.

In each of these cases, we have been able to identify specific sources. Sometimes, looser connections are made between speakers and messages, such as *newspapers said . . .* and *townspeople felt . . . .*

Many uses of source information in features do not make reference to an act of communication, and are instead stated authoritatively as facts:

Most Chinese still view fresh food as one of life's essentials.

The first sign of trouble came when chickens started dying on a farm near Yuen Long, in Hong Kong's rural New Territories.

Others have the authority of personal observation. In contrast with written news reporting, the feature article allows the explicit presence of the writer as 'I':

> When I got to the market at 9.30 one morning in June 1998 . . .

> In Rotterdam, in June, Jan de Jong had told me . . .

These features, some stronger than others, establish the authority of the writer and the evidentiality for the piece. There is a subsidiary value of diversity in the sources of evidence used, so that it is important that the writer does not get all the evidence from a biased source, and shows that all the angles have been examined thoroughly. The way in which sources are reported is a matter of choice, but it is up to the writer to show which pieces of evidence she or he has accepted as fact (and will therefore not always attribute to a source) and which need to be signalled as opinion. This process of choice helps to show the writer's point of view, since the different ways of reporting evidence show distance from, or alignment with, the different sources of information.

2 Discursivity

The notion of discursivity refers to the 'in-depth' nature of feature articles: what is presented is not just plain facts, but explanation and elaboration. A good way of seeing how this works linguistically is through rhetorical structure analysis, in which the text is described in terms of segments, often bigger than clauses or sentences, that link to one another in particular ways. These links are termed **rhetorical relations,** and they serve to describe not just what a chunk of language *is*, but what it is *doing*: explaining, describing, giving a reason, making a contrast, providing a counter example, explaining a purpose for something, and so on. Various frameworks exist in the literature for describing rhetorical structure. Winter (1994) and Hoey (1983) present a framework well-known in the UK Applied Linguistics tradition, while, more well-known in the USA and within disciplines such as computational linguistics (which uses rhetorical analysis a great deal for planning texts for computer generation) is Mann and Thompson's rhetorical structure theory (RST) (Mann and Thompson, 1987). What is presented below is a simple set of rhetorical relations, much cut down from the frameworks just mentioned, which should give a practical flavour of this kind of text description. On the left, I have named the relations, while a paraphrase of roughly what they mean appears on the right:

Temporal sequence	'This happened, then that happened'
Contrast	'This situation/event is unlike that one'
Cause/Result	'This event/situation caused that event/situation'
Elaboration	'To describe this event/situation in more detail . . .'

These relationships hold between segments of text, and provide the links along which readers can make sense of the article. In order to see how these rhetorical relations work in the feature, it is easiest to cut down and summarize the content of the article. We can then see instances of the different relations joining text segments. The first page or so of the *Guardian* article about Hong Kong 'chicken flu' can be broken down into the following segments of meaning, to convey the 'gist' of the story:

1   For all the Territory's modernity,
2   most Chinese still view fresh food as one of life's essentials.
3   The market is a vivid and lively place.
4   You'll not find any poultry market as vibrant today as they were until the last days of 1997.
5   Before then, you'd have found chickens, ducks, and all sorts of poultry.
6   In 1997, a lethal virus load was building up in the birds.
7   The first sign of trouble came in March 1997, when chickens started dying.
8   In all, nearly 7,000 birds died.
9   When a pathogenic strain of influenza takes hold in chickens, it's an ugly business.
10 The virus spreads through the bloodstream to affect every tissue and organ.
11 Apart from being thoroughly unpleasant, for the farmers involved it's economically disastrous.
12 To put an end to it in Pennsylvania, the US Department of Agriculture eventually had to slaughter 20 million chickens.
13 The virus responsible was isolated by Hong Kong's Department of Agriculture and Fisheries, and passed to Kennedy Shortridge, an Australian professor of microbiology.
14 He had been studying strains of flu in birds and animals for the past 25 years.
15 There are countless types of flu virus;
16 some are harmless, others are lethal.

We can first of all split this text up into five 'major' segments, or text spans, which I label below A–E, that are each made up of a number of smaller segments. The major segments can be summarized as follows:

A   1–5   Markets were vibrant before the virus.
B   6–8   The virus built up.
C   9–10   The effect of the virus on chickens.
D   11–12   Economic disaster caused by the virus.
E   13–14   Who found the virus.

The article pivots around the relationship between segments A and B, which we can term a relation of **temporal sequence** (before/after). C, D and E all, in fact, serve the same function: they **elaborate** upon B, since they say more

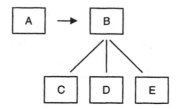

FIGURE 6.1   Schematic Rhetorical Structure for 'Chicken Flu' Text

about the virus. This set of relationships between text spans can be represented diagrammatically in Figure 6.1.

Although we have been able sensibly to split the text up into this five-segment structure, there are also relationships that exist among the elements of text that make up these five segments. A, the first text span, runs from segments 1 to 5, which describe the market, the reason for its existence, and introduce the fact that the markets were more vibrant before 1997. In detail, segment 1 makes the claim about modernity, and segment 2 contrasts this with a liking for fresh food. This relation of contrast (signalled by *for all . . .*) indicates that liking for fresh food is not modern (perhaps we would expect more packaged and convenience foods). This liking (2), however, is presented as having a causal relationship with segment 3: that the markets are vibrant. Segment 3 then contrasts, through comparison, with segment 4, which points out that, before 1997, the markets were *more* vibrant. Segment 5 elaborates on segment 4 describing how vibrant the markets actually were before 1997.

The next broad text span, B, runs from segments 6 to 8, which introduce the notion of virus build-up. Doing an analysis this way is not an exact science: what is to be aimed at is some agreement on the nature of the segments that exist in a text. There may be more than one candidate relationship between two segments. Note that, while the relationship between the two is mainly temporal, this whole segment also acts as a reason for the state of affairs described in segments 1–5, namely that the once-vibrant market had declined. Segment 6 claims that a virus build-up existed. Segment 7 elaborates on this, providing the origin of the 'trouble', while segment 8 describes the result: 7000 birds died.

Major segment C, 9–10, introduces the ugliness of the virus: segment 9 claims it's ugly, while 10 elaborates on how the virus spreads. Major segment D, 11–12, in its entirety describes another way that the virus is undesirable to advance the claims in 9–10. Segment 12 provides an elaboration giving evidence why 11 is true. The next major segment, E (13–14), elaborates further on the nature of the virus (who found it); 14 elaborates on 13, since it further describes the work of the microbiologist introduced in 13. C, D and E, then, perform similar functions, since they all describe aspects of the virus.

This analysis shows something of the method of rhetorical description that can be used to compare and contrast argumentative methods, and even to compare articles of different types. What is notable about the feature article, as compared to the structure of news articles, is the density of elaboration: evidence of the writer's exploration of different aspects of the same topic.

There is no one agreed set of rhetorical relations that all linguists feel to be 'out there', and you are invited to examine the references given earlier in this section to perform full analyses of texts. However, the lack of agreement as to what constitutes 'the' set of rhetorical relations should give you some courage in modifying existing frameworks, if the resulting rhetorical relations can be adequately justified by the text.

3 Point of View

What feature articles have in common is that they argue for a particular view. While it has been possible to demonstrate, in this book and elsewhere, that even news reports can convey ideological bias, it is part of the function of feature articles that they convey an opinion, rather than merely setting out the facts. In order to see in a simple example how opinion pervades the feature article, we can examine more closely the 'garden design' intro first examined at the beginning of the chapter. One way of beginning is to take an existing feature and try to rewrite it 'neutrally'. Here again is the original text of the intro to the 'garden design' feature:

> Far removed from the spacious areas that she usually designs, landscape architect Diana Bell faced a very different challenge when she transformed the tiny backyard of her mother's house. The plot measures just 26.8 square metres (32 square yards) and its triangular shape narrows as it goes away from the house. Unperturbed by these difficulties, she has created a wonderful garden that, according to her mother, 'always has something in flower'.

The following is my attempt to rewrite it as 'news', removing as far as possible material that is obviously evaluative or which conveys an opinion:

Garden Designer Designs Garden

Landscape architect Diana Bell has redesigned a triangular garden plot measuring 26.8 square metres (32 square yards) to make a flower garden for her mother. She usually works on larger sites.

Presented as news, there is a strong sense of 'so what?' about this information, a sense which I have perhaps mischievously accentuated through my choice of headline. It does not make news because it does not adhere to the news values discussed in Chapter 2 of this book. It does not make a good feature, either, because it lacks the 'angles' that the writer has taken in the original. First, we lose the sense of the difficulty of the site, conveyed in the original by *faced a very different challenge, tiny backyard, just* (26.8 square metres), *its triangular shape narrows*. *Backyard* also conveys something of the site's unattractiveness, which helps set the scene for the 'before-after' *transformation* that the article claims has taken place. This moves on to a sense of Diana Bell as a capable professional: *unperturbed by these difficulties*, doing something out of the ordinary, *far removed from the spacious areas that she usually designs.* The sense of *usually* was preserved to some extent by the news write-up, but 'spacious areas' conveys a sense of freedom and easiness of design that my 'larger sites' does not. After its transformation, the site is now *wonderful,* a claim to which her mother is quoted as adding her own evaluative testimony.

The feature text, then, is not neutral. Other signs of its lack of neutrality are the presence of the writer as narrator ('I', as we mentioned in connection with evidentiality above), and certain vocabulary uses. The 'Chicken Flu' feature, for example, has the following vocabulary (relevant items are underlined):

a <u>tangle</u> of strip-lights and ventilation ducts

the tile floor was <u>sopping</u> wet where it had been washed down

here and there lay <u>greasy</u> piles of red and yellow entrails

As we note in connection with advertising language later in this book, certain vocabulary items convey **affective meaning** – that is, the use of the word conveys a positive or negative evaluation on the part of the writer. Here, *tangle, sopping,* and *greasy* all indicate the writer's negativity towards the state of affairs. Fairclough (1989: 112) refers to these **experiential values** that words have, indicating ideological or personal beliefs. As Fairclough (1989: 116) also points out, language that seems to indicate opinion, too, may serve to establish relationships with the readership, in that they are expected to share the beliefs of the writer. Some elements may not seem evaluative, but when contrasted with a positive description, the writer's view becomes clearer. For example, the *Guardian* writer describes the Hong Kong market as *three floors of non-descript grey building*; compare this with the equally true alternative *modern three-storey building.* Similarly, *his birds . . . crammed tight in cages* could be rephrased *birds . . . snugly confined in carriers.* Even the description of the action of the virus can be rephrased to put an opposite 'spin' on it. As an onlooker, the writer is appalled and disgusted at the way the virus 'literally melts' chickens, but his words *the virus spreads through the bloodstream to infect every tissue and organ* could more neutrally be rendered as something like *the virus reproduces throughout the body.* For a discussion of the 'loadings' of words, see also Bolinger (1980), particularly Chapter 8. An excellent example of a text rewritten to show two completely different points of view is Edelman (1974: 300), reproduced below. The two texts, descriptions of psychiatric treatment of a patient, show a completely different ideological loading: one obviously favourable to the regime imposed, and one critical of it. It should not be too much of a challenge to guess which is which!

Text 1: deprivation of food, bed, walks in the open air, visitors, mail, or telephone calls; solitary confinement; deprivation of reading or entertainment materials; immobilizing people by tying them into wet sheets and then exhibiting them to staff and other patients; other physical restraints on body movement; drugging the mind against the client's will; incarceration in locked wards; a range of public humiliations such as the public posting of alleged intentions to escape or to commit suicide, the requirement of public confessions of misconduct or guilt, and public announcements of individual misdeeds and abnormalities.

Text 2: discouraging sick behaviour and encouraging healthy behaviour through the selective granting of rewards; the availability of seclusion, restraints, and closed wards to grant a patient a respite from interaction with others; enabling him to think about his behaviour, to cope with his temptations to elope and succumb to depression, and to develop a sense of security; immobilizing the patient to calm him, satisfy his dependency needs, give him the extra nursing attention he values, and enable him to benefit from peer confrontation; placing limits on his acting out; and teaching him that the staff cares.

The texts present point of view mainly through the selective use of vocabulary that has positive and negative connotations: for example, compare the noun phrases *seclusion* to *solitary confinement* and verbs *succumb to depression* to *commit suicide*. Note, too, that the elements in the list in the second text are predominantly cast as verbs: *discouraging, enabling, teaching, immobilize, satisfy, give*. These allow the text to present an image of the *agency* of the institution – of people doing things to help the patient. In the negative text, there are more nouns: *deprivation, incarceration, requirement, announcements*. These are things that exist, apparently without human agency, helping to create the impression of impersonality. A further analysis of these two texts is given in Fairclough (1989: 113ff.).

MAGAZINES AND THEIR READERS

There is a great deal of interest in the way that media texts – written and spoken broadcasting, publishing, advertising, and film – create and replicate beliefs and assumptions about society and the self in their readers, hearers, and viewers. In the discussion above, we saw something of the way in which feature writers convey their own beliefs in the form of point of view. In this section, we will look more closely at how assumptions about the readership are communicated, and how magazine features (and indeed advertisements, as discussed in Chapter 7) serve to create reader identities, as well as to reflect them. We will look first of all at magazine audiences, and the notion of 'common sense' in relation to the set of ideas and beliefs people bring to the interpretation of text, relating this to the discussion of ideology in general. We then look at how magazine content on the one hand, and linguistic forms in the text on the other, both serve to contribute to, and to exploit, this 'common sense'.

Magazines and Interest Groups

The experience of picking a magazine from a news-stand will make it clear to the casual reader that different magazines are intended to appeal to different audiences. Some of us, for example, may not linger long in front of the magazines on cars, hi-fis and computers, and may instead be drawn to the women's glossies; others will seek out specialist magazines on gardening, fishing or life in the country; still others will look for teen magazines, events and lifestyle magazines and men's magazines. A plethora of titles exist to address specific readerships, from professional nurses to turkey breeders, brides-to-be, company directors, darts players, or people interested in buying a house. Other magazines are intended to appeal to a more general readership, such as those that contain TV and radio listings (such as *TV Times* and *Radio Times*) and 'colour supplement' magazines that accompany newspapers at the weekend such as *Weekend* (the *Guardian* magazine), the *Telegraph Magazine*, *You* (the *Mail on Sunday* magazine) and the *Sunday Times Magazine*. As McCracken (1993: 257) points out in relation to women's magazines, however, what contemporary magazines have in common is a limitation of readership, either economically, or by special interest, or both. It is only in this way that advertisers can target known consumer groups. Specialization of content, then, allows advertisers to know, and shape, their readership. McCracken argues:

> The special-interest magazines often encourage their readers to think of themselves as members of a distinct group linked to certain modes of consumption. . . . Because of their commercial goals, the special-interest publications address readers with messages of pseudo-individualized consumption linked to the ideological roles expected of members of such groups. (1993: 257)

Readership, expectations of roles in society, and purchasing behaviour are therefore inextricably interlinked. It is this set of political and economic relationships that gives magazines a powerful role in shaping society and the individual: the choice of a magazine does not only influence that individual purchase, but much subsequent consumer behaviour as well.

In addition to issues such as circulation and target audience of magazines, it is worth considering how readers come into contact with them. It is easy to assume that magazines are always bought from the newsagent, news-stand or supermarket. However, many magazines are available by subscription, either exclusively or in addition to direct sales. Trade magazines and those associated with professional or special-interest organizations are very often available only by subscription (*Which?* magazine is one example). Other magazines appeal to an audience gathered together by location: local titles are one example, but in-flight magazines such as British Airways' *Highlife* reach an audience brought together through travel. Since rail privatization in the UK, 'in-flight' magazines are also available on trains. What all magazines have in common is an understanding of the characteristics of their readerships, however constituted. It is these characteristics that 'fit' the readership to the magazine, and to its advertising.

Mode of reading is also relevant. Readers vary from the 'accidental' reader in the hairdresser's, or the reader of the girlfriend's magazines, to avid subscribers. Not everyone who reads a magazine is a purchaser of it, as they are available in libraries or by informal lending as well as through deliberate purchase. An analysis of how people *use* women's magazines in particular as media can be found in Hermes (1995).

Attention has focused on women's magazines in particular as instruments of communication that serve to create reader identities. See, for example, Ferguson (1983), McRobbie (1991) and Talbot (1995); see also Mills (1995) for a detailed discussion of the replication of gender in texts of all kinds, and Fairclough (1989) for discussions on the interaction of text and assumptions in general. Benwell (forthcoming) gives a very useful perspective on the construction of masculine identities in men's magazines, while Tanaka (1998) is a linguistically-informed study of women's magazines in Japan. According to this view, texts are not seen as merely reflecting cultural norms and assumptions, but also as constructing them: they are a key part of the replication of culture in a political and economic context. In the reading process, readers are not simply seen as passive: Talbot (1995: 145) argues that they are 'actively involved in the processes of interpretation'. However, the resources that readers draw upon in order to make sense of the text – knowledge, beliefs, and assumptions – are not within their conscious control. Fairclough (1989: 2–4, 77–108) argues that the 'common sense' assumptions that are required to make sense of texts, although they may be basic assumptions that people treat as natural and normal, are themselves shaped by ideology. Through bringing their 'common sense' to the interpretation of texts, argues Talbot, 'readers are drawn into a kind of complicity with the texts they read' (1995: 145).

In order to see an example of this at work, we can look at some short examples from magazine features, examining what 'common sense' assumptions are required in order to make sense of them. The first text is from a promotional feature in a women's magazine:

Feast your eyes on the most gorgeous eyewear around from Valentino and you'll find the frames to suit exactly what you're wearing. (*Elle*, November 1998)

This sentence requires a range of assumptions to be in place for its interpretation. First, it is necessary to appreciate that *eyewear* and *frames* refer to glasses or spectacles. The word 'glasses' in British English has, at least in the context of magazines, come to have somewhat negative connotations, and this is even more true of *spectacles*: it is implied that the wearer is short-sighted and even, perhaps, slightly unattractive. The word *eyewear* has the function of locating spectacle-wearing in the realm of fashion, which brings with it a set of assumptions about the choice of glasses: that they should act as a form of self-expression, be subject to 'branding' and the association of aesthetic values and economic and social status, and that, like other items of 'wear', the wearer might even have the choice of several pairs. This is accentuated by the use of the adjective *gorgeous*, which emphasizes that appearance should be a criterion upon which glasses are judged, and the name of Valentino, which the reader assumes to be a designer: it is therefore relevant to believe that glasses designed by a named person – particularly by an Italian – are more desirable. The sentence has the form 'if you do this, this will happen', presenting the action of finding a pair of glasses as a desirable goal. Finally, it is implied by the phrase *to suit exactly what you're wearing* that glasses should be chosen to go with other clothing, rather than, say, for the shape, colour or material and its effect on the face alone. As a society of consumers, we are probably used by now to the notion of 'eyewear', particularly sunglasses, as a fashion item, and would not now be content with the correct lenses in the cheapest, plainest frames: arguably, it is the result of such promotion of glasses as a fashion item that has brought this about.

A second example comes from the magazine *The Lady*, a long-standing magazine (established 1885) which covers topics of general interest to a predominantly white, female and older readership. A piece of advice they are given is as follows:

> The general rule on present-giving is not to give the recipient something he or she gets and can afford, but to aim a peg or two higher. (*The Lady*, 3–9 November, 1998)

This sentence, taken from the introduction to a feature on Christmas, serves to communicate the explicit assertion that the presents given at Christmas should be more costly than the recipient would normally buy. In addition to this assertion, however, the sentence requires that the reader have certain beliefs that are applied to the text as the 'common sense' required for interpretation. Implicit, then, is the requirement that the reader supply (at least) the following beliefs: that Christmas is celebrated as a festival, that presents are routinely given as part of that celebration, that it is appropriate to think in terms of 'rules' governing such behaviour, and that presents are to be ranked 'high' or 'low' on some scale of worth determined by their monetary price.

Fairclough (1989: 83ff.) argues that all of these processes of supplying 'coherence' to the text by filling in the missing information, none of which is explicit in the text, and fitting the resulting meanings to our experience of the world, are ideological in nature. Ideology serves to project and legitimize particular power relations between individuals, or between sections of society. It is in this sense that readers are 'complicit' in Talbot's sense. Moreover, written texts such as these leave little room for negotiation: we cannot dispute the knowledge that is required for interpretation, but can only supply it. The most active form of rejection of the status quo assumed by the language of written media texts is to skip parts we do not like, or, ultimately, to decide that we fall outside the target audience of a publication and reject it as a potential purchase.

Mass communication, such as magazine publication, addresses an 'ideal' or 'implied' reader that characterizes their target audience as closely as possible. As Talbot (1995: 146) points out, actual readers may or may not have a great deal in common with the ideal reader, but when the fit is quite good, real readers take up the positions the text offers 'unconsciously and uncritically'. Fairclough confirms that this represents ideology working at its best:

> Ideology functions most effectively when its workings are least visible. If one becomes aware that a particular aspect of common sense is sustaining power inequalities at one's own expense, it ceases to be common sense, and may cease to

have the capacity to sustain power inequalities, i.e. function ideologically. And invisibility is achieved when ideologies are brought to discourse not as explicit elements of the text, but as the background assumptions which on the one hand lead the text producer to 'textualize' the world in a particular way, and on the other hand to lead the interpreter to interpret the text in a particular way. Texts do not typically spout ideology. They so position the interpreter through their cues that she brings ideologies to the interpretation of texts – and reproduces them in the process! (1989: 85)

Talbot (1995: 146) emphasizes that the communities of readership that are constructed by publications such as magazines are often illusory. For example, McRobbie (1978) describes the teenage readership of the now-defunct girls' magazine *Jackie* as being exposed to the values of a *'false* sisterhood' constructed by the magazine, which promoted the importance of appearance and emotional issues at the same time as accentuating rivalry and competitiveness as normal among girls.

There are two principal ways in which magazines position their interpreters: by magazine content, and through specific linguistic aspects of magazine text. Below, we look at each of these in turn.

1 Reader Positioning: Content and Image

Magazines construct identities for readerships through their choice of content, both textual and visual. For example, *SAAB Driver*, the magazine for members of the SAAB Owners' Club of the UK, contains predominantly first-hand, unedited descriptions of trips to SAAB car rallies, alterations and modifications performed by the owners on their cars, descriptions of new SAAB cars, and accounts of 'great finds': salvageable SAABs found in old barns and on scrap-heaps, for example. The readership of the magazine is constructed as people who treat their car as a hobby, rather than solely as a means of transport, who are predominantly male, who are technically proficient, who are competent on issues such as miles per gallon and performance, and who are divided as a group by the model of SAAB that they own. Women often feature as wives of members, rather than members themselves; and members who like the aesthetics of the car, have a low level of technical knowledge, and treat the car as a means of transport are less represented, partly because they do not write to the magazine, although it is likely that many such people are among the club's membership.

The readership of *Baby* magazine is similarly constructed: its content and presentation suggests that it is intended for women who are pregnant or who have recently given birth. Despite the fact that a roughly equal number of men as women, by definition, are also parents-to-be or new parents, and might therefore be interested in a magazine about babies, 47 images in the November 1998 magazine that involved babies were of women holding or in close contact with them, while only 10 were of men (of whom 3 were doctors or medical staff), and 4 images were of both parents in equal contact with a baby. Of the 10 images of men, around half the children involved were older than babyhood. The image of gender roles constructed by the magazine, then, legitimizes in women rather than men a set of interests associated with the state of pregnancy and early parenthood. Through the topics it covers, it also constructs women as health conscious, perhaps insecure or guilty about the balance of work and motherhood, having the role of primary carer in the family, keen on 'natural' approaches to nutrition, birth, and upbringing, and relatively affluent. How close these 'ideal readerships' are to the real readerships is hard to assess, but it is easy to see how the content of magazines, and representation of groups in them, helps to produce gender bias: in this case, men may own and work on a SAAB but participate in parenting as bystanders, while women may be totally occupied by a baby but not by a car.

2 Reader Positioning: Text and Language

We have seen so far that magazines convey assumptions about their ideal readers through their spread of content, as well as through the kinds of pictures they choose to include. The second major way in which magazines communicate reader positions is through conveying assumptions about them through linguistic means, treating information as shared, uncontroversial and 'common sense'. Some of this communication is done explicitly in what is said, but, as we shall see, much also involves the kind of information that the reader is expected to supply in order to make sense of the text.

There are several markers of assumed knowledge that serve to 'background' elements of textual content and treat it as uncontroversial. A common method is through **presupposition**. This has been mentioned earlier in this book in relation to news reporting, but it is of particular significance here. Presupposition is the use of linguistic forms that imply the existence of something, or some fact. If the reader is not already familiar with the presupposed information, he or she is required to **accommodate** it (cf. Lewis, 1979): that is, accept it as uncontroversial, already shared, or 'in the public domain'. As we saw in Chapter 2, some structures that commonly presuppose information are **definite** expressions ('this x', 'the x', 'that x'), **possessives** ('my x', 'your x') and **proper names**. For example, a feature in *Sugar*, in which pictures of celebrities have had speech bubbles added to them, contains many presuppositions of existence conveyed through possessives. The presupposing elements, or **presupposition triggers**, are underlined:

Sentence:	<u>Angela Griffin's new specs</u> allow her to have her first proper look at lovely boyfriend Will Mellor.
Presupposition:	Angela Griffin has new specs
Sentence:	Grant takes <u>his invisible pooch</u> with him everywhere.
Presupposition:	Grant has an invisible dog
Sentence:	<u>Natalie Imbruglia's latest man</u> is so dreamy, it's scary.
Presupposition:	Natalie Imbruglia has a latest man

A look at a quiz on sex and relationships in *That's Life* magazine (12 November 1998) reveals more presuppositions conveyed by possessives. In each case, the presupposition appears in a question, focusing attention on one element of the question and requiring the reader to accommodate the presupposed element: that is, to adopt a belief in the presupposition whether it is valid or not. For example:

> Does <u>your bloke</u> have a great physique?
> How old were you when you had <u>your first kiss</u>?
> Who is <u>Britain's sexiest politician</u>?

The presuppositions are, respectively, that the reader has a bloke, has had a first kiss, and can agree that Britain has sexy politicians.

Proper names are a common source of both presupposition of existence (we couldn't talk about Natalie Imbruglia without presupposing she existed, at least for the purpose of argument), but also assumed familiarity with the named person. While *OK!* magazine, for example, introduces some celebrities without assuming knowledge of them (*irreverent TV presenter Johnny Vaughan* and *Australian pop singer and former 'Neighbours' actress Natalie Imbruglia*), many are named without further explanation: for example, 'Mel B' (not *Spice Girl Mel B*), *Eddie Izzard* (not *the well-known comedian Eddie Izzard*) and so on. The use of names always presupposes existence of the named people or things, but using them without further explanation positions readers as apparently knowing not only that these people exist, but as being able to identify them, and knowing something about them.

The most productive source of presupposition of this existential kind is the use of definite expressions. The following examples are taken from *Sugar*:

> Sophie tries <u>the old touching your nose with your tongue trick</u>.
> Heidi and I have got <u>the glitter bug</u> in a big way.
> So Shaznay, what's <u>the one video you insist on having on your tour bus</u>?
> . . . for <u>that big night out</u>, slip into an Impulse Zen scented bath . . .

All of these expressions create an appearance of shared understanding that the named elements existed before being mentioned in the text. A second set of presupposing linguistic forms are those that presuppose facts. One presuppositional construction that we discussed in relation to sports commentary in Chapter 3 is the sentence form termed the ***it*-cleft**: this sentence type simultaneously focuses on one element of the message, and presupposes another:

> It was Cyril who many years later made the first orange-box cold frame.

> Presupposition: someone made the first cold frame
> Assertion: that person was Cyril

> It was on a shooting weekend at Sarah's ancestral home, Althorp, that Charles met her 16-year-old sister Diana.

Presupposition: Charles met her 16-year-old sister
                  Diana in some circumstance.
Assertion: the circumstance was a shooting
                  weekend at Althorp.

In each case, the asserted information is foregrounded as the import of the sentence, while the presupposition is conveyed as a 'known fact' (cf. Prince, 1978; Delin, 1992) and uncontroversial.

Other sentence structures, including two other kinds of **cleft construction**, have a similar effect. These are summarized below:

wh-clefts	What he did like was plants and gardening.
	Presupposition: he liked something.
reverse *wh*-clefts	That's why we're offering you not one, but all four of the Confessions books.
	Presupposition: we're offering you all four Confessions books for some reason.
wh-questions	What have you got on tonight?
	Presupposition: you have got something on tonight.
	Why does it happen?
	Presupposition: it happens (for some reason).
factive verbs	Verbs such as *realize, regret, understand* presuppose what comes after them:
	I regretted that I had forgotten him.
	Presupposition: I had forgotten him.

Features, then, can use all these devices for locating and placing readers within sets of beliefs. We will see how this works in tandem with an advertising message in Chapter 7.

SUMMARY

The chapter examined the range of types of magazine feature, before examining the structure of the 'in-depth' feature. It was suggested that magazine features espoused three main values: evidentiality, conveyed through a choice of devices including **direct** and **indirect speech** and the presence of the writer as observer; discursivity, conveyed by the use of particular **rhetorical relations**, in particular **elaboration** relations; and point of view, conveyed by the use of **affectively** marked vocabulary and the emphasis on evaluative elements. It was also described how magazines select and construct their readerships through covering topics, and conveying beliefs and assumptions that will appeal to certain readers. Advertising and features play an important role in this process. We looked specifically at how magazines convey assumptions about readerships through photographic images and the spread of topics covered, and through the use of linguistic markers of assumption, such as **presupposition** and vocabulary choice.

TOPICS FOR STUDY AND DISCUSSION

1. Using the list of types of feature at the beginning of the chapter, examine the distribution of the different kinds in several contrasting publications. What does the relative proportion of feature types demonstrate about the readership, and what do the assumptions of the publication demonstrate about the knowledge, beliefs, interests, and aspirations of its 'ideal reader'?
2. In a sample of features, what means can you find for each writer of establishing evidentiality? How diverse are the sources? What effect has this on your view of how authoritative the article is?
3. Apply the rhetorical relation analysis to different kinds of features. Do you find the relations exploited to a differing extent, depending on feature type? Do you have to add relations to the framework?
4. Examine the use of markers of writer's point of view, such as vocabulary choice and the use of particular themes, in features from different publications. Do you find a difference in the degree of subjectivity between different publications? How does this relate to your understanding of the magazines' readerships?
5. What 'common sense' background assumptions are readers required to supply in the following texts? Although the texts are in no particular order, it may be useful to begin with texts for which you believe yourself to be far from the target audience, as the required assumptions will be alien to you and therefore easier to spot. You could then work towards texts for which the required common sense is closer to your own, and therefore working more invisibly. You could of course add to these with your own examples.

(a) Your baby's first tiny mouthful of real food will open up a whole new world of taste for her. (*Baby* magazine, December 1998)

(b) With a little help from Richard Ashcroft and Beastie Boy Mike D, UNKLE have come up with the best LP you'll hear this summer. (*Loaded*, September 1998)

(c) To commemorate the thirtieth anniversary of the SAAB 99 it is proposed to assemble 99 model 99s for a run from Blair Atholl to John O'Groats on the ninth of September 1999. (*SAAB Driver*, October/November 1998)

(d) A shady position is no problem for *Clematis Montana* as it will smother a wall with white flowers in early summer. (*Gardeners' World Magazine*, November 1998)

(e) Four times British Hairdresser of the Year, Trevor Sorbie launched his new book *Visions in Hair* at Brown's in London's Great Queen Street with a champagne reception. (*OK!*, 13 November 1998)

FURTHER READING

Davis (1995) is a useful handbook for practising journalists, detailing the processes of writing for and production of magazines. Particularly useful is his chapter 'An ABC of magazine contents', which provides an overview of the range of different kinds of elements that make up a magazine and which may be of interest for linguistic description and comparison. Hennessy (1989) takes a similarly practical approach to the process of feature-writing for newspapers and magazines. Chapter 5 contains the list of different kinds of feature drawn upon earlier in this chapter. See also Chapters 7 and 8 for helpful descriptions of the structure of news and magazine features. Walker (1992) is a practical handbook on magazine design and layout, describing how textual and graphical content is effectively presented. Although this is intended for practical use, it gives an insight into the kinds of decision that are made in the positioning of information, and gives a sense of how magazines create the unique 'look and feel' that is their trademark.

Much has been written on the creation of masculine and feminine identities in magazines. See Heywood (1997) and Benwell (1998 and forthcoming) for discussion of masculine identity, and Ferguson (1983), McCracken (1993), McRobbie (1991), and Talbot (1992, 1995) for feminine identity. A useful overview of a range of features of magazine language is given by McLoughlin (2000).

For more on experiential vocabulary, read the chapter on advertising in the current volume, and see Fairclough (1989) and Bolinger (1980). Direct and indirect speech are described very clearly in Montgomery et al. (1992: 205).

7 The Language of Advertising

In this chapter, we look at one of society's most pervasive forms of discourse: the language that is used in advertisements. Much research has been done in marketing, media studies and linguistics on how the complex strands of the advertising message are integrated. Since this is a book about language, we concentrate on adverts whose message is substantially conveyed linguistically. First, we look at some of the important characteristics of advertising communication that have a bearing on the kinds of variety we can expect to find in advertising texts. We then take a simple structural analysis of print advertisements and look at the separate components, teasing out the factors in language that enable advertising to function as persuasive discourse. Finally, we take one particular framework for the analysis of adverts as ideological forms of communication – Fairclough's (1989) description of the 'work' that advertisements do in creating consumers, products, and relationships between them – and apply this systematically to expose further linguistic factors that help advertisements perform their functions effectively.

VARIETY WITHIN ADVERTISING COMMUNICATION

To begin our study of advertising as a diverse form of communication, it is worth noting the following, sometimes overlooked, facts:

- Advertising takes many forms, not just magazine ads, posters, and television ads, which may be the most obvious to the public.
- The aim of the advertising may not just be to persuade someone to purchase a particular product or service – it may be a complex or longer-term aim that does not include purchasing at all.
- Advertising is based on complex and sophisticated research into the characteristics of the target group of consumers.
- The one 'ad' that is noticeable to the general public is likely to be part of a larger promotional campaign that takes several different forms, and is spread over time, space, and different media.

All of these facts suggest that, in order to examine how advertising language works, any stereotypical view of advertising as consisting of broad-appeal posters or TV ads with 'Buy this now!' messages needs to be re-examined. In what follows, we will look first of all at the groups of consumers that advertisers can appeal to, and the information they use to discover, or even create, those groups. We then go on to look at the different media available to advertisers, the different goals that adverts can have, and the different approaches to persuasion that can be used in advertising.

CONSUMER GROUPING

In an age of social and geographical mobility, information about potential consumers of goods and services is ever more crucial to the success of a business. In order to target product development and advertising effectively, producers must find ways of fitting their products to consumers, and this requires access to an understanding of who those consumers are: where they live, what they will spend, what they know and believe, and what their needs and aspirations are. The field of market research has evolved in order to satisfy this need for information about consumers, predicting their future behaviour and securing competitive advantage.

Groups of consumers can be characterized in various different ways. The most obvious is to use some form of *demographic* description: that is, information based on the study of a population, usually using factors such as age, sex, region and social grouping. Advertisers may also use people's roles within their family unit: primary carer for children, single parent, single-person household, grandparent, for example. Stage of life is also relevant: the interests of couples without children in their late twenties will be different from those of people whose children have grown up and left home, or people who are in retirement. Moving away from demographic characteristics, psychologists have suggested that purchasing choices are affected simply by human needs, such as the need for companionship, status, love and belonging. Others worked on the idea that consumers self-identify with products, and buy when they can see a match with their own personality (see Brierley 1995: 31 for a brief overview of this work). *Psychographic* information is based on the idea that personalities can be segregated into characteristic traits, such as risk-taking, joining in and security-seeking. While it is controversial whether these traits are stable, or even useful, it is still the case that companies and agencies see personality traits and lifestyle habits as a means of targeting advertising campaigns, perhaps to activate certain sectors of the market at certain times. This summary by no means exhausts the methods that marketing researchers use to characterize populations (see Chisnall, 1992; Brierley, 1995; inter alia, for useful overviews of these research methods), but they do show how advertisers may characterize potential consumer groups. It is possible to read these groupings simply as facts about the population, but, as Fairclough (1989) argues, it is also relevant to see these groups as *constructed* consumption communities. These are idealizations of what people are really like, and advertisements based on these idealizations might therefore be argued to be performing ideological work in bringing these groupings into being through the messages they convey.

DIVERSITY OF ADVERTISING MEDIA

Advertising takes many forms: TV and cinema advertising makes use of the moving image, speech, music and written language; radio advertising uses music and speech, while advertising in newspapers and magazines and on posters relies on the visual design of the communication and written language. Other advertising may take the form of sponsorship of teams, events and activities, using public relations tools such as press releases and involvement in political issues, and merchandizing and sales promotion such as stands, packaging, shop signs, coupons, free samples and competitions. Advertising normally takes the form of a campaign which uses a mixture of these different methods, each targeted to deliver a particular message to a particular group at a particular time and place, and aimed at producing a particular kind of behaviour. How, and how much, language is involved in each of these advertising interventions varies enormously, and the balance with other kinds of information and design and the relative importance of each of the components is also crucial in the effectiveness of the communication. It is clearly impossible to approach all kinds of advertising communication in the scope of a single chapter, and since this is a book about language, we will concentrate on some forms of advertising in which language plays a key role.

DIVERSITY OF ADVERTISING GOALS

As Brierley (1995: 45ff.) points out, advertising is not only used to influence consumers to make a purchase. Some advertising is aimed at improving the image of a corporation (television advertisements for the visitors' centre at Sellafield Nuclear Power Station, for example, with the dual aims of prompting people to visit and find out more, and generally advertise the openness and approachability of the company), some towards social ends, such as improving the health and habits of a population (such as anti-smoking health promotion), reassuring consumers that a product or service is reliable and trustworthy (the introduction of the new bagless vacuum cleaning technology represented by Dyson cleaners, for example), to improve the general profitability of a whole market sector, such as milk or British Beef, to get the product or service talked about (the 'shock' advertisements produced by Benetton clothing during the early 1990s, one featuring a new-born baby still with umbilical cord attached, for example), or to transform the image of a brand (such as a re-launch of Skoda cars using engines and other parts engineered by Volkswagen).

ADVERTISING TECHNIQUES

Brierley (1995: 139ff.) presents a historical overview of the development of techniques in advertising. Earliest to emerge was 'reason why' advertising, which simply sought to convince the consumer by rational argument that she or he needed a particular product. The successor to this approach (although it is still used) was the notion of the 'unique selling proposition', which sought to distinguish a product unequivocally from its rivals. Both these approaches are based on the notion of the 'rational consumer' who makes decisions on the basis of information and comparison rather than on an emotional or impulse basis. This kind of advertising is rhetorical in nature, and language is therefore likely to play an important role. As Tuck (1976) has argued, however, the development of TV and radio as an advertising medium in the 1960s and afterwards opened up a different approach to advertisers, where moving images, music and voice quality could be used to create 'atmosphere' for an advertisement to a far greater extent. While this would not rule out a rational approach, it did enable a far more abstract association of products with lifestyles, occupations and moods to create a particular 'brand image' or 'emotional selling proposition'. This set of associations of brand with lifestyle may act more subconsciously than rationally based advertising, fitting instead with consumers' aspirations and beliefs about the kind of person they are, or want to be. In both rationally based and emotionally based advertising, language may play an important role, although what the language is doing, and how it is doing it, may differ substantially.

Having looked at some of the background that may help explain how advertising functions as a form of communication, its aims, and its techniques, we can begin to look at the way in which these features are realized linguistically.

THE STRUCTURE OF PRINT ADVERTISEMENTS

There are various ways to begin to analyze an advertisement, but the simplest way may be to look at a printed ad and its components on the page. Advertising on the printed page generally consists of four parts: a headline, body copy, a signature, and a slogan (see, for example, Vestergaard and Schroeder, 1985: 52; Toolan, 1988: 55). Each of these elements tends to have certain characteristics. The *headline* must be eye-catching or intriguing, sometimes even shocking. Carter and Nash (1990: 79) refer to headlines as 'titles', tracing the analogy between advertising and narrative: the headline is like the title of a story, and shares some of its characteristics. Headlines often interact with the images of the ad in a punning way, as in an advert for the American Express Blue credit card. The headline makes a pun on the image, which is of a couple sitting 'roasting' themselves in the sun: *Do the Sunday roast. And get paid for it*. Note that this contains two imperative verbs (*do, get paid*), a common feature of ad titles (see Carter and Nash, 1990: 78, for a discussion). Other common devices include allusions to titles of books or films, rhymes and **alliteration**, the repetition of consonant sounds, as with the *s* and *n* sounds in *noticeably smoother skin, now* (Nivea moisturiser), or with *n* in *Maybelline creates a whole new kind of natural*. The headline, coupled with the image, serves the advertiser's first aim of attracting attention to the ad, and if its meaning is not entirely obvious then it helps the reader become 'hooked', wanting to read on to have the mystery resolved. Headlines, too, are often **presuppositional**, in that they require a belief for certain information to be true, or for certain things to exist, if they are to be understood. Elsewhere we have discussed presupposition at work in news reporting and magazine feature-writing: it is not less prevalent in advertising. For example:

Why Guinot products are exclusively available from therapists

requires the reader to accept the belief that

Guinot products are exclusively available from therapists.

In the headline, it is the promise to tell the reason why, rather than the **assertion** of the fact, to which attention is directed. We will say more about presupposition later in the chapter, as it plays an important role in the construction of advertising messages in general.

The *signature* element of the advert is often a graphic that is the trade name of the product or company, perhaps a small picture of the product itself. The *slogan* is an element which often accompanies the signature. The following are some examples of slogans (the product names appear to the right):

Hungry? Why wait?	Snickers
You and Canon can.	Canon cameras
The Lynx effect.	Lynx body spray
More than just a bank.	NatWest bank
First for new technology.	Dixons
Serious performance.	Mizuno football boots

A variety of devices is in use here, and a range of syntactic forms. Some slogans are adjective phrases (NatWest, Dixons) which describe a quality or characteristic of the company (being first, being more than just a bank). Others are whole clauses (Snickers' two questions, Canon). Some are noun phrases, which refer to objects (Lynx, Mizuno). Note that the 'objects' described here are actually **abstract**, rather than **concrete**: an 'effect' (rather than Lynx body spray itself) and 'performance' (rather than the boots themselves). Through the slogan, an abstract quality or property can be associated with the product. Together with headlines, slogans often contain useful **ambiguities**: car ads are a case in point, with slogans like 'the car in front is a Toyota' (playing on the ambiguity of physically in front, and metaphorically in front), and 'Isuzu: it's where you want to be' (ambiguous between an interpretation in which you want to be inside the car, and one in which the car is able to go wherever you want).

Structural Characteristics of the Body Copy

In ads that rely on language (and not all do, as we noted above), the *body copy* does the main informative and persuasive work of the advert. This is particularly true of ads that employ 'reason why'-style argumentation, in which a cogent case is made for the consumer to buy the particular product. In these ads, a common structure adopted is **problem-solution**, a structure that is found in many kinds of texts (cf. Hoey, 1983). If the consumer can be made to accept that some situation in his or her life is a problem, then a solution is justified in the form of the product. Although problem-solution seems to suggest that the advert would have two logical parts, in fact there are three, as Carter and Nash (1990: 69) suggest:

1 Situation: some situation exists.
2 Problem: a problem is associated with that situation.
3 Solution: there is a solution (product or service).

The advertisement for a Nivea lip balm exemplifies this structure:

> Situation: Your lips are constantly exposed to the elements,
> Problem: making them extremely vulnerable.
> But, unlike other skin, they are less equipped to protect themselves.
> Solution: So to keep your lips soft and smooth, you need to moisturize and protect them, on a daily basis.
> That's why we have created Lip Care Essential, containing Pro-vitamin B5 and vitamin E. Just one of a range including Rosé, Sun and Repair variants, it's been specially formulated to care for your lips. Everyday.[1]

The 'solution' element in this advert actually has two parts: a 'common sense' solution, which does not mention the product, and allows the reader to accept the practice of moisturizing as a sensible one regardless of whether she buys the product or not. Once she has accepted this, the product is presented as a perfect way to do it. Note the use here of the **reverse wh-cleft** construction (introduced in the discussion of magazine features in Chapter 6): 'that's why we have created Lip Care Essential', which conveys the presupposition 'we have created Lip Care Essential for some reason'. Since the need for a moisturizer has just been presented, the use of the presuppositional construction improves the neatness of fit between the common sense solution which creates a need for some product, and Lip Care Essential as that product.

Often in advertisements sentences are short and even incomplete. Leech (1966: 90ff.) provides a very useful survey of the kinds of situations in which we might expect to find what he terms **disjunctive syntax**, including signposts, labels, and posters. He suggests that advertising uses a kind of disjunctive grammar that is virtually unique, in that it consists of 'sentences' which need not contain a main verb (1966: 93). This, in turn, means that other 'sentences' may consist of single elements or phrases of any other type. Some examples from different adverts are as follows:

Now.	(Adverb)
Beautifully.	(Adverb)
Every day.	(Adverbial phrase)
Pure.	(Adjective)

Deliciously different.	(Adjective phrase)
Midori.	(Noun)
A new kind of car.	(Noun phrase)
In three flavours.	(Prepositional phrase)

Dyer (1982: 144) suggests that one reason for disjunctive syntax in television advertising is shortage of time, but this does not explain the strategy in print advertisements. There are, however, other possible explanations. First, information that is broken up into smaller segments tends to suggest a conversational style. It perhaps mimics the short turns typical of face-to-face interaction between equals. We will have a lot more to say about conversational style in advertising below. Second, the information presented in this disjunctive way does not consist of statements. This means that there is no **truth value** to the information: it cannot be said to be true or false. But it will still be processed by the reader or hearer, just as it is unavoidable to think of elephants when reading the sentence 'Don't think of elephants'. What is happening, then, is not a 'reason-why' process of argumentation, but a set of associations between concepts. For example, an advertisement for Neutrogena soap consists of a photograph of a clean-looking blonde woman, a picture of the product, and the single word 'pure'. There is no statement that 'Neutrogena is pure', 'you/your skin will be pure if you use Neutrogena' or even 'this woman is pure'. The advertisement simply associates the concept of purity, the product and the woman.

A third reason for disjunctive syntax may be informational. Each small segment will be taken to have a separate information focus, usually at the end, in which salient or 'new' information appears, and so the more short segments there are, the more information foci there will be within the advertisement – the more distinguishable salient points. It is likely, too, that the full stops slow down the passing of the eye across the page. A final useful characteristic of disjunctive syntax is that the **connectives** can be used to relate the short segments together. Elements such as *and*, *so*, and *plus*, for example, can be exploited to give a sense of a logical argument unfolding, which can be very useful in 'reason why'-style advertising. Since typical information structure also tends to place new information at the end of the segment, connectives placed at the beginning will not be in a focal position: instead, they will be positioned as **themes**, which are elements that form the 'starting point' of each unit (themes are introduced in detail in Chapter 3). This may have the effect of making connectives part of the thematic material of the text, once more highlighting the impression of logical argumentation. If the connective method is simply the use of *and*, the effect may be of accentuating the number of advantages of a product, or reasons to buy it.

The body copy of an advertisement for the American Express Blue credit card is a good example of the disjunctive style.

Blue. A new credit card from American Express. It gives you money back, every time you spend. At least 1%. And a full 5% in November. Credited to your account each year. So whatever you do, Blue pays you to do more.

Want One?

> The introductory **APR** is just **9.9%** for the first six months. And you can transfer
> balances from other cards at the same low rate. So get one. Call 0800 700 111.

Only three of the 'sentences' are in fact grammatical sentences (*It gives you
money . . ., The introductory APR . . .* and *Call 0800 . . .*). Others contain
frequent **ellipsis** – the omission of grammatically expected elements. (Ellipsis is
very common in sports commentary: see Chapter 3 for some more examples.)
A more grammatically complete rendering of the first two segments, for
example, would be 'Blue is a new credit card from American Express'. The
elided element, therefore, is the main verb *is*. Connective material placed at
the beginnings of segments are *and* and *so*, which in writing usually connect
one clause to another within a sentence. In speech, it is hard to see what is a
sentence and what is not: perhaps it is more appropriate to expect texts like
this one to have the grammar of speech rather than the grammar of writing.
The effect of the placement of connectives in this ad, to conclude, is to
highlight a list of advantages in the case of *and*, and to emphasize the
conclusiveness of the argument for getting the Blue card with *so*.

THREE IDEOLOGICAL FUNCTIONS OF ADVERTISING

Fairclough (1989: 28) sees advertising language as 'one of the most populous
and pervasive modern discourse types'. By this, he does not mean simply that
there are a lot of adverts around, but that the discourse of advertising and
consumption become models that are drawn upon in other situations (1989:
198) so that advertising discourse tends to **colonize** other kinds of discourse.
We can see, then, the influence of the discourse of advertising elsewhere, even
in everyday conversation. This may take the form of simply quoting advertising slogans as a joke, but it may also permeate our thinking and reasoning
about the world in a much deeper way. Fairclough argues that this process of
absorption of advertising thinking and speaking into other areas of activity is
an ideological one. Through this process of absorption, we view ourselves as
consumers, rather than producers, in the world, who belong to particular
'consumption communities' that have been defined by advertisers rather than
by any inherent cultural experience, and whose beliefs, attitudes and values are
fundamentally shaped by the sets of consumption patterns seen in advertising.

A seminal work mapping out a means of ideological enquiry into advertising
is Williamson (1978). Concentrating particularly on language, Fairclough
(1989: 202) presents a useful framework for examining the ideological work
that advertisements do. The three elements of the approach can be summarized
as follows.

Building images: Advertisements have to establish an image of the product or
service by using concepts readily available to the target
audience, thereby involving the audience in building the
image;

Building relations: Adverts represent an interpersonal relationship between the producer/advertiser and the consumer. This relationship facilitates what Fairclough terms 'the ideological work' of the advert: that is, the establishment of trust, goodwill, or another relevant basis that will support acceptance of the product and consumer image, and therefore compliance with the message of the advert;

Building consumers: Adverts construct 'positions' for consumers that will give them a good fit with the product being advertised. Positioning of the consumer can be done by presupposing that s/he has certain knowledge, beliefs, aspirations, income, habits or possessions, or implying that s/he should have them.

In what follows, we will look at how language is used to build images, relations, and consumers.

BUILDING IMAGES

A key component of the way products and services are advertised, and their images built, is through the way they are named and described. The first thing that an advertiser can do to 'create' a reality for an advertisement is to use simple statements to **assert** facts about the world. Some of these may be verifiable facts about the product, as in:

Toyota Paseo has a driver side air bag, standard.

Other claims are more difficult to assess, often because they employ modal verbs like 'may', 'can', and 'could', as well as the **auxiliary** verb 'help'. Geis (1982: 71ff.) suggests that these verbs 'substantially weaken the claims they occur in'. For example, the following advertising claims all use *help*:

[Lipcote] will help keep your lips looking luscious all day long.

It's powerful enough to help beat spots.

Clear Complexion tablets contain natural active herbs that help treat your skin from within.

'Help' weakens the claim by implying that the product is just one of the things that will cause the desired result. 'Seems to' has a similar weakening effect:

With new All About Eyes, the look of under-eye circles lines and puffs seems to fade away.

Given the assumption of positive intention behind advertising statements, we are apt to assume more positive meanings than are logically justified. For example, the statement 'you can't buy a stronger painkiller' logically means only that no painkiller is stronger, but it also means that other painkillers could be as strong. The knowledge that this is an advert, however, is likely to predispose us to interpret any statement, however weakened or ambiguous, as positive approbation, since this is the way in which adverts typically work. Our knowledge of the text-type, then, sets up expectations that claims, statements, and associations of meaning will present the product in a positive light. This interpretation may often be favoured over the logical interpretation of the language.

Vocabulary

Vocabulary is clearly a central element in building the image of a product. Based on the discussion of aims and techniques in advertising presented in the first half of the chapter, we can predict that the vocabulary will have three general characteristics. It is likely to be *familiar*, *positive*, and *memorable*.

Familiar: If consumers are to identify with the product, and, as Fairclough suggests, even collaborate in 'building' the image through accessing concepts that are native to them, vocabulary should be familiar and everyday. This may be vocabulary that is particular to the consumption community being created or appealed to, and may exclude others.

Positive: Clearly, words that evoke positive associations are more persuasive than those that evoke negative ones.

Memorable: At least some elements of the ad must be memorable, clever, or appealing. This suggests some breaks from the 'ordinary' pattern are desirable.

We can look at these characteristics one by one, and find them at work in context. Several researchers have pointed out the familiarity or 'ordinariness' of words in adverts. Toolan (1988: 57), following Leech (1966), notes that the verb *can* is the most common modal verb found in advertising, as it conveys both possibility and permission. Leech (1966: 154) lists the most common verbs found in his sample of TV advertising, which include (in order) *make, get, give, have, see, buy, come, go, know, keep,* and *look*. Adjectives in the same sample were, going from the most popular, *new, good/ better/best, free, fresh, delicious, full, sure, clean, wonderful, special, crisp, fine, big, great, real, easy, bright, extra, safe,* and *rich*. Many of these are what Carter (1987) has termed **core vocabulary**: vocabulary that is neutral, and which can appear in a wide variety of different contexts. It seems as if ordinariness and normality, then, are what is being evoked here.

Selection of positive vocabulary in advertising draws upon a set of systems of meaning that provide many alternative ways of saying the same thing. For example, the following are all candidate synonyms, since they denote or refer to the same concept:

active frenzied lively hyper energetic frenetic vital

However, in important ways, these words do *not* mean the same thing as one another: we would prefer to think we had an *active* life, or an *energetic* and *vital* lifestyle, than a *frenetic* and *frenzied* one. These words, then, although they have similar conceptual meaning, have other differences in meaning that make them not true synonyms: indeed, many believe that there are *no* true synonyms, since there are no words that can be exchanged for one another in every context with no change of meaning. Leech (1990: 9ff.) terms the 'additional' meaning that differentiates sets of words such as these associative meaning. He breaks this down into several different categories:

Affective meaning: information about the speaker's or writer's positive or negative evaluation of the thing referred to. This can be conveyed by positive or negative descriptions, but also by tone of voice, facial expression, and so on.

Connotative meaning: meaning evoked by virtue of 'real world' associations with the concept referred to. For example, *teenager* may have a range of different connotations: lively, moody, delightful or hormonal, and friend or threat, depending on the experience and social group of the reader or hearer.

Collocative meaning: meaning that is derived from the placement of the word near others in frequent use: *fresh* may collocate with *fruit*, *flowers*, and *vegetables*, but not *babies*. So, it becomes part of the meaning of 'fresh', through usage, that the word does not apply to babies, but it does apply to some classes of edible or decorative things.

To look at these categories at work, we can see that advertising language, first of all, uses words that convey positive affective meaning. The words in the left-hand column were all found in magazine advertisements. Alternatives that indicate negative opinions through their connotations are provided on the right:

classic	dated, old-fashioned
modern	new-fangled
relaxed	idle, lazy
warm	stuffy, hot
romantic	sentimental, soppy
fresh	raw, immature
full	stuffed, turgid, compacted
clean	blank, featureless, sterile

As Leech (1990: 13) points out, positive connotations are often presented both visually and verbally. For example, an American advertisement for Lady Speed Stick anti-perspirant features a woman in sports-kit running, showing that the product works even during strenuous exercise, although this is nowhere claimed in the advertisement. It's a product for women, and some of the print is in pink, presumably reflecting that it is designed to appeal to a female market and so is linked to a 'feminine' colour. Positive connotations are used in the language, too: almost universally in anti-perspirant advertising, the function of the product is referred to as *protection*, which has highly positive connotations. The collocations of *protection* in advertising, in fact, are rather different from those in casual conversation. A search of a small computer corpus of magazine English reveals that *protection*, in the world of the magazine, appears in the context of sex (1), sun (9), sanitary (2), underarm (1), insult (1), income (1), weather (1), environment (1), data (1), and roads (1). The same search on a corpus of conversational English found collocations with the environment (5), consumers (2), military (1), crime (3), drugs (1), police (2), of children (1), against attackers (1), data (1), insurance (1), and of professionals at work (2). While a small corpus analysis is not conclusive, it does seem that the portrayal of protection as a notion in everyday conversation has to do more with protecting the environment against threats, and people against dangers such as crime, attack, and drugs, than it does with protecting against sweat, the sun, and sanitary emergencies. What is clear, though, is that the conversational usage seems to expect *people* (like police and politicians) to protect others, rather than things (like sunscreen, sanpro, or anti-perspirant). The advertising norm therefore borrows from other contexts the idea of anti-perspirant as an animate agent warding off something highly undesirable. This is an example of **personification**, a device also used in poetic language: treating things and ideas as if they were human. Another very common example is the use of *care* in association with skin products and detergents in advertising, implying that something like washing-up liquid has emotions.

The speed stick advert suggests that the product will not 'fade'. Expected collocations for 'fade' are *light* or *colour*, which makes a link with the pink-coloured page, but also suggests lightness for the product. Finally, the term 'anti-perspirant' is itself a **euphemism**: a polite term used to cover something unpleasant or taboo: 'perspiration' has acceptable connotations, while 'sweat' apparently does not. (The opposite of euphemism, **dysphemism**, is the use of rude or taboo terms to discuss something that normally has neutral or pleasant associations. This is found less in advertising, for obvious reasons.) Bolinger (1980: 16) discusses euphemism at length, giving many examples from advertising: hair *rinse* (not *dye*), *crafted* (not *manufactured*), and *simulated* (not *imitation* or *fake*); see also Allan and Burridge (1991).

Other features that build the image of the product are **gradable adjectives**: in the anti-perspirant advert, for example, the product is described as 'the longest lasting Lady'. Here, *longest* is the **superlative** of the series (and so better than the comparative *longer* or the absolute *long*).

We have looked at ways of evoking positive associations in relation to products, and at the use of 'core' vocabulary to evoke familiar concepts. However, as we noted above, adverts have to be memorable, and vocabulary choice can also be used to achieve this. Many of the techniques used to make ads memorable are also shared with literary, and particularly poetic, language. These can make use of any level of linguistic structure, and sometimes several at once. Exploitation of **sound** is a common device. For example, an ad for Mizuno football boots uses alliteration, which we have already noted is prevalent in ad titles. Here, it appears in the headline, *the pride, the passion, the performance.* An ad for Galaxy Caramel chocolate bar uses assonance (vowel sound repetition) on 'a': *Galaxy Caramel . . . Accidents can happen.* Note that these devices work not on the repetition of letters, but the repetition of sounds: *ph* can therefore alliterate with *f*, while *pound* can be assonant with *down.* A second level of linguistic structure in which inventiveness can take place is that of **orthography**: the spelling or appearance of words. Unusual word segmentation (or lack of it) such as *Bodyspray* is included in this category, as is *MacUser* (unusual capitalization to show word boundaries where none are distinguished by spaces). Different fonts and font sizes, colours, and unusual spellings are also used to draw attention to words (*Frijj* milkshake and *Imanance* cosmetics, which is not quite English and not quite French, for example). The morphology or shape of words is also used to good effect, often through the coining of new words using parts of old ones. A nail varnish advertisement, for example, includes the neologism or new coining *Nailslicks*, and the creative combination *shiny-wet* to refer to the finished appearance of the nails. Syntax can be unusual and even ungrammatical, as in *Active Clothing High Technology* (a clothes company slogan). A common device is to use parallelism, or repeated similar grammatical structures. These may be brief, as in *New Look New Woman* (a magazine) and *twist it, use it* (a perfume). The same perfume ad also uses parallelism in its body text:

0% Shrinking Violet. 100% Pure Chipie.

An advertisement for chocolate uses a more extensive parallel structure:

For the taste of a real chocolate bar with
half the fat of milk chocolate, eat Flyte.
For the taste of most reduced-fat chocolate bars,
eat the box.

These are just some of the devices that are employed in creating positive and memorable associations through language, and 'building the image' of the product.

BUILDING RELATIONS

One of the key techniques that is used in much modern advertising is the inclusion of features of face-to-face conversation. Three reasons have been suggested in the linguistics literature for why this might be done:

1   to create 'ordinariness'
2   to create a personal relationship
3   to downplay power differences

Myers (1994) discusses the use of conversational style as a means of creating 'ordinariness' in advertising: if ordinary people are using and talking about a product, the activity of 'selling', or being told something by someone with a vested interest, is downplayed. As Myers (1994: 112) notes, 'everyday talk is not selling anything'. The language of advertisements therefore needs to be as 'ordinary' as possible, and not much is more ordinary than everyday conversation between equals. However, in order to achieve ordinariness in this type of discourse, several obstacles need to be surmounted. The first is that advertising is impersonal, mass communication. Fairclough (1989: 128) suggests that at least one conversational device, that of direct address to the reader/viewer using 'you', constitutes 'simulated personal address . . . to remedy increasing impersonality'. People do not like to feel that they are being addressed as part of a mass audience, as individuality is something that is culturally highly valued in Western society. Fairclough (1989: 62) uses the term 'synthetic personalization', which he describes as 'a compensatory tendency to give the impression of treating each of the people "handled" *en masse* as an individual' (and see also Williamson, 1978: 50). A second problem is that everyday relationships between friends are usually ones of equal power and authority. Fairclough (1989: 37) views the advertising relationship as inherently unequal, since there is no two-way communication between advertiser and consumer, and advertisers are cast as the 'knowers' of information. He suggests that one of the aims of advertising is to simulate an equal power relation, rather than one in which authority and power lie with the advertiser. Just as people like to feel that they are individuals, they also do not like to be talked down to and told what to do. Adopting a conversational style helps to avoid this sense of inequality.

In order to see some of these conversational features at work, we can look first of all at some examples of magazine advertising. The following is an example of social advertising from the UK's Health Education Authority (August 1999):

> After cleansing,
> exfoliating, toning and
> moisturising,
> how about a bit of
> poisoning?
> Considering the care with
> which you choose your
> face creams, perhaps you
> should consider this:
> every cigarette contains
> 4000 toxins, many of
> which your blood stream
> carries right into the
> structure of your skin. So
> how do you cleanse there?
> Er, the cream people are
> still working on that one.
> **Quitline 0800 002200**

This text occupies about an eighth of a magazine page, and appears in the very bottom right-hand corner with the Health Education Authority logo at its right. One very basic way that this advertisement involves the reader in an apparently conversational, equal relationship is to use direct address. Direct address is when the reader or hearer is 'spoken to' as if they were present, and is often characterized by the use of 'you'. In addition to direct address, the advert makes reference to shared knowledge about the habits of the consumer (that she cleanses, tones, and moisturizes, for example, and that she chooses face creams with care). Face-to-face interaction is also mimicked by the use of 'how about' (a common form of invitation or suggestion), the rhetorical question 'So how do you cleanse there?', which is a common device in everyday discussions and which seems to invite suggestions, and the formulaic hesitation 'Er'. Hesitation, of course, is not an expected feature of printed text: see below for more on features of conversation in print (and see the discussion of characteristics of unplanned speech in sports commentary in Chapter 3). A close peer-group relationship is evoked, too, by the use of the phrase 'still working on that one', which is a common everyday expression of British thirtysomethings and below, along with its stablemate 'I'll get back to you on that one' (usually meaning *I don't know* or *I haven't done the task you asked me to do*). Here, then, the use of 'still working on that one' is ironic, and is used in everyday parlance to mean that the work isn't being done at all. The use of the direct language of face-to-face interaction with someone of a similar age and social group implies a close relationship between the 'advisor' (the advertiser) and the reader. Brown and Levinson (1987) note that the use of 'in-group identity markers' such as a shared vocabulary is a way of claiming solidarity with an interlocutor through evoking a shared experience with them, and this seems to be the case here.

Myers (1994: 112) suggests that **turn taking** is a feature of conversation that is regularly evoked in advertising. This is, of course, most obvious in advertisements where interactions are featured, most usually on film, TV and radio. One way of including conversation is to use an indirect address technique, in which the viewer is cast as an eavesdropper in a conversation that takes place between others. This can be done in print, as in the following ad for One 2 One mobile phones:

IF I WANT to make lots of calls during the day won't it be really EXPENSIVE?

No. Because we offer what we call a One 2 One Diamond Service which means you only have to pay 12p per minute all day, every day.

This dialogue takes place between a potential consumer and the phone company, without direct address to the reader at all. Another example does not make clear the distinction between the 'turns' in the conversation, leaving the reader to work out who is speaking. An advert for Johnson & Johnson moisturizer involves a range of strategies of address. The headline appears to be addressed to the reader:

Has something come between you and your skin care?

The body text, however, begins with words that are apparently attributable to the woman pictured in the main image of the ad, accompanied by a baby:

> Nurse him at 3am, get up and go to work, **don't talk to me about a five-step beauty plan**. I don't have time.

If she is answering the question of the headline, perhaps the headline is directed at her, too.

The next 'voice' may be a continuation of her speech, but may be the advertiser. If it is the advertiser speaking, then the woman of the ad *and* the reader are being addressed:

> Here at last is PURPOSE dual-treatment moisturizer from Johnson & Johnson – the one, simple way to soft skin. It's wonderfully light, it won't clog your pores, it has no fragrance, it has just the right sunscreen, dermatologists love it.
>
> Take 15 seconds and put it on. You're beautiful. Tired, but beautiful. Kiss the baby for us.
>
> Have a life. And beautiful skin, too.

The second paragraph of this ad is highly ambiguous, since it is not clear whether 'us' is the advertiser, the Johnson & Johnson company, or the mother and baby speaking to the reader. However, the **gaze** implied by 'you're beautiful . . .' seems a masculine one, which would suggest the voice implied is not the woman featured in the ad. If this is the case, the addressees are both the woman in the ad, and the reader. This advertisement, then, has the features of an overheard dialogue:

Advertiser:	Has something . . .?	[to reader, to woman]
Woman:	Don't talk to me about . . .	[to reader, to advertiser]
?:	Here at last is PURPOSE . . .	[to reader, (to woman)]
Advertiser:	Take 15 seconds . . .	[to reader, to woman]

The ambiguity of this third turn works to good effect as it combines the authoritative voice of the advertiser with the friendly voice of the busy woman advising her peers. The reader is uncertain as to her role in the 'conversation', but this ambiguity is perhaps more inclusive than the purely 'overheard' conversation offered by the One 2 One ad.

A series of animated adverts appeared in the early 1990s featuring animal characters modelled by Nick Park from Aardman Animations, the creator of the Wallace and Gromit characters. The approach adopted was to take tape recordings of ordinary people talking about the electrical appliances in their homes, and use drastically edited-down versions of these soundtracks as the basis for the animation. The result was the use of natural speech in the advert, following on rather in the tradition of the 'vox pop' soap powder advertisements of the 1960s in which housewives were asked to comment on the whiteness of their wash. The following advertisement from the campaign features two pigs, a mother (M) and son (S), in their bathroom:

```
 1   M:      that's why we like electric showers don't we (.)
 2           sponTANeous that's what I like about [
 3   S:                                         [ mYEAH
 4           I'm all muddy and scampering around and
 5           mum goes GET IN THAT SHOWER so I goes (.)
 6           oh YEAH SHOWer (.) nnneeeeeaoow straight
 7           upstairs and into t'shower [4 sylls overlap]
 8   M:                                 [ yeah well what
 9           I like about it especially in summer is that (.) hhh
10           it's quick (.) and you save money n you don't have
11           to put the HEATing on
12   S:      BRILLiant what they can do with technology today
13   Voice:  For all your creature comforts (.) shower electric.
```

In this advert, the two pigs are addressing an interviewer, rather than the viewer: this is demonstrated by the presence of a model microphone apparently pointing towards them. Note that, even in the editing-down that has had to take place to get from a 2-hour interview into 30 seconds, features that show that the speech is natural rather than scripted have been preserved, for example, the markers at the beginning of turns such as 'mYEAH' and 'yeah well'. As Myers (1994: 112) notes, these are 'words that make sense only in response to another remark or immediate action'. He refers to this as evidence of **turn packaging**, namely the fact that turns are built to address other turns in the conversation and need to be marked as such. Other ordinary conversational features are also present, even though this leaves the speech 'untidy'. For example, the son first interrupts the mother at line 3, and then she overlaps him at line 7. The overall effect is of natural conversation, because it *is* natural conversation.

We are also given the impression that we have come in on a conversation that has been going for some time. The advert opens with a sentence type known as the **reverse wh-cleft**: *that's why we like electric showers don't we*. It is as if the first utterance is answering a question, perhaps from the invisible interviewer, and gives a sense that this conversation began before the TV viewer arrived. This construction serves to presuppose the information in the clause-like part of it: here, 'we like electric showers for some reason' is presupposed as already available from the previous discourse. Of course, this is not available to the viewer, who is left simply to absorb the information and catch up as well as possible. This impression is heightened by the use of *that* at the beginning of the sentence, which refers back to something the viewer has not heard. Conversational style, then, can be used either to include the viewer, or to cast them as an onlooker. As Brierley (1995: 145) points out, however, adverts need to talk to the consumer, so even in indirect address advertisements there is usually some element, however minimal, which does address the reader or viewer directly. Here, it is the voice-over: '*For all your creature comforts, shower electric*'. The *you* here is the viewer, so the advert is ultimately directed to the consumer.

Another advertisement in the series features a tortoise 'athlete' who is describing his central heating system. A key feature of his voice is its lack of intonation: it is not an excited, stereotypically advertisement-style voice, but is in fact rather flat. In addition, he speaks hesitantly, with many pauses and some **false starts**:

ah ah an ath-a-lete (.) like me (.) has to be able to to come in (.) f f(.)rom doing a training (.) g run and be warm (.) in all the rooms (.)

The impression of 'ordinariness' is achieved, then, despite the fact that the interlocutors are pigs and tortoises made of modelling clay, by the naturalness and quality of the voices.

It is relevant to note, here, that attitudes to accent play an important role in how people will react to advertisements. Advertisers regularly choose accents that will 'fit' with the product: Boddington's beer, for example, is advertised on UK television using a voice with a Manchester accent, while Hovis bread adverts have long used voices from Yorkshire to create an image of rural innocence and honesty. The Creature Comforts ads (discussed above) use a range of voices, including Scottish, Midlands and North of England. Stereotypically, regional accents such as these are often felt to be associated with positive values such as being down-to-earth, good with money, sociable, and wise, rather than having a particularly high status in terms of social aspirations. Voice contrast is also noticeable in audible advertising, particularly the contrast between characters and voice-overs. Often, the advertising message that recommends a purchase is conveyed using a more authoritative voice than the preceding conversation. The person may be a different sex, and is likely to use an accent than does not clearly evoke a particular region of origin. The relationship set up between the voice-over and the consumer is often very different in terms of power relations to the relationship of equality that has been established by the advertisement characters.

Interpersonal information that sets up a relationship between advertiser and consumer is also carried by the mood of clauses, in particular, the use of **imperatives** and **interrogatives**. Toolan (1988: 54) describes 'an intimate, interactive addressing of the reader, with ample use of interrogative and imperative forms, in a conscious effort to engage the reader rather than simply convey information' as one of the main emphases of advertising language in the printed press. Questioning the reader or hearer, or telling or asking them to do something, necessarily involves the other person. Examples of imperatives are underlined in the following extracts from magazine adverts:

Define and conquer	(Max Factor mascara)
Make the perfect recording for your perfect place	(Sony MiniDisc)
Get your teeth whiter	(Rembrandt toothpaste)
Join Tony Soper for an Island Odyssey	(Noble Caledonia Holidays)

Similarly, questions demand answers, and the use of an interrogative (question) form presupposes the existence of an interlocutor who is in dialogue with the speaker, as in the following examples:

Relationships, share prices, your career. Wouldn't it be nice to have a bit of stability for once?	(Nissan 4-wheel drive car)
Has something come between you and your skin care?	(Johnson & Johnson moisturizer)
Not going anywhere for a while?	(Snickers bar)

The following example, from an advert for Diadora football boots from *Loaded* magazine, is actually ambiguous between an imperative and an interrogative:

Remember playing football against a brick wall . . .

It is not clear whether the reader is being told to remember (imperative reading) or asked whether he remembers (interrogative form). This ambiguity between two common advertising devices serves to reinforce the direct address, although perhaps to make the reader think harder about the message as well.

BUILDING CONSUMERS

We noted above that much advertising focuses on the individualization of the consumer, differentiating them from the mass. When an advertisement addresses *you*, however, it is really addressing an imaginary subject: the advertiser does not really know you. As Williamson (1978: 50) suggests:

. . . for this is not 'you', inherently; there is no logical reason to suppose that the advertisement had 'you' in mind all along. You have to exchange yourself with the person 'spoken to', the spectator the ad creates for itself. Every ad necessarily assumes a spectator: it projects out into the space in front of it an imaginary person composed in terms of the relationship of elements within the ad. You move into this space as you look at the ad, and in doing so 'become' the spectator . . . .

Fairclough (1989: 206ff.) describes a 'subject position' set up for the reader, in which the reader assimilates the kinds of beliefs needed to interpret the advertisement as a kind of 'common sense'. In this section, we look at how language creates the framework of beliefs, associations, aspirations and assumptions that enables advertising to create consumption communities, and communicate to readers or viewers that they are part of them.

A first step in establishing the nature of the identities desired for readers or viewers is to examine the situation: on TV, ads are scheduled to come at certain times of day and in the breaks between certain programmes when it is known that different categories of people will be watching. If you print an ad on the back of a till receipt, it will be seen only by people who use that store, while a bus advertisement will clearly reach a regional audience across all social groups wherever the bus goes. In magazines, we can see the spread of interests presupposed by the publication by looking at the range of advertisements that appear. For example, *Sugar* magazine, which is aimed at teenage girls, has in one issue ads for Tampax tampons, Shockwave hair gel, Hi-Glow hair mascara, VO5 Hot Oil hair conditioner, Solo debit card, Frizz-Ease hair de-frizzer, Benetton eau de toilette, Chipie perfume, Bourjois lipstick and C&A clothing. The reader, then, is assumed to be someone who is female and very interested in her appearance. In comparison, the *Telegraph* magazine, which accompanies a major national newspaper with a predominantly over-55 male readership, has adverts for the Jeep Cherokee 4×4, Audi cars, De Beers diamonds, Sainsbury's apples, NFU Mutual insurance, Debenhams Clinique make-up, Vauxhall cars, Gucci watches, Intel Pentium computer chips and Nissan cars. The reader is clearly expected to be a householder who is at the stage of life where large considered purchases are made, and who has buildings and possessions to insure.

When we look at the nature of the advertisements for these products, the general message also conveys a number of assumptions about the consumer. In *Sugar*, for example, the reader is someone who is negotiating a difficult world. She is inexperienced. The message of the Tampax ad is that the reader is likely to be a first-time user and may find tampons difficult to insert correctly, but she will find things improve with practice. The Solo debit card emphasizes the freedom of 'paying with plastic', without allowing her to run up an overdraft (her first card?). She is also imperilled by problems with her hair. The hair gel ad describes the horror of 'morning hair'. The VO5 ad describes how hair might be damaged by blow-drying, styling, sun and wind. The Frizz-Ease product shows how 'problem' frizzy hair can be made either curly or straight. On the positive side, she is also a party animal, or wants to be. This is shown by the activities pictured in the lipstick, perfume, and clothing ads, where people are dancing and cuddling up to one another.

Further positioning of the reader is done through choice of vocabulary, using terms that will be familiar to the reader, or will be made so through the advert. The *Sugar* ads contain **colloquial** and 'in-group' words, such as *snogging*[2] and *blisserama* (Tampax), *top!* (Poppets sweets), and *totally party* (stick-on nails). It is not particularly important whether these words are in current use in the target group: readers will subscribe to them as words that *some* in-group is using, and perhaps aspire to join the in-group. Similarly, colloquial grammar may be used: the hair mascara ad, for example, contains non-standard dialect in the form of the sentence 'don't need no boy to turn me on', which contains the double negative common in many regional and social dialects.

Perhaps the most pervasive positioning devices are those expressions that **implicate** meanings that are not stated explicitly. It is part of the natural processing of language to draw inferences from what is heard or read. **Conventional implicature** occurs when, through the use of a particular word or phrase, an implication is drawn. For example, 'You've been at the booze again' implies 'You were at the booze before'. Advertising language often contains these implicature triggers such as *again*. An excerpt from the Tampax tampons advertisement in *Sugar* magazine is a case in point (an advertisement

FIGURE 7.1   Tampax 'All the Best Things in Life . . .' Ad

from this campaign is also analyzed in Goddard, 1998, which will be useful for comparison). The advertisement is reproduced in Figure 7.1.

The general argument of the ad is that the first kiss can be a disappointment, as boys are enthusiastic rather than skilful, but patience wins out. Likewise, attempts to use tampons for the first time can be unsuccessful, but the reader should persevere. The ad is very wordy, but an extract from the advert that encapsulates the argument runs as follows:

1: The first snog is a hideous disappointment. [. . .]
2: Now we're well aware that your first experiments with tampons may have been equally disappointing.

Sentence 2 conveys several implications. The second sentence implicates, through the use of *we're well aware that*, proposition 2a:

2a: Your first experiments with tampons may have been disappointing.

Note that, because of the use of the modal verb *may*, sentence 2 also allows 2b:

2b: Your first experiments with tampons may not have been disappointing.

So the reader is positioned as someone who may or may not have been disappointed while trying to use tampons. Sentence 2 also implicates 2c:

2c: Your first use of tampons was an experiment.

Geis (1982: 43) suggests that the effect of conventional implicatures such as these in advertising is to suggest that the implicated propositions are not controversial, and should be accepted as true by the reader. If things went absolutely fine, and the user felt confident and expert, however, 2c may be difficult to accept. In addition, through *first* as a trigger, sentence 2 also implicates 2d:

2d: There were other experiments with tampons.

The reader is therefore not only cast as inexpert, but as trying repeatedly.
   One final assumption of 2 is not an implicature, but a **presupposition**. This form of conveying meaning is stronger than an implicature, and stronger even than an assertion: as we have seen, presupposition requires the reader or hearer to accept the truth of a proposition whether or not the sentence that carries it is itself true. The presupposition trigger in sentence 2 is the expression *your first use of tampons*. The use of the possessive *your* presupposes that you *had* a first use of tampons. This gives rise to presupposition 2e:

2e: You have used tampons.

To see how strong presupposition is, try contradicting a sentence containing the presupposition trigger. The presupposition will remain true, even if you succeed in contradicting the sentence that carries it:

A: <u>Your first use of tampons</u> was a disappointment.
B: No it wasn't!

Even when B disagrees with A's sentence, proposition 2e remains true.

An important piece of positioning, then, is to construct the reader, through conventional implicature, as somebody who has already used tampons but is inexperienced. But there are more implicatures to unpack. The presence of *equally* in sentence 2 also implicates 2f:

2f: Some other experience was disappointing.

Here, then, the reader is asked to accept as non-controversial that she has already had a disappointing experience. What disappointing experience? This must be the 'first snog' referred to in sentence 1. However, sentence 1 did not assert or presuppose that the reader has had a first snog: it does not say 'your first snog', which would do this, but 'the first snog'. What is presupposed by sentence 1, then, is only 1a, and not 1a^a:

1a: There exists a first snog.
1a^a: You have had a first snog.

To interpret the world as seems to be required by 2f, however, the reader apparently *should* accept that she has already had a first snog. The use of *first* in sentence 1, too, triggers an implicature in the same way as the *first* in sentence 2, namely 1b:

1b: There is a series of snogs.

The message of the advertisment is that the attempts at snogging will be successful ('. . . and you're there. Blisserama') and that attempts to insert a tampon correctly will also be. But in order to make sense of the message, the reader has been required to accept a range of implicit propositions about herself: that she has used tampons, inexpertly or unsuccessfully, on a number of occasions, and that she has snogged with boys, unsuccessfully at first, but then successfully. Little or none of this was asserted explicitly in the advertisement, but was conveyed through presupposition and conventional implicature.

Presupposition is so important in reader/hearer positioning in advertising it is worth looking at some more examples. Presupposition as a device requires the presupposed proposition to be accepted not only as non-controversial but as unarguable. There is the additional meaning that, if this fact is not already known to the reader, it is a 'known fact' in the public domain, already available to some community of readers. So '*how to spot a tension headache*' presupposes there is such a thing as a tension headache, and also conveys the assumption that the advertiser expects the reader – or the community of readers to which the reader is expected to belong – to already know this.

As in the case of the Tampax advertisement analyzed above, it is clear that, in many cases, the beliefs of the reader do not necessarily quite match those that presuppositions require us to accept or, to use the technical term, to **accommodate** (see the discussion of presupposition in Chapter 6, relating to magazine features, for further examples and applications of this term).

These feelings can become clearer when reading publications that are clearly not meant for you as a target reader. For example, if you have no children, reading magazines for parents of new babies will reveal some presuppositions it is impossible to accommodate:

> The new Britax travel system.
> All you need for your baby's journey into childhood.

Non-parents will not be able to accommodate the presupposition conveyed by *your baby*, since it presupposes that the reader has a baby. Some other presupposition examples from advertising include the following:

Possessive adjective:	Reveal <u>your best skin</u>.
Presupposition:	You have best skin.
Definite article:	<u>The lengths you go to</u> for pleasure.
Presupposition:	You go to some lengths for pleasure.
Demonstrative adjective:	<u>This great new feeling</u> can last and last.
Presupposition:	There exists a great new feeling.
how-questions:	How much chocolate mocha supreme will it take to get you into these jeans?
Presupposition:	It will take some amount of chocolate mocha supreme to get you into these jeans.
why-question:	Why let cramps get the best of you?
Presupposition:	You let cramps get the best of you for some reason.
when-question:	When are you going to take the Crunch Test?
Presupposition:	You are going to take the Crunch Test at some time.
Wh-cleft:	What surprised me was how much my doctor could do for me.
Presupposition:	I was surprised about something.
Reverse *wh*-cleft:	That's why you can trust Vital.
Presupposition:	You can trust Vital for some reason.

Presupposition and implicature, then, are powerful ways of establishing meaning without asserting it, and thereby making it one of the claims of an advertisement.

FURTHER READING

Goddard (1998) is a readable and very thorough exposition of the language and visual imagery of advertising, and is an excellent next stop for those wanting to take their study of advertising further. This book contains an interesting historical overview (1998: 86ff.) of the development in explicitness of sanitary product ads (during the 1930s, 1950s and 1990s), including the Tampax advertisement from the same campaign as the 'snogging' ad discussed above. Cook (1992) and Myers (1994) are also highly recommended as general studies of advertising language. Cook (1992: 131ff.) has a clear and thorough section on the use of parallelism in literature and advertising. Dyer (1982) is an older, but still useful, overview of advertising practice and methods, and contains a useful chapter on advertising language (1982: 139ff.).

The visual rhetoric of advertising – how images are used, and how image, text, and the gaze of the viewer combine in making the message – is of course a vital component of advertising communication. Goddard (1998) contains a good introduction on the use of images in advertising, and how consumers relate to them. Dyer (1982) provides a useful and readable discussion in somewhat more detail of the positioning of products and people in ads. Vestergaard and Schroeder (1985) discuss both language and image in targeting particular groups of consumers, while Williamson (1978) presents a highly detailed and complex discussion of how products and meanings come to be associated through both word and image. Messaris (1997) is a more recent book-length study of the contribution of visual images to advertising, and provides a useful analysis of recent trends in visual communication. Finally, Cook (1992) contains a discussion of how a large number of different media – music, images, speech, and writing – combine in the advertising message. Nilsen (1979) presents a systematic overview of how 'play' at many linguistic levels creates memorable and positive product names.

Further reading on **discourse markers** such as *well, and, but, so,* and *because* and their many functions can be found in the detailed book-length study by Schiffrin (1987). Schiffrin (1999) is a shorter article on the function of *oh,* while a useful discussion of **turn taking** is given by Ten Have (1999: 110ff.). Ten Have also contains a very useful bibliography on conversation analysis in general, with a number of seminal references on turn taking.

Leech (1966) was the first to identify a range of linguistic characteristics of what he termed 'standard advertising English', and explains these clearly and accessibly. In particular, he outlines a range of grammatical features of advertising English, including the characteristics of direct and indirect address, clause structures, cohesion and vocabulary. Even if advertising more than thirty years later may not adhere to these 'standard' features to the extent it did in the mid-1960s, some advertisements still do, and some even use them ironically. Toolan (1988) can be seen as an extension and brief revision of Leech's approach. Tanaka (1994) presents a useful **pragmatic** approach to advertising.

A discussion of the use of different accents in advertising can be found in Myers (1994: 90ff.). For a good general introduction to accents and dialects, see Wardhaugh (1998: 21ff.). Hughes and Trudgill (1996), and the accompanying recordings, are a good source of information on the range of British accents, particularly their phonetic differences. Freeborn (1993: 59ff.) gives a helpful set of short extracts of dialect forms of English, and hints on how to describe them grammatically. Milroy and Milroy (1993) is a more detailed analysis of a range of British dialects, going from their sound right through to the kinds of differences that can be found in sentence formation and text structuring. A summary of research into attitudes to different varieties of accents is given in Fasold (1987, Chapter 6).

The differences between speech and writing are discussed in overview in Freeborn (1993: 76ff.), while Halliday (1989) is a subtle and complex book-length study of the topic.

TOPICS FOR STUDY AND DISCUSSION

1. An article in the magazine section of the *Independent* newspaper (7th August 1993) describes mail-order collectibles – sets of thimbles, dolls, plates, and figurines, for example, ordered by mail and collected over several months or years – as 'a £50 million industry that defies logic'. If it *does* defy logic, how do you account for the wordiness of the ads? Is this 'reason-why' advertising, or does the language function in some other way? What is the persuasive element in the language?

2. Examine some copies of different newspapers and magazines and identify which elements of the adverts constitute direct address to the reader, and which are indirect. What features do you find occur most regularly to signal that either mode of address is taking place? Do you ever find a 'pure' indirect address advert, in which *no* direct appeal is made to the reader? Do you find that direct and (mainly) indirect address patterns occur regularly with any particular kinds of product?

3. Identify the features of conversation that occur in a range of advertisements. Do you find that the conversational approach occurs more often with some kinds of products, or in some kinds of publications, than others? Which products or publications use adverts in which the conversational approach is irrelevant? Why do you think this is?

4. Record some TV and radio ads, taking careful note of the voices that are used throughout. What kinds of voices are used in the body of the ad, and how do these compare to any final voice-over? What kind of relationships are established with the viewer or hearer in each case, in terms of intimacy, warmth, power, authority? Is regional accent a factor in the shaping of these relationships?

5. Examine the use of different fonts to perform different functions in magazine adverts. Is there any useful generalization you can make about how fonts establish different 'voices' and therefore relationships in the ads, in a similar way to the previous item?

6. Do advertisements in women's magazines function differently from those in men's? Compare two adverts of a similar nature, or even for similar products. Is there a different level of reliance on linguistic persuasion? How are consumers 'built' in each case? Are there differences, too, in the product characteristics that are emphasized and presented as attractive?

7. Not all advertisements are for the same kind of product or service. Brierley (1995) distinguishes three broad types: fast moving consumer goods (frequent purchases such as food, toiletries, household consumables), consumer durables (considered purchases such as carpets, cars, washing machines), and services (such as holidays, travel, financial products, banking, advice, and health services). Using a selection of

advertisements for each kind of product, can you say how product differences influence the nature, language and placement of advertising?
8. The point has also been made that advertising language is very like literary language, particularly the language of poetry (Leech, 1966, Toolan, 1988). Taking examples of both, can you distinguish them linguistically? What are their similarities?

SUMMARY

Advertisements are a diverse genre of communication, ranging across different media, and targeting different groups of consumers. A first look at the structure of print ads revealed a structure of headline, body text, slogan, and signature. Slogans are often **alliterative** and **presuppositional**, and may play with language in other ways, such as using unusual syntax. A common structure in the body text is **problem-solution**. Sentences are often **disjunctive** and incomplete. Fairclough's three-part framework for analyzing advertisements was applied. Building the image of the product involved making positive claims, some of which are not interpreted in ways their logic would suggest, using positive, memorable, and familiar vocabulary, and using language play. Building relations involved invoking ordinariness, particularly using the structures and features of face-to-face conversations between equals. Relationships between advertiser and consumer were also constructed through the choice of regional and social accents, and through direct address using **imperative** and **interrogative** forms. Building the consumer was done through the spread of topics in a particular publication, sharing vocabulary, and in particular the non-explicit meanings that are conveyed through conventional **implication** and **presupposition**.

NOTES

1   Readers will note that 'everyday' as one word is an adjective, as in 'The Language of Everyday Life'. Adjectives modify *nouns*. To be strictly grammatical in Standard English, an adverbial phrase, 'every day' (two words) would be used here, which modifies an action (the caring for the lips) by decribing when it is done. However, I have seen the use of the adjective 'everyday' performing the adverbial function sufficiently frequently to suggest that this may be a linguistic change in progress, although many will still judge it to be incorrect.
2   *Snogging* is a long-standing colloquial term in British English for prolonged kissing.

8 Researching the Language of Everyday Life

The aim of this chapter is to help you get started, as straightforwardly as possible, on a project involving naturally occurring language. It includes information about how to arrive at a useful design for a study, how to plan and carry out your data collection, and how to treat the data once you have it. Suitable references are included throughout that will enable you to read up further on the issues involved in capturing language in the wild. You are particularly advised to follow up these additional references for anything beyond a study at a fairly introductory level.

FINDING A SUITABLE SUBJECT FOR STUDY

If you are working for an assignment, your individual topic will, naturally, have to conform to the various criteria that your tutor will have set, depending on the content of your course of study. The advice below is intended to help you pick out a topic similar to those dealt with elsewhere in this book: a situation in which spoken or written language are in some way characteristic of a particular everyday situation. It is assumed that one of the aims of your study will be to capture through close linguistic analysis the features of the language that reflect the situation, arriving at a closer description of both the language and the features of the context in the process.

From your reading so far, you will have begun to appreciate that we are simply surrounded by texts: the advice here is intended to help you pick out an area about which there will be something interesting to say, and perhaps to look more closely at your own everyday communicative environments to widen your choice beyond what immediately suggests itself.

How does an analyst go about studying language in context? There are many approaches, but a simplified way of doing things is to approach the subject in one of the following ways:

- Select a genre of discourse, such as *newspaper advertisements* or *dentist-patient interaction*, and discuss the linguistic features that contribute to its overall effect;
- Select a particular linguistic feature, such as *tag questions* or *silence*, and analyze the meaning of this feature alone, either across a range of genres or in one or two genres;

TABLE 8.1   Mix-and-match Table for Project Design

Issues	Linguistic features	Types of discourse
power	core vocabulary	political speeches
personalization	presupposition	dental consultations
social groupings	'fancy syntax'	legal documents
authority	intonation	poster advertising
ideology	connotation	websites
politeness	transitivity	chat shows
hearer 'positioning'	unplanned discourse	official forms
shared knowledge	vocabulary choice	police interviews
formality	questioning	problem pages
mode	indirectness	magazine features
intimacy	rhetorical structure	romantic fiction
age difference	turn taking	product instructions
image building	silence	telephone sales
colonization	speech errors	tutorial discourse
status	metaphor	art class
gender	orthography	sports training
humour	graphic devices	scientific discourse

• Select a more general issue, such as *initiative* or *politeness*, and analyze the linguistic features that correlate with this, either in a single text type or across a range.

Combining these three approaches, however, can generate very strong project ideas. To work out how this might be done, you could use a mix-and-match table based on text type, linguistic features and general issues. Table 8.1 is an example, using concepts and features that are touched on in the literature and in this book. Using the tips in the rest of this section, however, you may wish to construct your own table. Not all the combinations will yield interesting or even possible studies, (spelling in chat shows, for example, will not work), but the process will get the creative juices flowing and several possible projects should arise.

For your own table, you could consult the glossary for other examples of both general issues and linguistic features, and supplement these with your other reading. Specific suggestions for ways of thinking creatively about text types that occur in particular situations are given below, dividing the space of discourse into three areas: written, live spoken, and broadcast-spoken.

WRITTEN LANGUAGE

To find an interesting topic involving written data, a useful start is to think about your everyday life – this will be general advice for any topic, written or spoken. For written texts, however, it is helpful to note down over a couple of days whenever you encounter a written text. Here are some examples:

cereal packet	shampoo instructions	junk mail
bank letter	chequebook	names of cars
signpost	newspaper	magazine
bus ticket	car manual	graffiti
official form	essay/assignment	textbook
library info	textbook	leaflet
TV subtitles	Ceefax, Teletext	advertisement
e-mail	poster	web page
food labelling	health leaflet	prospectus

Some of the possibilities may not be very promising – bus tickets, for example, might prove rather limiting for a study. Some will be too general, and could usefully be broken down into further subcategories: in this book, for example, it will be noticed that 'newspapers' and 'magazines' were considered too broad a category for useful study. You might therefore like to break these down into component parts, such as editorials, advertisements, problem pages, news reporting, features and so on.

Either perspective could be enlightened, too, by the use of comparison between two kinds of data, perhaps closely related (for example, advertising posters compared with magazine advertising; instructions compared with the packet information for particular products). More distantly related texts are harder to write about since they don't suggest obvious comparisons. You could, however, move between **modes** for comparison, rather than comparing two types of written texts: an interesting topic might involve, for example, comparison of spoken and written advertising (TV vs magazine), or e-mail vs written mail, e-mail vs telephone conversation between intimates, or a printed newspaper compared with the same newspaper's website.

SPOKEN LANGUAGE

It is often difficult to be sufficiently objective about your everyday life to see something in it that might be the basis of an interesting project about spoken language. The most successful projects, however, are often those that you as a researcher can get really close to, and are therefore the things that you might at first overlook. Here are some possibilities:

1   Do (or did) you, or a close relative or friend, have a job that involves you in interaction? (It would be difficult to imagine one that didn't.) Working in a supermarket, bar, restaurant, a bank, a public service of some kind, for money or not, places you in a good position to get valuable data.

2   Do you do a hobby or sport? Think of the verbal element involved. How did you learn how to do it (the language used in training or learning)? What is the language used in performing it (directions, judgements, scoring, commentary)? How do you and others talk about it, either during or afterwards?

3   What are the regular interactions you are involved in during your everyday occupation? Keep a simple diary for a day or two, jotting down when and where you talk to people. This may include using public transport, buying lunch and coffee and other service interactions during the day (shops, at work, library, telephone services you might use), quite apart from whatever you do as your 'main' occupation.

4   If you are involved in an institution (and this includes colleges and universities) try to find out what kinds of interaction take place in order for it to run itself. The most obvious to you may well be teaching interactions such as lectures and tutorials, but apart from this it's like any business: it has financial, training, informational, and other management requirements all of which require staff to interact with each other and with people outside. You might, for example, ask a secretary or administrator in your department what kinds of interaction make up their day, and then perhaps follow up contacts with some of the people your chosen person talks to and ask them the same question.

5   What kinds of interaction are involved in running your non-working life? What about the bank, phoning up to get things done to your flat or house, getting things cleaned or fixed, ordering goods and services either by phone or face-to-face?

The above list should get you thinking about a number of situations that might be interesting to study. Think about how the people involved know the rules they need to follow in the interaction in order to behave appropriately. These are normally subconscious, and often the people involved couldn't tell you what the rules are. As a linguist, you may well be able to work them out, and explain what regulates the elaborate verbal dances that people carry out, perfectly and subconsciously, every day.

If the situation involves an institutional representative, it may also help to see if you can gain access to materials that are used to train them in their role: sales assistants, for example, are frequently given training that explicitly instructs them on the verbal element of their job.

BROADCAST-SPOKEN LANGUAGE

We will assume that 'broadcast' includes terrestrial and satellite TV channels and radio. An assumption behind all the spoken data used in this book, too, is that the language is unscripted, and therefore shows conversational features that are unplanned (as far as is possible in the context). We will therefore rule out the scripted parts of news broadcasts, TV drama, magazine programmes, soaps and radio plays, but can include talk shows, 'vox pop' documentaries, live interviews on television and radio, live comedy videos and so on. Many of the kinds of discourse included are planned as to timing and topic – including the floor contributions on many talk shows – but not scripted, which should give access to some spontaneous speech features. Of course, the language of scripted broadcasts is interesting in itself, but will not be considered further here.

A rich source of spoken data exists in electronic form in computer corpora, a section on which can be found later in this chapter. Carter and McCarthy (1997), in a book based on the CANCODE corpus of spoken English, present a range of transcriptions of spoken language from 18 different situations, and very useful commentaries on them.

As with written data, a more interesting topic often arises out of some 'crossing' of types of data – using comparisons between two types, for example – or selection of specific features for study, rather than a straight and perhaps unfocused description of your chosen data. What is interesting about the situation you have chosen? How do participants cast themselves by the way they speak? Who sets the agenda? Do agendas clash in any way? How do participants negotiate with one another to gain the floor? How do facilitators such as chat show hosts control the situation? Does everyone have equal rights to speak? Do they answer one another's questions directly? Many of these characteristics of interaction are based on the negotiation of power relationships between speakers, and these factors are often particularly important where the topic is emotive or controversial and when time is limited. Both these factors are often relevant in political interviews and TV talk shows, for example.

PLANNING THE PROJECT

Before going into the intricacies of data collection, it is important to spend some time planning what the aims and scope of the project are, and what sub-tasks it will involve. This should be done paying close attention to the aims and scope of your assignment, consulting your tutor for additional guidance. Every institution has its different aims, but here are some characteristics that would be expected of more or less any piece of research:

- Well-chosen and accurately transcribed data.
- A hypothesis or set of expectations that express the project's aim, detailing what you expect to find.
- A good grounding in relevant literature you've been able to find for yourself.
- Clarity of organization and expression.
- A clear indication of its own limitations.

While this list may seem onerous, it's an important guide to planning the project, rather than just a set of points to attend to at the writing-up stage. The guidance in this chapter should help you choose the right data: its accurate transcription (if it's spoken) is of course important, as is clear indication of how and where you got the data. You should also make clear what you expected to find in the data: all the better if this expectation is grounded in your reading. If, for example, you are interested in comparing the different forms of advertising appearing in women's and men's magazines, you may have quite well-founded expectations about the predominant motifs that each will use. You may, for example, decide to read about advertising language, and about 'male' and 'female' language, and then state what you expect to find. If your expectation isn't borne out by your study, this is still a finding, albeit a negative one.

EXPLORING RELEVANT LITERATURE

It is a good idea to begin your preliminary look at the literature before you complete the collection and transcription of data, since what you read can help shape your study. For example, if you decide upon chat shows, you may find that conversational management interests you: interruptions and turn taking, for example. You will then want to take care to transcribe these features carefully. If you are interested in metaphor in news reporting, you will need to collect a sample of newspaper reports (perhaps comparing one event between different publications) that contains more than just a couple of metaphorical references. If you are looking at something as big as rhetorical organization, such as in written advertisements, you will need more adverts than you would if you were looking at, say, vocabulary. Generally, the larger the phenomenon, the less frequent it is, so you will need more data to find it, and even more to get a good sample of it.

Your library and your tutor will be able to give you tips on how to find relevant literature on your particular topic. It is, however, very worthwhile to use the World Wide Web as a means of searching for information, and to use sources such as CD-ROMs as well as traditional paper-based library holdings at your institution. Two resources that are particularly relevant in linguistics research are the CD-ROM databases produced by the Modern Languages Association (MLA) and the CD-ROM abstracts database known as the Linguistics and Language Behavior Abstracts (LLBA). Both contain large numbers of linguistics references to books and articles, and can be searched using keywords and phrases. A little practice with either can yield two or three central references either to print out or save on a disk, and either can usually be found in your library or ordered through inter-library loans, if you have access to this facility in your institution. Even if your library has neither LLBA or MLA, you can still use a 'search engine' on the World Wide Web – a program that searches any set of World Wide Web pages on the internet for anything matching a description you give (Yahoo, Lycos and AltaVista are the names of some search engines). Keyword searches will yield anything from useful references to other students' course notes. As a general rule, World Wide Web references should be treated like any published source: you should give the address of the page you used (its URL or Uniform Resource Location) in your bibliography. Ask at your computing advisory service or library information desk for information on using any of these resources.

The ability to find relevant references yourself is evidence of a valuable research skill, and one which will improve both the quality of your project and the impression it makes. Take care to cite your sources clearly and correctly, using the form that your institution requires. It's helpful to start a bibliography right at the beginning of your study, on a computer if possible, including full references to anything you've looked at, which can then be weeded out to include just the references that you cited in the final version of the project. Looking through your bibliography is a good ego-boost during the writing process, and keeping full references saves much precious time at the end of a project, when looking for an elusive reference, perhaps to a page in a book that's now out of the library, can take hours.

SCOPE OF THE PROJECT: LIMITATIONS, STATISTICS, AND 'PROOF'

It is assumed here that the scope of your project is something between a few weeks and a few months. Although the guidelines given here will still hold good for larger endeavours, planning a corpus of data that will be amenable to quantitative analysis – that is, that will yield reliable results through counting – is a larger undertaking and will require expert guidance as well as the use of references on statistical sampling techniques. In your project, you may well need to count things – for example, you may wish to know if male participants use fewer hesitations per turn than female ones in a chat show, or if one newspaper uses more polysyllabic words than another. It is always helpful to use percentages to display these results, since these control for texts of different lengths. For example, if one text contains 132 examples of something, and another contains 47, it will be helpful to know if this comes out at 32% for both of them when compared with the number of words. However, if there are only three examples of something in a ten-word text, the use of statistics can appear to disguise the triviality of this result at 33%. When there are only very few examples of something, don't just give a percentage: state exactly how many examples you found, and how large the data sample was, to give the reader a proper idea of the scale of your study and findings. As a general guideline, if you have less than 30 of anything, you should be aware that yours might be an unrepresentative result, and you should be suitably diffident about this when reporting it.

It is always heartening to see in a project that the writer, student or not, understands the limits of what they have found, and how likely it is to be indicative of what will be true of other texts of the same type. For this reason, it is helpful to include a section describing what you would have done given more space and time, and outlining your understanding of the limitations of your sample. Within the space and the time allowed for you to complete your project, you should not expect to be able to *prove* anything. In fact, 'prove' is a word that scientists use with care, if at all. You can, however, state clearly whether or not your data supported your legitimate expectations and whether you felt that any of your results were due to peculiarities of the data you collected. If you feel disappointed that you cannot be conclusive about your hypothesis and its success, it is worth remembering that large-scale linguistic projects which attempt to do this are often planned in terms of three years of one or two people's time, (and full-time, at that!) to collect, transcribe, and analyze the data.

PLAN B

It is a good idea in the early stages to have a plan B, even if you are completely sure you want to carry out your plan A. Things can go wrong, especially when you are gathering your own live data. It is helpful if plan B is something that you can switch into at an early stage, and does not have the same difficulties as plan A: if, for example, your plan A involves taping teachers and children in a primary school in your area, and timings are hard to negotiate, it makes sense for your plan B to be something quicker and more accessible – something from TV, for example, or some easily available written texts. Take advice from your tutor and take note of how far other students on your course have progressed with their data collection and transcription so that you can work out when is a good time to abandon plan A as a lost cause. This will avoid the situation of you still chasing your data when everyone else is writing up their results.

DATA COLLECTION

Once you've decided on an area to study, you will of course need to collect the data. For some kinds of analysis of spoken interaction, taking observation or field notes of your chosen situation may be sufficient: see Graddol et al. (1994: 174ff.) for a description of some methods and situations in which this may be appropriate. For a close analysis of the detail of interactions, however, I am assuming that you will want to report on actual texts and discourses in full. Below, information is given both on collecting your own data, and on using data available from on-line corpora (existing computer data banks).

There are many theoretical pitfalls involved in collecting and transcribing data. If you are attempting a long project at higher than an introductory level, it will be helpful for you to review some of the biases that may creep in through recording, sampling, and transcription. Ochs (1979) and Stubbs (1983: 218ff.) are useful references in this regard.

HOW MUCH DATA?

I'm afraid that the best answer to this question is 'how long is a piece of string?' It's a question frequently asked, especially in view of considerations such as those dealt with in the previous section. It all depends on what you're studying, and the scope of the project you are attempting. As a general guideline, five minutes of conversational data would take an experienced transcriber about an hour to complete: allow longer if you are a novice. Before you begin your project, it's a good idea to attempt to transcribe five minutes of conversation, if you intend to attempt a spoken topic, since this will give you a good check on what's going to be viable in the time you have.

Another variable is what you intend to focus on. If you intend to do a comparison between two kinds of data, you'll obviously need more than one sample of both. If you intend a genre study of a particular text, you will perhaps need three or four examples of the text type, but this depends on length. A study of service encounters in shops, for example, may find that at an ordinary till it's possible for more than 100 encounters to occur within an hour, so using 20 or 30 of these is perfectly possible. TV advertisements are longer, so anywhere between six and ten of these might suffice. Whole conversations may be arbitrarily long, so two or three may be enough. Check with your tutor for guidance. Another tip is that you may wish to transcribe *examples* of what you're interested in, but base your observations on informal impressions of a larger corpus. So, you may listen to or read your data several times over and form the impression that a certain speaker performs a certain agenda-reinforcing manoeuvre repeatedly, or that a certain rhetorical structure occurs several times in different examples of the same genre. You might then transcribe the sections in which this takes place in order to pay particular attention to them, quoting one example in the text and referring to the others. Another way of cutting down an impossibly long transcription task is to concentrate on certain key sequences of talk: conversation openings and closings, for example, or certain topic segments.

Obviously, using data from a pre-existing source such as an on-line corpus will give you more time to do analysis, but you have less control over the form of the data and less knowledge about the situations in which it was collected. So, if your study is on newspaper language and you want to compare two newspapers, you need to know exactly which newspaper each article is from. An on-line corpus may not necessarily tell you this.

GATHERING WRITTEN DATA

Gathering written text is mainly a matter of tracking it down. If you are using newspapers, it's worthwhile finding out if any library nearby receives newspaper editions on CD-ROM, since these can be searched by date and by keyword and you can then save onto disk and/or print off the articles you want. Many libraries keep back editions of newspapers and other periodicals. If you need special materials, such as training materials or other written texts only available to certain professions, it makes sense to use a personal contact, or contact the relevant professional organization.

An area of confusion that sometimes arises is the thorny issue of copyright. All texts (including computer files, tapes of conversations, published written texts of any kind) belong to somebody, and, in the UK at least, the author's or publisher's copyright over it lasts for 70 years after the death of that 'author'. Any kind of copying of any text potentially infringes copyright. However, if you wish to copy a text for research purposes (make a copy of a newspaper article, for example, to analyze the language) then this *probably* constitutes what is called 'fair dealing' under section 29 of the 1988 Copyright Act, which allows copying for the purposes of private study, criticism, review and such purposes. 'Fair dealing' has never been tested in court, and is not actually defined in the Act. So, it is important to copy as little as possible, and to cite fully the sources of any text you wish to analyze. If you are unsure about whether what you plan to do constitutes 'fair dealing', or any other copyright issue, you can get advice from your library, or consult a reputable source on copyright such as Jones (1996).

If the written texts you use as data have been published in any way, include in your text or as an appendix precise references to when and where they were published. If there is any possibility of your work reaching public view (in a collection of papers, for example), you will need to clear copyright for any of the written text you wish to reproduce. This will involve contacting the original publisher and asking permission. For a project that is simply to be submitted to a College or University, however, copyright clearance is not required.

GATHERING LIVE, SPOKEN DATA

For projects involving spoken discourse, I will be assuming that you are recording a situation of the kind already described in this book: the person in my mind here is a student (undergraduate or postgraduate) who probably won't have done such a thing before. I'm also assuming that you don't have enormous resources in terms of advice and equipment and that you won't need a recording that's going to be of broadcast quality: just something that's good enough for you to transcribe effectively. If your needs are different from this, you may still find this section of use, but you should probably take more local advice, especially about equipment.

Since gathering live, spoken data involves close co-operation with others, it is worth spending a little more time on the factors that will help ensure the success of a data-gathering exercise. It might therefore help you to consider them when you make your choice of topic, and try to choose something that has the following characteristics:

1 Familiar situation: a knowledge of the situation that will enable you to record practically and unobtrusively, avoiding the physical and emotional pitfalls that are inherent in the situation.
2 Inside contact: someone (perhaps yourself) who is connected to the situation in which you are intending to tape, who can be counted on to ensure that you get what you want; and
3 Control over time: how soon you can get your data, and/or how much control you can have over when it's collected.

If you have the choice, it's very much easier to gather your data from a situation with which you are familiar and are already a regular participant, or where a *close* friend or relative is in that position: you are, in very important ways, already 'in', and will be able to work out not only the most likely points of interest from a social or linguistic point of view, but the most practical way of recording the data while disturbing the natural course of events as little as possible. Perhaps most importantly, you'll be able to see how the collection of data can be done without offending anyone involved.

Because your project is likely to represent an intrusion of some kind, however minor, you may either be refused access, or mutually convenient access might be so hard to organize that it takes forever to finally get into a position to record. The closeness of your link with the situation you are trying to record really helps here: the closer the link, the less likely it is to become protracted or, worse, to fall through (if you don't know them, your priorities are less likely to be adopted as theirs).

Prior to Recording Live, Spoken Interaction

The cardinal rule is get *permission* from anyone and everyone who might have any interest in the interaction. If everyone involved is an adult who is in law capable of consent, then it's often enough just to ask the people involved. However, people who are representing an institution in some way (for example, sales representatives, waiting staff or teachers) may well need to ask their superiors: in general, it's a good idea to make sure your subjects have permission from the level immediately above them. Ask your tutor if your College or University has any rules of its own about data collection, and whether, for example, written permission needs to be gained from the place you are going. A letter from your tutor, too, may help you identify yourself. If you want to collect data in a situation in which some participants are not deemed to be capable of giving consent (children and minors, people in certain kinds of institutions, people with certain disabilities, for example) then you should accept the guidance of their responsible teachers or carers. Make sure you know who is, in law, able to give permission for your intended subjects: again, ask your tutor to check up if you are not sure. In schools, you may well need to get parental permission for the children you are hoping to record and/or interview: the head teacher will guide you on this point. In caring situations (medical, for example) or in any place where children are looked after, you should always make sure you check with an institutional representative before approaching anyone: don't expect just to walk in and out. Build it into your plans that this process will take time, and be prepared even to be refused access, despite your best preparations.

Perhaps the biggest problem with recording naturally occurring talk is the Observer's paradox, a term coined by the sociolinguist William Labov. The paradox is that the very act of observing natural speech will make subjects self-conscious about it, and make them speak less naturally. This obviously means that recording needs to be done with the minimum of attention being drawn to it. Rather than recording obtrusively, you may need to wait elsewhere and ask the people after the recording is done for permission to use the data. In a public situation such as a shop, however, any approach to someone else's clients or customers must be done in close consultation with management in the store or institution you are working in. Some places will be happy for their representative to ask permission, and you must ensure you have a means of making a note of which interactions you have permission to use and which not. Some places have a pre-existing warning displayed in their literature – some phone services, for example – that tapes may be made for training purposes. Check with your institutional representative whether any such arrangement comfortably covers you, or even whether training tapes exist that you could use. You can offer your tapes for training use if that brings you within this agreement.

However, it may also be important not to divulge too much to potential subjects and people who may speak to them about what specifically you are interested in within the data you are recording, as this will make them self-conscious about their behaviour. It may be useful to imply that you're interested in the content of what people are saying, rather than its form, or to divert attention onto another participant. For example, one study of tutors speaking to students was helped by the students thinking that the tutor was the object of the researcher's attention, and the tutor thinking that the students were. Most self-consciousness evaporates after a few minutes due to the overriding demands of the interaction, but you can obviously help by being unobtrusive – absent, if possible – and not fiddling with the equipment to remind people of it. If you think that some subjects have remained self-conscious throughout the interaction – through continued reference to being on tape, for example – you should discard that particular data.

Apart from asking your subjects' permission, it's sometimes necessary to maintain confidentiality about what appears on your tapes. Check with your contact person whether this is the case: even some relatively innocuous situations may need to remain confidential since they involve the revelation of names, addresses or financial details. If this is the case, you can reassure your subjects that any names that appear on the tape will be changed in the transcription. You may need to hand in your tapes to your tutor with your project, but in this case you can ask him or her to respect their confidentiality. You can also offer to hand tapes back after the project is finished.

You can be generous with your findings once you have finished: offer the participants access to the data, if you think it may be of interest, and a copy of your report. People are often interested in how they sound on tape and may have their own uses for work tape recordings, although it's important to make sure that control of the tapes resides with the subjects themselves: don't use your recordings for any other purpose than that which you made clear to those involved.

Recording Equipment for Live, Spoken Interaction

In what follows, I will be assuming that you are making an audio, and not a video, recording of your material. This, of course, means that you will not be able to comment on aspects of gaze, gesture, posture and other elements of non-verbal communication except through informal note-taking at the scene. If you are thinking of using video, and of looking at non-verbal communication, a good starting reference is Graddol et al. (1994: 174ff.), who discuss ways of including non-verbal information in transcripts.

Your College or University may well provide, and instruct you on, suitable equipment for making your recording, particularly if students or researchers there regularly record live speech for various purposes (marketing, social sciences, linguistics, psychology and media studies, for example, all have regular needs in this area). Take advice from your tutor and/or technician on equipment, therefore, and, if you need to, contact the Audio-Visual Services section of your institution to see if they can offer advice or lend equipment. (Different places are set up differently, and it will almost certainly be the case that this section has a different name.) The information given below could supplement your existing knowledge, but is mainly intended for people starting from scratch with relatively little advice on equipment, or who may even need to supply their own.

What You'll Need

What you will need will vary according to the situation, so it may help to think of a few quick examples to focus the mind on how recording might be set up. Whether your subjects are moving around or stationary will be important, as will the level of background noise. Here are a few situations:

Retail sales: two or more shop assistants are walking around the shop floor all day, and you need to get their speech on individual tapes.
Group discussion: a smallish circular group, round a room or table, where most participants are going to contribute and you want to record them all.
Interview: your data consists of you or someone else interviewing one or two people, and you want these voices on the tape.

There are some fairly hi-tech ways of recording all of these, and if you are in an institution where ample advice and equipment are available to you, you might want to skip the rest of this section. If you want to rely on a few fairly simple pieces of equipment, you will find this section useful.

A suitable basic kit is as follows:

- A cassette tape recorder;
- One or more suitable microphones that attach with a lead;
- The right adapter to connect the mike and tape recorder;
- Either spare batteries or a mains adapter;
- Cassette tapes.

If you need to record more than one person on the same tape, you will only need one tape recorder, but you will need either a suitable microphone that will capture them all (best for a quiet, stationary situation) or several microphones and a small mixer to connect in several mikes to the same tape recorder. If you don't mind if your people are on different tapes (you are collecting several different interactions simultaneously, for example) you will need more than one complete set of equipment.

Tapes and Tape Recorders

The best kind of tape recorder for a job like this is small and simple: effectively a personal stereo that records. These are often found in large electrical shops and are sold as business tape recorders for people to record letters for dictation and so on. It's best to choose one that takes standard cassette tapes rather than micro cassettes, so that you can play back the tapes on other machines if need be. Don't be afraid to try out different machines: take a blank tape to the shop and talk to the machine. It is worth getting something with good recording heads, and the difference between brands in this respect can be astounding. If you are going to use a plug-in external microphone – the set-up recommended here – make sure the machine has a microphone input to plug it into. Other useful features might include a 'Voice Activated' facility, where the machine will only record when it hears something (this saves tape, but doesn't allow you to note the length of pauses). A jack for an external power source can also be useful if the tape recorder isn't going to be moved during recording, so that you don't have to rely on batteries. Finally, choosing a tape recorder with a numerical tape counter can be useful as it provides you with a way of referring to parts of the tape and finding things on the tape quickly. In 1999, all this could be had for around £35.

Unless you have specialist equipment that is able to make use of really good tapes, mid-range cassettes are fine. It is up to you whether you prefer 60-minute tapes or longer: the longer the tape, the less you will need to disturb long interactions, but it will take longer to wind back and forth as you are transcribing and finding things on it.

Microphones

Using a micro cassette recorder or normal cassette recorder without an external microphone (very few of these have microphone inputs, using instead their own condenser mikes) can be adequate for some favourable recording situations. Often, however, using the recorder's own microphone will mean that you record motor noise, and the lack of a distant mike will mean that you are more restricted with positioning your situation – to change a tape, for example, you will need to intrude into the middle of the interaction to retrieve the tape recorder.

There are various kinds of external microphone that you can use, depending on the situation. These vary in price a great deal, and can be very expensive. You can often get good advice on microphones from specialist sound shops – the kind where they sell amplifiers, mixing desks, and other electrical goods. The choice in high street shops tends to be very limited, but the exception seems to be Tandy, who stock all the kinds of mikes listed below. These are all active microphones, meaning that they have their own power source and must be switched on and off independently.

1   Tie-clip mikes: these are tiny microphones, operated with a watch-style battery, which clip to a tie, lapel, or top pocket. These are designed for one speaker, but you may find that in close interactions – till sales, for example – that the mike picks up more than one person satisfactorily.
2   Boundary or pressure zone mikes: these look either like a flat plate with a box sitting on it, or a lozenge shape, and are designed to sit flat on a table or to hang on a wall. They have a wide range (a small room, for example) and can be used for a group of speakers.
3   Directional mikes: these are the mikes used by news interviewers on the street and by lead singers, often on a stand. They are good for directional work: two speakers close together, or one speaker with the mike pointed directly at them.

Going back to the specimen situations listed above, the tie-clip mike would be chosen for close retail sales work, especially if the person was mobile around the room (and would therefore need to carry the tape recorder in a pocket or clipped to a belt). The group meeting and interview could both be captured with a boundary mike placed on a table in the middle of the group or hung on a nearby wall, while the interview could additionally be managed with a directional mike, perhaps placed on a stand, between the two or three speakers. The instructions for each mike will include a diagram of the 'catchment' of sound that you can expect: consider this when you set up your situation.

   Before you record, test out all the equipment at home and, if possible, do a trial run in the same environment to test if everything's working. It may be that too much background noise, poor microphone positioning, or the working or movement patterns of the interactants mean that you need to reconsider the set-up. Most mistakes with recording are simple ones, and this recording checklist may help you to avoid losing valuable data:

• Is the microphone switched on?
• Is the tape speed, where alterable, set correctly?
• Is the power supply switched on, or batteries fresh?
• Is voice activation, where fitted, set correctly, either off or to the correct trigger volume?
• Are all adapters pushed in snugly?
• Is the tape the right way round?

Remember to switch microphones off when you've finished using them, or the batteries will drain. It's also a good idea to remove batteries from the cassette recorder when you're carrying it around, to prevent it switching itself on in your bag.

USING ON-LINE CORPORA

There are many corpora now available for use on-line. On-line corpora contain thousands or millions of words of ready-transcribed written or spoken text, and, being on computer, can be searched for particular words or phrases. Some are held as plain text, some are annotated in various ways (annotated with part-of-speech information, for example), and some have more than one different version. Not all of them contain complete texts.

The ones briefly described below require an individual or University subscription in order to use them. By far the best information about them is obtained by looking at their Home Pages on the World Wide Web. URLs for some that are likely to be of interest are given below. If you see one that you think would be very useful, check with your tutor whether your institution currently subscribes to it, or whether a subscription could be bought.

A popular way of analyzing corpora is through using concordance software, which searches for every occurrence of a given word or phrase and lists it within several words of context, resulting very quickly in a huge number of instances of the element you are looking for in its natural habitat. This can be a very useful tool for looking at vocabulary, metaphor, and the popular uses of words and phrases. A very useful study using concordance methodology for analyzing textual meaning in a range of text types is Stubbs (1996). The book also includes brief details of a range of linguistic corpora (1996: xvii). Wray et al. also provide advice on using linguistic corpora (1998: 213ff.).

Two long-standing popular corpora are the London-Lund Corpus of Spoken English and the Lancaster-Oslo-Bergen (LOB) Corpus of written English. Information about these and a range of other corpora can be found at the International Computer Archive of Modern English (ICAME) at the University of Bergen in Norway. Their website is at: http://nora.hd.uib.no/whatis.html

The British National Corpus contains over 100 million words of written (90%) and spoken (10%) language, composed of extracts from 4124 texts in 1980s and early 1990s British English. It includes a large amount of published material from a wide range of sources, casual conversation, but also educational and informative events (such as lectures, news broadcasts, classroom discussion), business events (such as sales, interviews), public events (such as sermons and speeches), and leisure events (such as club meetings and radio phone-ins). It can be bought on CD-ROM or accessed through an annual subscription. For full information, see the website at: http://info.ox.ac.uk/bnc/ This site also includes useful pointers to other corpora, including ICAME.

A more recent corpus of spoken English is the CANCODE corpus (The Cambridge-Nottingham Corpus of Discourse in English). This was still under development at the time of writing, but data from the corpus and a description of it can be found in Carter and McCarthy (1997).

The Collins Cobuild Bank of English contains 320 million words at the time of writing, and contains written and spoken texts. In their words: 'Written texts come from newspapers, magazines, fiction and non-fiction books, brochures, leaflets, reports, letters, and so on. The spoken word is represented by transcriptions of everyday casual conversation, radio broadcasts, meetings, interviews and discussions, etc.' See: http://titania.cobuild. collins.co.uk/index.html for more information. This corpus can be bought in its entirety, or a subset of the corpus can be accessed on-line. Finally, Longman publishers have a range of corpora that they use for compiling dictionaries and textbooks. For information about these, see: http:// www.longman-elt.com/dictionaries/lccont.html

PRESENTING THE DATA

Written Language

For written texts, it is often sufficient to number the lines and use the text 'as is' from its original source. It's often a good idea to include the whole text, with whatever layout and pictures it came with, to give a good idea of how the text was intended to be consumed. Give close and precise details of the sources of all your data, perhaps in a table in the project appendix. If your data is too large to be included tidily – if it's taken from a newspaper, for example, and is beyond A4 size – then it may help to reduce it on a photocopier so that it can be included without appearing to be an ungainly bundle.

Spoken Language

The transcription conventions adopted in this book were introduced in Chapter 1. They are simple ones, repeated here for convenience:

FL	speaker name
A, B	speaker identifier
(.) or (pause)	very short audible pause
(2 secs)	timed pause
[	beginning of overlapped speech

Some methods of transcription are far more complex, depending on what it is you want to capture. An additional list of useful features is given in Table 8.2.

When you present transcribed data, you should always give a key to the conventions you have used, even if you think these are commonplace. For more on transcription, see Wray et al. (1998: 201ff.).

This chapter does not cover non-verbal elements that you might wish to include in your transcription, such as gaze and gesture and pointing. For suggestions on how to transcribe these (as well as discussion of what they mean), see Beattie (1983) and Graddol et al. (1994). Your transcription

TABLE 8.2   Transcription Features

Symbol	Definition	Example
=	**Continuous utterances** Utterances that run on from one another without a break	K: You got your BCG= C: = uh huh
::	**Extended or prolonged sounds** Sounds that are prolonged beyond their normal length	K: Oh I'll just sit and cry:: (.) do:n't hurt me: (.) do:n't let me see what you're do::ing
h	**Audible aspiration** 'hh'ing (exhalation) during an utterance	L: Now I didn't say that to her because that might confuhhse her
.h or ˙h	**Audible inhalation** Intake of breath	S: A Norfolk word is it, ˙hhhhhh (.) I see
underlining	**Distinctive pitch change** Incidences of emphasis that involve a marked change of segment over which pitch change moves	L: Oh: how lovely

should, of course, capture the features you are interested in talking about, but need not cover all the possible transcribable elements. It is worth planning in advance, therefore, the features you wish to cover before you transcribe. You may also wish to consider whether it's likely you will wish to use the data again for another purpose before deciding on the level and features of the transcription. For further information on transcription conventions, see the references on presentation and sample transcription of spoken data at the end of this chapter.

WRITING, PRESENTATION, AND ORGANIZATION

One of the joys of carrying out a practical piece of research is that there are always parts that are easy to write: whatever your hypothesis or the stage of your analysis, for example, you can always write the section about how you recorded and transcribed your data. Again, writing will need to be done according to the guidelines given with your assignment, and it's always helpful if you can inspect a previous successful project along the same lines. Dividing the writing-up into clearly delineated sections, however, is a great help in writing, since each section will have a clear function and content. If you plan word-length effectively, no time is wasted writing parts that are too long and then editing them back down again. Neither do you have to write in sequence. In fact, it's often helpful to write the introduction and conclusions last, since you often won't know what will survive in the final version. Once you have finished the main body of the text, the introduction and conclusion can be written to fit your content and direction of argument precisely.

Pay great attention to any style sheet that's given out for projects of this kind, and follow it closely. Don't give in to the temptation to decorate your work with the variety of fonts and pictures that your computer offers to you: readers are rarely impressed with these, since they tend to distract, and perhaps give the impression that your main concern has been for something other than intellectual content. Instead, label diagrams clearly, give good 'signposting' of your argument in terms of why you're telling the reader what you are telling them, and indicate sections clearly with numbering and/or bold or italic type. Don't make sections too short: if you subdivide section 3, for example, into sections 3.1, 3.2, and 3.3, it's probably fine to then subdivide those subsections into sections 3.1.1., 3.1.2, 3.1.3, and so on, but if you find you are writing section 3.1.2.1 and it has only five lines in it, that's an indication that you've broken it down too far. Three levels of subdivision are generally the most you will need, even for a PhD-length study. In general, keep fonts in the same family: the bold, italic, and underlined version of the same font should be enough for your needs (although again observing any local style rules that apply). A typesize of 12 points is about as large as fonts need to get in running text, and 9 points about as small as anyone can comfortably read. If you hand-write your project, it's obvious that doing so neatly will make a good impression. It's helpful to provide a key to any conventions you use for transcription or citation of data (do your curved brackets mean the same as someone else's square ones?). Large portions of transcription are usually preferable as an appendix, with line numbers in the text for ease of reference. Shorter examples can be included in running text, but it's helpful to indent and number them so that they stand out. Find out from your tutor if your data is meant to be included in the word-count: it generally isn't, but different tutors may have different practices.

Planning Guide

It may help you to use the frameworks given in Tables 8.3 and 8.4 for planning in the early stages of the project, and communicating, where relevant, with your tutor about what you plan to do. It will help to do a full one for plan A, and fill in at least the first few sections – without the references and main sections of the project – for plan B, as an aid to thinking clearly about your backup plan. Using an outline like this will give you a much better idea of what you're aiming at, and where your project might gain some marks.

FURTHER REFERENCES

An excellent overall guide to designing and carrying out projects on language is Wray et al. (1998). This book covers everything from choosing a topics to

TABLE 8.3   Project Planning List

Project planning list
Topic or title:
Situation and subjects:
Specific linguistic features:
Hypothesis or expectations:
Outline description of data:
Plan for preparing data:
Key references:
Main project sections:

study and research methodology, to referring correctly to sources, transcribing data, and using computers in your research. Stubbs (1983) provides very useful notes on collecting conversational data and sociolinguistic methodology (see in particular Chapter 11). Useful guidance on transcription conventions can be found in Beattie (1983), Button and Lee (1987), Schiffrin (1994), and Wray et al. (1998). Butler, in Wray et al. (1998: 254ff.), also provides a very useful first introduction to the use of statistics in a language project.

Glossary

All the main ideas and linguistic features that are discussed in the book are included in this glossary. Words and phrases that are underlined refer to other glossary entries that give related information. Words and phrases in **bold type** refer to the text types dealt with in this book (interviews, advertising) in which the subject of the entry is mentioned or discussed.

Abstract vs Concrete Nouns   Abstract nouns are those which refer to things that cannot be observed or measured, such as *love, idea, argument*. Concrete nouns, conversely, refer to observable, measurable, tangible things that are available to the senses, such as *table, tree, insect*. Abstract and concrete nouns in **advertising** slogans are discussed on page 127.

Accommodation   A process by which hearers or readers are expected to accept that information presented as a presupposition is true, known or uncontroversial, even though it may be new to them. For example, in the familiar sentence *The management regrets that no responsibility can be taken for coats left in this cloakroom*, the information after *regrets* is presupposed. However, the sentence is clearly intended to inform the reader, who is required to accommodate it as true and unproblematic. A discussion of accommodation in relation to presuppositions in **advertising** appears on page 146.

Action-orientated   see task-orientated

Actors   see agency

Active voice   see passive voice

Adjective   Adjectives describe nouns or pronouns, expressing some attribute of the thing referred to. Examples are *a big room, a nice meal*, where *big* and *nice* appear before or premodify the noun; or *the room is big, the meal was nice* where the function of the sentence is to predicate some property of the noun.

Adjunct   Adjuncts are elements that modify either the action of a verb, or a whole clause. They can describe when, where, how, or when the action took place, for example: *on Friday, under a tree, suddenly, because it was easier*. A useful discussion of adjuncts is given in Crystal (1996: 156). Adjuncts are mentioned in relation to **sports commentary** on page 54.

Affective meaning   Affective meaning is the component of word meaning that gives information about the feelings of the speaker – positive or negative – about the thing referred to. For example, while referring to someone's house as a *home* is neutral or slightly positive, calling it a *dive* is negative. Similarly, again in relation to houses, *compact* has positive affect, while *cramped* is negative. Affective meaning is discussed in Leech (1990: 14ff.). Here, it appears in the description of **news reporting** on page 33, and **magazine features** on page 112.

Agency   The agent of an action is its doer. This is a semantic issue, rather than a syntactic one, so where in the sentence the agent is referred to makes no difference. The sentences 'Archie lit the candle' and 'the candle was lit by Archie' both have the same agent (Archie) although the <u>subject</u> is different: 'Archie' in the first case and 'the candle' in the second. See also <u>transitivity</u> and <u>passive</u>. A discussion of how agents, or 'actors', are presented in **news reporting** appears on page 28.

Alliteration   Alliteration occurs when a sequence of <u>syllables</u> has the same consonant sound at the beginning, such as *the lazy lump lounged by the lake* (alliteration on *l*) or *round and round the ragged rock the ragged rascal ran* (alliteration on *r*). Note that alliteration takes place between sounds, not letters, so that *physics* and *festival* can alliterate. There may be many alliterating words, or just two. Alliteration is mentioned in relation to **advertising** on page 126.

Alternative question   An alternative question is one that supplies both or all of the answers, leaving the responder to choose one: for example, *do you want soup or salad?* Alternative questions obviously constrain the responder to certain kinds of behaviour, since the expectations of the questioner are so clear in the question. Alternative questions are used in **interviewing**, discussed on page 90.

Ambiguity   Ambiguity occurs when a word or syntactic structure has more than one meaning. For example, the sentence *Anthea was drawing the curtains* is ambiguous between her sketching them with pencil and paper, pulling them closed, or pulling them open. In practice, the meaning of ambiguous sentences is often made clear when they appear in their context, but they may be used either for the purposes of humour and innuendo, or for a writer or speaker's real meaning to remain vague. Ambiguity in the language of **advertising** is discussed on page 127.

Anticipation   Anticipation is a type of <u>speech error</u> in which a speech segment that should come later has appeared too early in the utterance, anticipating the production of the later segment. An example is *rebute the computer* instead of *reboot the computer*, where the element that sounds like 'you' of 'computer' has been anticipated. This is discussed in relation to the <u>unplanned discourse</u> of **sports commentary** on page 50.

Assertion An assertion is the element of the content of a sentence that is treated as the claim that the sentence is making. A contrast is often made between assertion and <u>presupposition</u>, where presupposition can be seen to be information that is supposed already to be part of the context, while assertion is the novel content that the sentence communicates. So, in the sentence *John regrets he failed his driving test*, the presupposition is that John failed his driving test, while the assertion is that he regrets it. Similarly, in the sentence *my husband has been run over*, the presupposition is that the speaker has a husband, while the assertion is that he has been run over. The use of assertion in **advertising** is mentioned on page 131.

Assessment A conversational <u>move</u> in which a speaker evaluates another speaker's contribution and gives an opinion on it. This is a move that interviewers typically avoid: see the discussion of **interviews** on page 97.

Authority Authority is often discussed in the context of one speaker having more power than the other, usually because of the position they hold in an institution and/or in the <u>speech event</u> that is currently taking place. Authority results in speakers having their opinions respected, their claims believed, or their wishes complied with, and their role in managing and even 'policing' the way the interaction gets upheld. Authority is discussed in relation to **instructions** on page 64.

Auxiliary verb Auxiliary verbs are <u>verbs</u> which can 'help' full verbs. The main examples of these in English are *be*, *have*, and *do*, but there is an additional set of modal auxiliary verbs: *may*, *might*, *could*, *would*, *should*, *will*, *can*, and *must*. The modal auxiliaries must appear with a full verb, as they cannot act alone (there is no full verb 'to must', for example). In Modern Standard English, the auxiliaries are the only verbs that can have a negative attached to them: *haven't*, *aren't*, *don't*, *wouldn't*, *may not* (*mayn't* is not now common), *shouldn't*, *won't*, *can't* and *mustn't*. To negate a full verb, an auxiliary must be used (so, *didn't know* rather than *knew not*, *didn't go* rather than *went not*). The appearance of modal auxiliary verbs in **advertising** is discussed on page 13, in **instructions** on page 25.

Back-channelling This useful term found in <u>conversation analysis</u> refers to speakers' production of formulaic utterances such as *mmhm*, *mmm*, *aha*, *yeah*, and *I see* during the course of another speaker's <u>turn</u>. These are not intended as attempts to take a turn in the conversation, and are not interpreted as such. However, they do not always indicate agreement: a speaker can provide a good deal of apparently positive back-channelling *mmms* and 'yeahs' throughout another speaker's turn and then contradict them with *yes, but . . .* once they have finished. Back-channel is discussed in relation to **interviews** on page 93.

Behavioural process see <u>process types</u>

Circumstances The term 'circumstance' originates in functional grammar to describe expressions that give information about how, where, why, or when the process expressed in a clause took place. Circumstances may describe extent (*a long way*) or duration (*for half an hour*), place (*in the house*) or time (*at three o'clock*), manner (*by car, with a stick*), reason, or purpose (*because he was tired, to get the lid off*). These and other types of circumstances are described in detail in Halliday (1985: 137ff.), the seminal textbook on functional grammar.

Clause A clause is the basic grammatical structure from which sentences are made. A sentence may consist of a single clause, as in *we went to the cinema*, or more than one, connected in various ways. Simple conjunction with *and* or *but* can give a two-clause sentence such as *we went to the cinema and enjoyed the film*; while subordination, the inclusion of one clause within another, can give more grammatically complex structures such as *we went to the cinema that was nearest*. Here, *that was nearest* is a clause in itself, but expands the description of the cinema and forms part of it. A useful description of clause is given in Crystal (1996), which covers the main basic components of clauses in English.

In the discussion of **advertising** on page 129, it is pointed out that the clause is the smallest thing which can be said to be true or false (words or phrases cannot be true or false, as they do not make claims about the world).

Clause structure Clauses in English minimally consist of a verb (such as *Go!*). However, even in these cases we assume the presence of a subject (such as *you*), giving a basic subject-verb structure. Clauses may additionally have an object, as in *I like you*, or two objects, one direct (the element most directly affected by the action, abbreviated dO) and one indirect (abbreviated iO), as in *I sent a letter* [dO] *to Naomie* [iO]. Note that it is also possible to have these elements the other way around, with the direct experiencer of the action postponed: *I sent Naomie* [iO] *a letter* [dO]. Many other clause structures are available in which elements are placed in a different order: inversions and preposing constructions are two. For an excellent and detailed description of clause structure, see Quirk et al. (1985: 723ff.).

Cleft construction This is an umbrella term for a group of sentence forms that are equivalent in basic meaning to an ordinary active sentence, but which are different in pragmatic meaning. An active sentence such as *Arlette added the milk* has a range of corresponding cleft forms:

It-cleft	It was *Arlette* who added the milk
	It was *the milk* that Arlette added
Wh-clefts	the one] who added the milk was *Arlette*
	What Arlette added was *the milk*
Reverse wh-clefts	*Arlette* was the one who added the milk
	The milk was what Arlette added

Cleft constructions are formed by extracting one element to form the clefted constituent (either *Arlette* or *the milk*, the clefted constitutent italicized in each case above) and presenting the rest of the information in a relative clause. This has various effects, including conveying the assumption that the material in the relative clause consists of a presupposition, and is either already known, or knowable, by the hearer. This is not necessarily the case: in the *it*-cleft, *It was then I knew that Alphonsine had made off with the crucible*, the presupposed information (I knew that Alphonsine had made off with the crucible) is not already known by the reader (you). This is conveyed as an assumption for you to accept, while what is being focused on by the use of the cleft is the time of the discovery. Clefts also convey a sense of uniqueness about the clefted constituent: *then* in the example above has the meaning of *then and only then*. In the Arlette examples, it appears to be emphasized that the person adding the milk was Arlette and nobody else, or that the milk and nothing else was added by her. For a useful description of the discourse functions of *it*-clefts and wh-clefts, see Prince (1978). *It*-clefts are sometimes referred to simply as clefts, or as 'predicated theme' constructions; wh-clefts are referred to as 'pseudo-clefts', and reverse wh-clefts as 'inverted pseudo-clefts' or 'reversed pseudo-clefts'. Clefts are discussed in this book in relation to **magazine features** (wh-clefts and reverse wh-clefts: page 119) and **sports commentary** (*it*-clefts: page 54).

Collocation   Collocation describes the habit that words have of appearing with (collocating with) other words. For example, we might think the word *minor* means the same as *small*, until we look at the collocations of *minor*: it tends to appear alongside words like *offence, crime, road, accident, problem*, and *incident*. This suggests that part of the meaning of *minor* is concerned with official, and potentially negative, events. We would not then say *a dozen minor eggs, please*, or *minor trees dotted the horizon*. These usages both reflect and construct what minor means in English beyond the basic connotative or referential meaning. Carter (1987: 52ff.) describes how more neutral vocabulary such as the word *fat* has a large number of collocates: *fat man, baby, chicken, salary* and *book*, for example, while the less neutral term *plump* has far fewer: *plump babies, people* and *chickens*, but not *plump book* and *plump salary*. Because of these regular usages, we would say that part of the meaning of *plump* is that it usually refers to animate objects, while this is not a restriction on the meaning of *fat*. The ability to produce unusual and surprising collocations is often prized in literary writing. For example, the unusual collocation of a *blind door* is perhaps more arresting as an image than a *closed door*, while a cat with *reticent fur* communicates more about the cat than if its fur were *soft* or *black*. The more collocates a word has, the more central and neutral a vocabulary item it is. We refer to these central, neutral words as core vocabulary. Examples of collocative meaning at work in **advertising** are given on page 133.

Colloquialism   Colloquial language is language which is associated with informal situations (see informality). Because it has these strong associations, it can be very effective when used in more formal contexts. For example, Stubbs (1996) notes the use of colloquial language in a courtroom in order to catch the attention of the jury, making particular phrases memorable. Stubbs notes the judge's use of the phrases *jolly fishy, hoodwink, a pack of lies* and *cheeky old sod.*

Colloquialisms can also be a sign of conflict in a discourse. Fairclough (1989: 68, 136) notes that the failure of a school pupil to adopt formal, non-colloquial language when speaking to a head teacher shows his refusal to adopt the conventions of the discourse situation. Colloquial language is mentioned in relation to **advertising** on page 142.

Colonization The tendency of a dominant kind of discourse to influence language and thinking in other situations. Fairclough (1989: 36) uses this term to describe cases such as the discourse of commodification (where the salient items are objects to be bought and sold) colonizing the discussion of more abstract ideas: *I don't buy that explanation* and *How are you going to sell your plan to him?* are some of the resulting metaphors and ways of seeing the world. Colonization is discussed in relation to **advertising** on page 130.

Conjunction This term, more specific than connective, is used to describe a small class of elements that are used to link clauses together. Conjunctions can be of two kinds: subordinating or co-ordinating. Subordinating conjunctions introduce clauses that cannot act independently and are known as subordinate. This is the function of *although* in *Although it was late, John decided to drive home.* Other examples of subordinating conjunctions are *whereas, so, if, since, that* and *as long as.* Co-ordinating conjunctions link two clauses of equal status, and are far fewer in number. The most common ones are *and, but* and *or.* For a useful discussion of both kinds of conjunction, see Crystal (1996: 176ff.). The use of conjunctions in **sports commentary** is discussed on page 40.

Connective A general term used to refer to elements whose purpose is to link together words, phrases or clauses. Examples are *and, but, however, so, or* and *although.* The use of connectives in **advertising** is discussed on page 129. See also conjunction.

Connotation The element of meaning that is derived from expected characteristics of what is referred to. For example, one British chain store sells a range of shoes called the *footglove.* One relevant connotation of *glove* is that gloves are usually an excellent fit, and this connotation is clearly part of the reason for naming the shoes after them. Similarly, some sanitary towels are advertised as having *wings.* The connotations of the word *wings* might be flying and freedom, since we think of bird wings when we interpret the word. These sets of associations between words and connotations may be specific to particular social groups, or quite general across cultures. Connotation is discussed in relation to **news reporting** on page 33.

Conventional implicature Conventional implicature is a kind of meaning that is attached through convention and usage to particular words and phrases. For example, the use of *but* conventionally implicates a contrast between two things, so that an utterance *but you just came in!* even without surrounding context, suggests that there is an additional implication such as a contrast with going out. The use of *even* in *we've even finished the biscuits* implicates a chain of events that are being compared or evaluated (*we've finished the biscuits as well as . . .*). Independently of context, items such as *even* and *but* serve the function of triggering additional inferences on the part of hearer or reader which can give rise to quite complex argument structures. Conventional implicature is discussed extensively in the interpretation of the meaning of **advertising**, beginning page 142.

Co-ordinating conjunction   see conjunction

Core vocabulary   Some words in a language are more neutral, central, or 'core' than others. For example, the word *eat* has this neutral status in English, and many possible alternative terms exist: Carter (1987: 35) lists *gobble, dine, devour, stuff* and *gourmandize* as examples. All these terms could be seen to have additional or associative meaning beyond what is conveyed by *eat*. Core terms are less specific than their non-core counterparts, and can therefore appear in a wider range of contexts. The neutrality of core terms means that they do not have particular overtones of negative or positive (compare *eat* and *stuff* in this respect), and are unlikely to be restricted to a particular social situation (compare the neutral term *eat* with the formality of *dine* and *gourmandize* or the informality of *stuff* and *gobble*). The use of non-core terms in various contexts will convey less neutrality, and more specificity of meaning, than the use of core terms.

   Core vocabulary is discussed in relation to advertising on page 132. For an excellent description of how vocabulary choice operates in a piece of political writing, see Carter and Nash (1990: 61–8, 129–37).

Definite/indefinite article   Articles are types of determiner. The definite article in English is *the*, in contrast with the indefinite *a* or *an*. The use of the indefinite article is mentioned in relation to **news reporting** on page 26.

Definiteness   A definite noun phrase is one that features a definite determiner, signifying that it is expected that the concept referred to can be retrieved by the hearer or reader from the shared context. Examples are *the dog, the Balkans, this house, that animal* and *your shoe*. Definites are contrasted with indefinites which specify something that cannot be identified uniquely: *some shoes, a dog, an argument, any politician*. The role of definite noun phrases in **advertising** is discussed on page 146, **news reporting** on page 25, and in **magazine features** on page 118.

Determiner   Determiners are elements that appear before the noun, performing the function of determining the interpretation of the noun in terms of its number (the determiners *many, few, all, half, some, one* and *a*, for example), or its definiteness. Definite and indefinite articles are kinds of determiners.

Direct/Indirect object   see object

Direct/Indirect speech   These terms refer to the way in which speech is represented in written form. Direct speech is enclosed within quotation marks, and is accompanied by a reporting clause such as *he said* or *she remarked*. Indirect speech is the reporting of speech without quotation marks, including the speech more fully into the syntax of the sentence by using some marker of subordination, such as that, as in *he told her that he was leaving in the morning*. The 'direct' version of this would be: *'I'm leaving in the morning', he said*. See Montgomery et al. (1992: 205ff.) for a full description of ways of reporting speech. Direct speech is examined in the current volume in relation to **magazine features** (page 106), while ways of incorporating the speech of others into **news reporting** are discussed on page 24.

Directive   Directives are utterances which ask, tell or even hint that another person should perform some action. Directives are discussed in detail in the treatment of **instructions** beginning on page 60.

Discourse   A stretch of text or speech longer than a single clause. The term also came to mean 'a way of speaking about something', or an ideological standpoint from which a subject is addressed.

Discourse marker   Discourse markers are linguistic elements that serve to give clues about discourse structure, and are used by speakers to organize the discourse. For example, a teacher may often begin a class or a new activity with the marker *right*; while someone answering a question will often begin with *well*. Markers show where different structural elements of discourse begin and end, thereby enabling other speakers to know how to respond (for example, by taking a turn), and how in general to interpret the information. Other examples are *right, anyway* and *now*.

Disjunctive syntax   Discussed in relation to **advertising** on page 128, syntax is referred to as disjunctive when it is composed of fragmented text elements, either loosely related or unrelated to one another, and featuring a good deal of ellipsis. Disjunctive texts require greater effort on the part of the reader to retrieve the coherence of the overall message, which is largely left to inference. The 'sentences' of these texts may often not contain a main verb, and may be composed of single words or short phrases that do not have a clear relationship with any clause structure. It is often perceived that what is missing from such texts are conjunctive elements such as *so, but, although, however, because* and so on, which make explicit links between text elements and make the retrieval of an argument easier.

Dysphemism   see euphemism

Elaboration   Elaboration is a term which is often applied intuitively to a technique of argumentation in which a person further explains or amplifies something that has already been said, and may do this repeatedly. In the analysis of rhetorical relations in texts, elaboration is used to refer to a relation that holds between one text segment and another, in which the elaborating text segment provides further information describing, explaining, or exemplifying another segment. Elaboration is discussed in relation to **magazine features** on page 109.

Eliciting exchange   see exchange

Ellipsis   Ellipsis refers to clause structures that are syntactically incomplete, and which therefore require the reader or hearer to supply the missing element, or at least appropriate shared knowledge, for their full meaning to be retrieved. Ellipsis is noted with respect to **advertising** on page 130, and **sports commentary** on page 42. In addition, the monologue produced in the step aerobics **instructions** is highly elliptical: see data on page 73.

Equative   Equative constructions are sentences that feature some form of the copular or 'joining' verb *be*, and that apparently serve to equate one element with another (as in *my tie is the one with the spots on it*). The equation is only apparent, because the sentence does not really equate two distinct objects in the world (two separate ties), but the description *my tie* with the observable object *the one with the spots on it*. Equatives frequently serve to link descriptions with observable objects, as in *coming up the inside is Dazzlin Lady* (see **sports commentary**, page 54).

Euphemism   Euphemisms are words or phrases that are used in order to avoid other, less acceptable, expressions. The replaced expression may be taboo, too impolite, or too overly direct for the situation. Examples are *misappropriate* as a euphemism for *steal* and *go before* as a euphemism for *die*. Dysphemism is the opposite of euphemism: it is used with the intention of implying something offensive about what is referred to, such as calling someone a *bitch, louse* or *snake*, for example, when the person referred to is technically none of these. Euphemism is discussed in relation to **advertising** on page 134. Allan and Burridge (1991) provide a book-length overview of the derivations and use of euphemism and dysphemism, while Bolinger (1980: 116) discusses euphemism in relation to advertising. Beard and Cerf (1992) take a tongue-in-cheek look at 'politically correct' vocabulary, much of which can be seen as euphemistic.

Event   Events are 'happenings' that take place (the *vase broke*, for example) or 'doings' that have an agent or doer (as in *Anthea shut the window*). They may be instantaneous or 'atomic', as in both the cases just given, or 'extended', as in the *paint dried* or *Jack ate his dinner*. Events are part of the apparatus used in the analysis of **news reporting** beginning on page 16.

Event structure   Event structure is the order in which happenings take place in the world: what eventualities took place before, during, or after one another. This is discussed in relation to **news reporting** of chains of events on page 16.

Eventuality Eventuality is a collective term used to refer to both <u>events</u> and <u>states</u>. The term is used in the analysis of **news reporting** on page 17.

Exchange Exchanges have been identified as units in spoken interaction that consist of a number of <u>moves</u>. The exchange acts as a 'chunk' of conversation in which speakers provide moves that satisfy the requirements of an opening move such as a question or a greeting. The exchange extends until the next opening move. Exchange types discussed in this book include eliciting exchanges, greeting exchanges, and informing exchanges (see the discussion on page 89 in relation to **interviews**). For a useful discussion of exchanges, see Eggins and Slade (1997: 222).

Existential presupposition see <u>presupposition</u>

Experiential values This term is used by Fairclough (1989) to describe the capacity inherent in vocabulary to convey the ideology or opinion of the speaker or writer. For example, someone who describes a friend as having *coloured* or *tinted* her hair is likely to have a more positive opinion of this practice (or its result) than someone who describes that friend as having *dyed* it. Note that the term partially overlaps with the notion of <u>affective meaning</u>, which refers only to a meaning component based on personal opinion, rather than ideology. Experiential values are discussed in this book in relation to **magazine features** on page 112.

Face, Face wants Face, as defined by Brown and Levinson (1987), is of two kinds: positive and negative. Positive face relates to our need to be approved of; negative face to our need to carry out our business unimpeded. Face wants are people's wishes to have both of these needs attended to in interaction with others. Face is the keystone of the theory of politeness articulated by Brown and Levinson. It is discussed in this book in relation to **instructions** on page 65.

Factive verb see <u>presupposition</u>

False start A false start is a kind of <u>speech error</u> in which a speaker begins, and then re-begins, a speech segment. It is mentioned in the discussion of **sports commentary** on page 50.

Field The notion of field is part of the three-part description of <u>register</u> (discussed in Chapter 1, page 4, and in relation to **instructions** on page 78). To describe the field of a discourse type, its nature, purpose, location, participants and subject matter are specified.

Field-specific vocabulary Field-specific vocabulary is vocabulary that clearly belongs to a particular subject matter or discourse purpose. For example, a text that features the vocabulary item *cold front, depression, high pressure area, mist* and *heavy rainfall* belongs to the field of weather forecasting. Field-specific vocabulary is discussed here in relation to **sports commentary** (page 40) and **instructions** (page 78).

Finite verb   A finite verb is a verb that carries tense and number information, and is usually the main verb in the clause. So, for example, in the sentence *he asked to stay*, the verb *asked* is finite. The verb *to stay* is non-finite, as it does not do the work of conveying tense and number. For a fuller description of finite and non-finite, see Crystal (1996: 58). The notion of finiteness is used in relation to **sports commentary** on page 47.

Free indirect speech   Free indirect speech is a way of reporting (or inventing) the speech of others in a way that blurs the distinction between the narrator and the speaking character. It does not use quotation marks, but still remains in the third person. So, for example, *Was there a way round it? What should he do?* is an example of free indirect speech. In free direct speech, quotation marks would be used and the character would refer to himself as *I*: '*Is there a way round it? What should I do?*' A useful discussion of free and non-free, direct and indirect speech styles appears in Montgomery et al. (1992: 205ff.). It is discussed in this book in relation to **magazine features** on page 107.

Gaze   Gaze is used in linguistics and sociology to refer simply to where a person is looking. This is discussed in relation to **advertising** on page 138. However, the term is also used metaphorically to describe the 'ideal onlooker' or person whose perspective is being adopted. For example, it is possible to describe women's fashion as a product of a male gaze.

Goal   The term goal is used in the discussion of the transitivity of a clause to describe the recipient, experiencer, or thing directly affected by a process. So, in *he closed his eyes*, the goal is *his eyes*; in *Jonathan tore the paper*, the goal is *the paper*. This notion is described in detail in Halliday (1985: 101ff.), and is relevant to this book in the discussion of **news reporting** on page 28.

Gradable adjective   see adjective

Greeting exchange   see exchange

Hearer-interested   This term refers to texts or interactions in which linguistic choices are made based on the assumption that it is the hearer or reader, rather than the speaker or writer, that benefits from the text. This is discussed in relation to **instructions** on page 64.

Hyperbole   Hyperbole is a figure of speech in which emphasis is created by overstatement, as in *I've got tons of work to do*.

Hedge   Hedges are elements that serve to distance a speaker or writer from responsibility for the claims he or she is making. For example, *sort of* can be used to soften a negative statement like *it's boring* to *it's sort of boring*. Modal auxiliary verbs such as *may*, *might* and *could* are also used as hedges: on refusing an invitation, for example, the refusal can be hedged by saying *I* *might have something else on that night*, which still apparently leaves open a possibility, rather than *I'm busy that night*. Other hedges include *like, kind of, perhaps, maybe* and many other elements that bring the truth of the assertion that is being made into doubt. Hedges are discussed in relation to claims in **news reporting** on page 25.

Ideology   Ideology is a set of beliefs, or entire belief system, through which a group or culture views the world. Ideology is relevant in most of the chapters of this book, but is discussed most explicitly in relation to **news reporting** on page 25.

Imperative   The imperative is one of the three major sentence types or clause structures in English (the other two being interrogative and declarative). It consists of a verb in imperative form (*Go! Sit! Drive!*), and optionally other elements. The imperative is used to convey <u>directive</u> intent (getting someone to do something), although many other constructions can also serve this function (see the discussion of directive use in **instructions** beginning on page 60). Imperatives are discussed in this book in relation to **advertising** on page 140.

Implicature   A way of describing the non-literal meaning that is understood by means of conversational or conventional principles applied to what is said. For example, when someone says *It's cold in here*, this is literally an observation about the temperature in the room. However, the utterance will almost universally be understood by hearers that the speaker means that the window or door should be closed or that a heater be switched on. This non-literal meaning is said to be conversationally implicated (or a conversational implicature). Conversational implicature was first proposed by the philosopher H. P. Grice to account for the gap between what is said and what is meant, suggesting that a set of conversational principles or 'maxims' applies to interaction which, if broken, gives rise to additional, non-literal meaning. For a full description of Grice's maxims and their role in creating implicatures, see Grice (1975). A second type of implicature, conventional implicature, refers to the conventional meanings of words or phrases that is, again, not always logically warranted. For example, Levinson (1983: 127) notes that *and* and *but* are, in logical terms, identical in meaning, but that it is part of the conventional meaning of *but* that it implies some kind of contrast between the two elements it conjoins (therefore, *the dog is brave and obedient* does not imply a contrast, but *the dog is brave but obedient* does, perhaps referring to the additional inference that its bravery may lead to it attacking people). See the chapter on **advertising** (page 142) and **instructions** (page 64) for an application of these ideas to texts in this book.

Indefinite article   see <u>definite article</u>

Indirect speech   see <u>direct speech</u>

Informing exchange   see <u>exchange</u>

Initiation   A type of conversational <u>move</u>, such as a question, statement, or greeting, which is used to begin a conversational <u>exchange</u>. Initiation is discussed in relation to **interviews** on page 179.

Interrogative   Interrogative is the term used to describe the syntax commonly used for questions, consisting of an inversion of <u>subject</u> and <u>verb</u> (for example, the statement *You are going out now* becomes the question *Are you going out now?*) Interrogatives are discussed in relation to **advertising** discourse on page 140.

Intonation   This term refers to the melody or 'tune' with which speech is articulated. This is generally understood to consist of three different components: the height of the <u>pitch</u>, the range of pitches that are used in the whole tune, and the directions (falling, rising, level) of the changes in pitch. Intonation is discussed in relation to **sports commentary** on page 51.

Inversion   Inversion is a <u>clause structure</u> in which the <u>subject</u> appears after, rather than before, the <u>verb phrase</u>. *Outside stood a little angel*, for example, is the inverted correlate of *a little angel stood outside*. See Green (1989: 131), whose example this is, for a description of the varieties and functions of inversions. Inversions are discussed in relation to **sports commentary** on page 53.

Inverted pyramid   This is a term used in the analysis of **news reporting** (see page 00) which describes the practice of elaborating on the content of the story in more and more detail as a text progresses. The small tip of the pyramid, therefore, will be the first part of an article, summarizing the news in one or two lines. The next level, which takes up slightly more space, goes into more detail about circumstances and participants in the story. This expansion goes on until, at the 'base' of the pyramid, the most detailed description appears.

It-cleft   see <u>cleft construction</u>

Material process   see <u>process types</u>

Mediation   This term refers to the role of a dominant speaker in an interaction in structuring the talk: for example, s/he may mediate what topics are discussed, when turns are taken, and/or who speaks. Mediation is discussed as it is performed by the chair of a panel in **interviews** on page 86.

Mental process   see <u>process types</u>

Metaphor   Metaphor is a highly pervasive and often hidden process of creating analogies between one thing and another, a strategy by means of which a known situation or understood entity is superimposed upon an unknown one in an attempt to understand it. This is not simply a process of drawing a parallel (suggesting that one thing is like another), but a means of seeing one thing as another, thereby carrying over a whole set of <u>associative</u>

meanings between the situations. So, for example, if a government minister suggests that a situation has to be *met head on*, rather than *by the back door*, s/he is applying spatial metaphors: one apparently derived from combat and creating an image of an aggressive and brave approach, and the second relating to buildings such as houses, creating an image of furtiveness and clandestine behaviour.

Mitigation   Mitigation is the process of limiting, diluting or making indirect something that may threaten another speaker. In the context of **instructions** (page 63), the notion is applied to strategies through which the instruction-giver may limit the challenge presented by telling someone else what to do, perhaps through joking, being indirect, or making the action seem optional.

Modal verb   see auxiliary verb

Mode   Mode is one of the three elements that makes up the description of register (see also tenor and field), all of them combined serving to capture the features of a situation which are reflected in language to make up a discourse 'type' or register. Mode refers to the manner or means of communication, such as face-to-face or on paper, in a planned or unplanned way, through broadcast or personally, through images, gestures, or some combination of means. Mode is often simply used to mean 'speech' or 'writing', but a mode analysis of any text shows this to be simplistic. Mode is introduced in more detail in the **introduction** to this book (page 4) and is mentioned in relation to **sports commentary** on page 57.

Modification   Modifiers are words that serve to extend, restrict, or otherwise alter the meanings of other words which they accompany. In the noun phrase *the dark room*, the adjective *dark* premodifies the noun *room*; in the noun phrase *the train which was late*, the relative clause *which was late* postmodifies the noun *train*.

Move   Moves are the components of conversational exchanges, and may be of various types. For example, an initiating move opens an exchange, and may be a question or a statement; a responding move should, in an orderly exchange, refer to the initiating move, and a follow-up move may optionally come next. A simple such structure might be: *A: You OK? B: Yeah. A: Good.* To relate moves to the notion of turns in an exchange, turns may consist of one or more moves. Moves and exchanges in **interviews** are discussed on page 89.

Multi-unit turn   A turn in spoken interaction that is made up of several components with different functions. For example, a speaker may begin a turn with a greeting, ask a question, explain the reason for asking the question, and then go into a longer description of something evoked within the reason, before another person is given the floor to respond. This gives a turn with several identifiable sub-components, a situation frequent in **interviews** (see page 93), either because the interviewee is granted very long turns, or sometimes because the interviewer tries to do more than one thing within the scope of a single question.

Narrative   Narrative is the recounting of a series of events, usually in the past tense, in which an attempt is made to establish relationships of various kinds between the elements of the narrative. There may be a series of different kinds of components in a narrative: stating the facts may be broken up by description, evaluation, etc. Labov (1972) has made a study of the natural tendency of people to tell stories in a certain order and with certain broad components: this is discussed in relation to **news reporting** on page 14. The term narrative is also used in the analysis of an aerobics workout in the discussion of **instructions** on page 76. Here, it refers to a discourse move in which the instructor describes what the participants should be doing at the time at which they are doing the action. Gray (1992) gives a useful description of narrative in a literary sense, while Montgomery et al. (1992: 177ff.) contains a detailed discussion of narrative in prose and film.

Negative face   see face

Neutrality   Neutrality is a general term used for situations in which speakers or texts are free from bias of ideology or personal opinion. In practice, this is very hard to achieve, but there is a discussion of speakers' attempts to achieve it in **interviews** on page 99.

Newsmark   see news receipt object

News receipt object   This term refers to a group of utterances that are used to acknowledge another speaker's contribution of new information to the discourse (or information which the hearer wants to treat as news). They include exclamations such as *oh*, *really* and *no*, uttered with appropriate intonation. They are discussed in relation to **interviews** on page 98.

News values   A set of factors that, together, make a news story 'newsworthy'. According to Bell (1991), some of these values are that good news stories have to be negative, recent and geographically close to the consumer. A discussion of news values and their relationship to the arrangement and slant of news stories is given in the chapter on written **news reporting**, page 12.

Nominal   Nominal is a general term for a noun or noun phrase. Nominals are discussed in relation to written **news reporting** on page 23.

Nomination   A technique for achieving turn taking in multi-party discourse by which a speaker chooses who will speak next by naming them explicitly. This is exemplifed in the discussion of **interviews** on page 88.

Non-fluency phenomena   A general term for unintentional and non-meaningful occurrences in speech such as hesitations, false starts, speech errors, unintentional pauses, stammers and other speech 'noise'. This is discussed in relation to **sports commentary** on page 51.

Noun A category of word, the most obvious examples being words that refer to concrete objects such as *computer* and *rock*. Many nouns are <u>abstract</u> (referring to things that cannot be touched or observed directly). Nearly all nouns in English inflect for number (*computer, computers; child, children*), and all except proper nouns (*Canada, Dave*) occur with <u>determiners</u>. All can appear with other material inside <u>noun phrases</u>.

Noun phrase A non-verbal element within a clause structure that can occupy one of the major syntactic roles, such as subject, or direct or indirect object. This may consist of a single noun (such as *Dave* in *Dave ran the water*) or may consist of more material (*Sally's friend Dave; that guy Dave I was telling you about*).

Object Any <u>noun phrase</u> that is not the subject of the sentence is a candidate for object. An object may be the <u>goal</u> or recipient of the action of the main <u>verb</u>, but need not be. Objects may be direct or indirect: in *John gave the book to me, the book* is the direct object, and *me* is the indirect object. The question of which is which is not entirely settled in contemporary grammar: see Trask (1993: 140).

Observer's paradox A term that describes the paradox that it is not possible to observe something in the condition that it would be in if it were not being observed. This is a problem for anyone who wants to observe something in its 'natural state', since the very act of observing it may make it (anything from a virus to a human being) act differently. This is mentioned on page 160 in relation to conducting a **research project** on language: it is relevant here because it is very difficult to be sure that speech that is being tape-recorded is 'natural'.

Open question see <u>closed question</u>

Orthography This term refers to the way in which text is written or spelt. See **advertising**, page 135.

Participant Participant is used as a general term to refer to people taking part in a conversation, or people or other <u>agents</u> named or described in a text. It is used in a specifically grammatical sense to refer to the elements that take part in particular types of <u>process</u>. So, in <u>material</u> processes such as *give*, the participants are <u>agents</u> (the doer) and <u>goals</u> (the done-tos). These terms are drawn from functional approach to language study, and are described further in Halliday (1985: 102). We use them in relation to **news reporting** on page 27.

Passive voice, passive construction Ordinary sentence structure in English is <u>Subject</u> <u>Verb</u> <u>Object</u>. In a sentence like *Sarah broke these plates, Sarah* is

Subject, *broke* is the Verb, and *these plates* are the Object. When the Subject is the <u>agent</u> or 'doer' of the activity described by the verb, as it is in this case, we refer to this as the active voice, or say that the clause itself is active. In some sentences, however, the <u>noun phrase</u> which was Object in this 'basic' structure is placed first, in Subject position, as in *these plates were broken by Sarah*. Sarah, while still agent of the action, is no longer subject of the clause. Once it is placed in this position, it is possible to delete the agent entirely: *these plates were broken*. In an ideological analysis of language, it is possible to view agent deletion as a means of removing the agents of action from attention, and possibly directing blame elsewhere. Henley et al. (1995) report that the use of the passive voice in newspaper reporting of crimes of sexual violence has the effect of making those crimes more acceptable to readers, removing the perpetrators from the focus of blame. Clark (1992) examines passive voice and its interaction with how perpetrators of crime are named in news reporting. Trew (1979) discusses the use of these constructions in newspaper reporting of political events. Active and passive voice are discussed in this book in relation to **news reporting** on page 29, **instructions** on page 60, and **sports commentary** on page 55. A further useful description of the active–passive distinction is given in Quirk et al. (1985: 156ff.).

Personification   Personification is a device whereby thoughts and feelings are attributed to an inanimate object. Describing shampoo or washing-up liquid as 'caring', for example, qualifies as personification. This is discussed in relation to **advertising** on page 134.

Phrase   A language element with a recognizable function that may be one or several words long. A verb phrase will have a <u>verb</u> as its main and defining element, but may contain many other elements as well; likewise, an adjectival phrase has an <u>adjective</u> as its head. The reason for including single words as potential phrases is due to the fact that even single nouns always have the capacity for further expansion: for example, *houses* could expand to *these houses* or even *these houses on the right*. There is a useful generalization of function to be had by calling all three noun phrases, since all perform a similar function in a clause.

Pitch   Pitch perception is based on the speed of vibration of the vocal folds used in producing speech. Fast vibration produces an effect of high pitch, and slow vibration produces low pitch. Great differences in the pitch of adjacent elements are heard as emphasis or stress, so a sudden high- or low-pitched syllable is heard as emphasized in comparison to its context. The **pitch contour** of an utterance refers to the sequence of pitches that make up its distinctive melody (see intonation). A speaker's **pitch range** – the range of pitches they can physically produce – is pre-set physiologically, with men's pitch range lower than women's, but within a single utterance or discourse we can talk about the pitch range selected for that particular purpose, which is the span between the lowest and the highest pitches actually used. **Pitch compression**, the use of a restricted range from the lower part of the natural pitch range, can be used to signal that the speaker is reaching the end of an utterance or topic. Pitch is discussed in relation to **sports commentary** beginning on page 51.

Planned discourse   see <u>unplanned discourse</u>

Positive face   see <u>face</u>

Possessive adjective   Possessive adjectives are a restricted class of adjectives that <u>premodify</u> nouns by describing possession by someone or something. They are *my, your, his, her, its,* and *their.* These belong to the class of <u>definite determiners</u>, and are also <u>presupposition triggers</u>. Their function is discussed in relation to **news reporting** on page 25, in **magazine features** on page 118, and in **advertising** on page 146.

Possessive pronouns   These are like <u>possessive adjectives</u> in that they indicate possession of something, but differ in that they do not premodify a noun. Instead, they stand in place of a noun, as in: *Whose is this cup? It's his/hers/theirs/yours/ours.*

Pragmatics   Pragmatics is the study of meaning beyond what is literally conveyed by the sentences of a language. The business of pragmatics is to examine what sentences and utterances mean to their speakers and hearers in a context, looking at how factors such as inference, shared knowledge, presupposition, implicature and information structure go together to make up the actual, rather than literal, meaning of what is said. For a further introduction, see Salkie (1995), and Green (1989).

Pre-allocation   see <u>turn type pre-allocation</u>

Premodification   see <u>modification</u>

Preposing construction   Preposing, also called fronting, constructions are clauses that place an element normally expected elsewhere to the front of the clause. Examples are *De-caf, I ordered* (preposing an <u>object</u>), and *Near the river a church stood* (preposing a <u>prepositional phrase</u>). See Green (1989: 13) for a discussion of preposing and related constructions such as <u>inversion</u>.

Preposition   A restricted set of words (known as closed class words, meaning that they cannot easily be added to within the grammar of the language) such as *with, by, from, to, for,* and *under.* **Prepositional phrases** consist of a preposition with a <u>noun phrase</u>, as in *under the sink, through the window.*

Presupposition   Presupposition is the use of a syntactic construction that has the effect of presenting information to a hearer or reader as if it were already known, true, factual, or uncontroversial. There are two broad types of presupposition. Factive presupposition presents facts or whole propositions as true, as in *John admits he did it*: here, *he did it* is presupposed. A similar effect of the truth of the information would be achieved by replacing admits with *regrets*, *realizes* or *knows* – all of which are known as factive verbs. Notice, however, that the effect of the information being necessarily true disappears when we replace the verb with *thinks* or *believes*, which do not convey presupposition. The second kind of logical presupposition is known as existential presupposition: in this case, the presupposed information is not a fact, but a reference to a thing as if it definitely exists. We get a pre-supposition of existence from phrases such as *the dog* in *put the dog out*: in normal usage, there has to be a dog. We know a presupposition is at hand through the use of syntactic presupposition triggers. The chief description of presupposition in context is given in relation to **magazine features** on page 118. Presupposition is also discussed in relation to **news reporting** on page 25, **sports commentary** on page 55, and **advertising** on page 144.

Presupposition trigger These are syntactic clues that presupposition is taking place. Examples include it-clefts (*it was John who realized first* pre-supposes someone realized first), definite noun phrases (*the* in *the tree on the horizon* presupposes that there is such a tree and a horizon), and possessive adjectives (the *my* of *my black jacket* presupposes that the speaker has a black jacket). Other presuppositions include factive verbs (see presupposition entry for a description of factiveness) such as *realize*, *regret*, and *know*. A dis-cussion of presupposition triggers in **magazine features** appears on page 118.

Problem-solution structures The problem-solution structure is a general organization of text common in text types such as **advertising** (pages 126–30). This discourse strategy consists of presenting a problem first, perhaps, for advertising purposes, emphasizing its negative aspects, and then presenting a solution such as a product that can be bought as a remedy. See Carter and Nash (1990: 69) and Hoey (1983) for a discussion.

Process types The notion of process is current in functional linguistics to refer to what Halliday (1985: 106) refers to as the 'goings on' reported by a clause: the 'happening' that is taking place, often specified by the verbal element of the clause. Processes may be of several different kinds: mental processes such as thinking, material processes of doing, relational processes of being, behavioural processes, and verbal processes of saying. These are discussed in some detail in relation to **news reporting** on page 27.

Pronoun Pronouns are elements that stand in for nouns, but which require information from the context to be understood: for example, the personal pronouns *he*, *she*, *it*, and *they*. Other classes of pronouns include reflexive pronouns (*myself*), demonstrative pronouns (*this*, *that*), relative pronouns (*that*, *which*, which introduce relative clauses), interrogative pronouns that appear within questions (*who? what?*) and indefinite pronouns (*anything*, *something*).

Proper noun, name Proper nouns or proper names are the names of specific people (such as *Churchill*, *Tony Blair*), places (*London*, *Edinburgh*), publications (the *Guardian*), occasions (*Christmas*), and so on. These do not have determiners, and cannot usually be made plural. Proper names are discussed in relation to **magazine features** on page 118 and in relation to **news reporting** on page 25.

Purpose expression Purpose expressions are phrases or clauses that describe why a certain action has to be done, usually in the context of an instruction. For example, one might be asked to push a lever *to make frothy coffee, so that the drain can clear freely, in order to release the mechanism*, or *for easier cleaning*. Some purpose expressions give information that constrains the way the accompanying action is done: for example, *cut the paper to make two triangles*. This expression not only tells the reader why the paper should be cut, but how. Purpose expressions are discussed in the context of **instructions** on page 72.

Referent The referent of an expression is the thing, idea or concept that it refers to. The use of particular constructions that postpone having to identify a referent is discussed in relation to **sports commentary** on page 42.

Register A way of describing how language is intricately related to the situation in which it is produced. The standard Hallidayan notion of register has three components – field, tenor, and mode – elements which are intended to capture characteristics of the subject, purpose, relevant social relationships, and manner of transmission which give different kinds of discourse their distinctive flavour. Register is discussed in more detail in the **introduction**, beginning on page 4, and used in relation to **sports commentary** on page 40.

Relational process see process types

Relative clause Relative clauses are subordinate clauses which function as modifiers within noun phrases, as in *the man that I saw* (where *that I saw* is the relative clause, introduced by the relative pronoun *that*).

Replanning Replanning is a phenomenon that frequently occurs when complex syntactic constructions are entered into that a speaker cannot finish, sometimes from lack of concentration but more usually because of the changing demands of the communication they are trying to construct. For example, the sentence *what he's trying to do . . . he's running up the far side* shows that what might have been a wh-cleft has been replanned in midstream, either to communicate the originally planned content more effectively, or perhaps to say something quite different. Replanning is discussed in relation to **sports commentary** on page 50.

Reporting clause In reporting the speech or thought of others in direct or indirect speech the reporting clause is the clause-like element that signals speech is taking place, as in *she said, he thought, Bill wondered, expostulated Mike*. This may occur before or after the speech or thought itself. Free direct or indirect speech omits the reporting clause. Attribution of speech is discussed in

news reporting on page 24; reporting clauses are mentioned in the analysis of **magazine features** on page 106. For further reading on direct and indirect speech, see Montgomery et al. (1992: 205ff.) and Quirk et al. (1985: 1022ff.).

Reverse wh-cleft   see cleft construction

Rhetorical relations   This general term describes the links that are constructed between segments of discourse that allow us to understand the general form of argument or rhetorical structure of the text. For example, in the text *Max fell because John pushed him*, the rhetorical relation between the two elements is one of cause, signalled by because. However, rhetorical relations are not always signalled: *Max fell. John pushed him* is also an acceptable text, and the reader is invited to infer the relation for him or herself. The structure created in the text by the discourse segments and their interrelationships is known as rhetorical structure. Several frameworks that attempt to describe and enumerate rhetorical relations are available, including Winter (1994) and Hoey (1983), and the framework known as Rhetorical Structure Theory or RST (for example, Mann and Thompson, 1987). Rhetorical relations are discussed in relation to **magazine features** on page 108.

Salient   This general term refers to information that is current in the discourse, often linked to psychological states of attention or short term memory. Salient items, for example, are sometimes defined as those elements that can currently be referred to by a pronoun.

Second story   This term originates within conversation analysis and refers to an informative turn or 'story' that is given as the second turn in a conversational sequence, perhaps in response to a related 'story' by the first speaker. They are discussed in relation to **interviews** on page 98.

Self-selection   A term originating in the discussion of turn taking in conversation analysis, referring to a situation in which a speaker appoints him or herself as next speaker, without waiting to be invited either by name or by somebody looking at them (these are both forms of selection in which the power to choose is exercised by the current speaker). Self-selection is mentioned in relation to **interviews** on page 86.

Sound   Carter and Nash (1990: 119–29ff.) give a good summary of various sound effects in poetry. Many of these principles can be applied to any variety of discourse, particularly text types in which 'word play' of some kind is valued, as in **advertising** (see page 126).

Speaker-interested   see hearer-interested

Speech errors   Speech errors are unintended disfluencies in speech, sometimes referred to as 'slips of the tongue', which are very revealing about how speech is processed in the mind. For example, the speech error termed 'perseveration', where a previous speech segment is reproduced accidentally in a later word. An example is the phrase *snack on a small piece* accidentally produced with a perseveration of the 'sn' sound as in *snack on a snall piece*. The most famous producer of speech errors known as 'spoonerisms' was William Spooner, who was reputed to reverse consonant sounds on nearby words, as in *town drain* for *down train*. Speech errors are discussed in this book in relation to **sports commentary** on page 49. See also Crystal (1987: 258ff.), Fromkin (1973).

Speech event The notion of speech event was originally due to Hymes (1962), who used it as a way of describing events involving language that are recognized by their participants as serving particular functions, having particular rules and expected ways of proceeding, and being made up of particular kinds of language used in particular ways. Hymes' aim was to describe the uses of language in a way that could equally be applied in all cultures, however unfamiliar to the analyst, and that would yield relatively full descriptions of practices of language use that were as free as possible from cultural bias. Speech events are discussed here in relation to **interviews** on page 81.

State A state is a type of eventuality with no clear agent or doer, but which occurs, or holds. States do not have clear results, and it is not easy to say when they begin or end. For example, *being in love, sitting,* and *living in Birmingham* are all states. Many states may hold at once, and they may certainly hold while events are going on at the same time. States are part of the set of concepts used to analyze **news reporting**: see page 16.

Subject The grammatical subject of a clause is, in 'ordinary' unmarked clause arrangements, most often the agent of the action reported by the clause. Subjects exhibit a large number of special properties that make them more 'controlling' of the grammar of the clause than, say, objects. One useful test for subject is to construct a tag question for the clause: so, for the clause *John was running away*, the appropriate tag question *wasn't he* refers to *John*, the subject. In trickier sentences, such as *These boots were given to me by Mary*, the tag question *weren't they* correctly singles out *these boots* as subject even though in this case Mary is the agent of the giving.

Subject positioning Subject in the non-grammatical sense is a term used to refer to the way that individuals operate within society depending on the social constraints that they are subjected to. Fairclough (1989: 38ff.) sees individuals as social agents, but suggests that their actions are determined to some extent by their need to negotiate with types of discourse that they are faced with. We can say, then, that people (subjects) are 'positioned' by any text or discourse that they take part in as speakers, hearers, readers or writers. This notion is discussed further in relation to **instructions** on page 66.

Subordinate clause Subordinate clauses are any clause that is a constituent of another clause, and is therefore embedded within it or subordinate.

Subordinating conjunctions may be used to do this: for example, *because, although, when, while, after,* and so on. So, *John was running away while Bill was loading the dishwasher* has the second clause, *Bill was loading the dishwasher,* as subordinate clause. Subordinate clauses are referred to in relation to **sports commentary** on page 41.

Superlative   see gradable adjective

Syllable   A syllable is a 'beat' of a word. 'Beat' has a single syllable, 'onion' has two, 'syllable' has three, 'biology' has four, and 'deactivated' has five.

Task-, action-orientated   Task- or action-orientated language is language that is very closely linked or dependent for its interpretation on action that is taking place at the time. The language is often orientated towards getting the reader to do something, and this has many implications for its form. Instructions (see page 59) are predominantly (though not exclusively) task-orientated.

Technologization   This is a term used by Fairclough (1989: 211ff.; 1992: 55, 215ff.) to refer to the application of specialist knowledge, often derived from sociological or related study, to certain types of discourse in order to gain control, power, or advantage in the interaction. In its mildest form, such knowledge can be derived from 'how to' manuals on writing and speaking (for example, after-dinner speeches, interview technique), but there are cases in which highly sophisticated knowledge derived from the study of human behaviour can be applied to train people in how to act or speak, as in the training of sales staff in ways of speaking that will ensure a sale. This term is applied to **interviews** on page 84.

Telegraphic   Telegraphic language, so called because it was employed in telegrams, which were billed by the word, is a type of language which has many elements missed out for brevity or urgency. The elements missed out are often function words – the grammatical 'glue' that holds sentences together – or things that are easily inferrable. The telegraphic language used by a step aerobics instructor is discussed in the chapter on **instructions,** page 68.

Temporal sequence   Temporal sequence refers simply to the order in which things occur in time. It is important in the description of **news reporting** (page 16), where the organization of the events in the written report is very different from their temporal sequence.

Tenor   Tenor is a term that belongs to the tripartite categorization that makes up the description of register. The tenor of a text or discourse refers to the information it conveys about the interpersonal relationships between the speakers, or between writer or reader; its relative formality, and the social characteristics of the speaker(s) or writer(s). Tenor is introduced in more detail in the **introduction** to this book (page 4) and is discussed in relation to **instructions** on page 66.

Tense   Tense is the term used for the markings in a language that convey temporal (time) information. In English, tense marking takes place on verbs, and accounts for the difference between *he goes, he went,* and *he will go.* Tense is mentioned in relation to **sports commentary** on page 46.

Theme   A term from functional linguistics, theme (and its complement, rheme) is used to describe how clauses are arranged as messages. Theme is defined as the 'point of departure' of the message, and usually appears in first position in the clause. According to Halliday (1985: 38ff.), clauses are organized by speakers and writers in order to put what is wanted as theme in this position. To use Halliday's examples, in *the duke has given my aunt that teapot,* the theme is *the duke* (the rest is rheme), while in *that teapot the duke has given to my aunt,* the theme is *that teapot.* In the first case, the theme is also the subject of the clause: this is the normal state of affairs. However, in the second case, the theme is not the clause subject. This arrangement is known as marked theme. Thematic organization of clauses is discussed in relation to **sports commentary** on page 53, and **advertising** on page 129.

Time-critical utterance   These are utterances which depend for their interpretation on their positioning in time, as in the countdown to a space launch, for example. **Sports commentary** is often time-critical: see page 46.

Tones   The notion of 'tone' captures the idea that languages have a few basic meaningful 'tunes'. In English, these tones work at the utterance level, differentiating , say, a question (rising tone) from a statement (falling tone). Some languages, such as Chinese, Thai, and many West African languages, use tone to differentiate a range of meanings for words. Tone is applied in this book to **sports commentary**, page 51.

Transitivity   This notion has been developed within functional linguistics, particularly by Halliday (see, for example, 1985: 101ff.). Transitivity refers, according to Halliday, to 'the different types of process that are recognized in the language, and the structures by which they are expressed'. Transitivity is therefore a notion that operates at the level of the clause, and it refers to how the clause elements (the processes expressed by verbs, the people and things expressed as participants in those processes, etc.) are arranged in relation to one another. The notion of transitivity is explained in detail on page 26 in the chapter on **news reporting**.

Truth value   Truth value is a term borrowed from logic and the mathematical study of language. The basic unit of meaning on this approach is the proposition: for example, the meaning conveyed by a statement such as *John runs.* All propositions require a truth value. Usually there are two possibilities, true or false. This notion is applied to **advertising** on page 129.

Turn packaging   Turn packaging refers to elements such as *yeah, well, right, so, ok,* and *but* that act as indicators of the relationship between the speaker's turn and the preceding discourse. For an application of this notion in **advertising**, see page 139.

Turn taking Speech events in which more than one speaker participates generally operate through the speakers taking turns to 'hold the floor'. The basic rule in English-speaking culture, according to Sacks et al. (1974), is 'no gap, no overlap': that is, we stick broadly to a pattern in which we don't leave large gaps between utterances, and we try not to talk over one another. Who speaks next can be negotiated between speakers. For example, a speaker can nominate someone else explicitly, or a speaker can select themselves by starting to speak at the appropriate moment; the kinds of turn that can be taken (answering a question, rather than initiating a new topic, for example) may also be constrained or even pre-allocated. Often, turn taking is regulated by the more powerful participant, or by some outside mechanism such as the order of proceedings in a courtroom (in which case, a powerful participant may enforce the turn taking conventions agreed by the institution she or he represents). The relative freedom of individuals to speak, and other related matters such as pauses between turns, interruptions, and overlaps between turns, is a very fertile area of study for those interested in how the patterns of spoken interaction can reveal the power structure inherent in the discourse. Turn taking is discussed in this book in relation to **sports commentary** (page 48), **interviews** (page 86), and **advertising** (page 137).

Turn type pre-allocation This is a situation that occurs often in formal contexts in which it is decided beforehand, either explicitly or by some understood convention, which speakers will have access to what kinds of turns in an interaction. So, for example, in a TV quiz show, the studio audience know that they are not permitted to shout out answers unless explicitly called upon, and that questions are directed at the team or person doing the quiz. The audience predominantly, therefore, do not have free access to the turn type 'answer', and do not have any access at all to the turn type 'question'. A similar situation prevails in **interviews**, discussed on page 86.

Unmarked theme   see theme

Unplanned discourse This is discourse that is not scripted, and which is produced spontaneously. It may be that the event it accompanies (as in the discussion of **sports commentary** on page 41) is quite well planned, but the language itself is not.

Verb Referred to in schoolbooks as 'the doing word', verbs express processes, actions, states of affairs and events.

Verb phrase The verb element in a clause structure, consisting of one or more elements: in *I don't know* the verb phrase is *don't know*; in *I should have been going to open the shop*, the verb phrase is *should have been going to open*.

Verbal process   see process types

Wh-cleft   see cleft construction

Wh-question   Wh-questions are those which feature a wh-word, such as *What are you doing? Why are you here? When are you leaving?* These allow a relatively wide range of choices from the responder, more so than yes-no questions. Wh-questions are frequently used in **interviews**, discussed on page 90.

Wh-word   Wh-words are a category of words most of which begin with *wh*: *who, where, what, why, when* but also *how*. These are clearly key components of questions, and are discussed as such in relation to **interviews** on page 90.

Yes-no question   Logically, a question whose answer is constrained to the negative or affirmative, such as *Do you live near here?* Yes-no questions contrast with wh-questions, which, while also constraining the answer, give more room to elaborate. The use of yes-no questions in **interviews** is discussed on page 90.

Bibliography

Allan, K. and Burridge, K. (1991) *Euphemism and Dysphemism*. New York and Oxford: Oxford University Press.

Atkinson, J.M. (1982) 'Understanding formality: the categorization and production of "formal" interaction', *British Journal of Sociology*, 33: 86–117.

Bach, E. (1986) 'The algebra of events', *Linguistics and Philosophy*, 9: 5–16.

Beard, A. (1998) *The Language of Sport*. London: Routledge.

Beard, H. and Cerf, C. (1992) *The Official Politically Correct Dictionary and Handbook*. London: Grafton.

Beattie, G. (1983) *Talk: An Analysis of Speech and Non-Verbal Behaviour in Conversation*. Milton Keynes: Open University Press.

Bell, A. (1991) *The Language of News Media*. Oxford: Blackwell.

Bell, A. (1994) 'Telling stories', in D. Graddol and O. Boyd-Barrett (eds), *Media Texts: Authors and Readers*. Clevedon: Multilingual Matters: Open University Press. 100–18.

Bell, A. (1998) 'The discourse structure of news stories', in A. Bell and P. Garrett (eds), *Approaches to Media Discourse*. Oxford: Blackwell. 65–104.

Bell, A. and Garrett, P. (eds) (1998) *Approaches to Media Discourse*. Oxford: Blackwell.

Benwell, B. (1998) 'Is there anything new about these lads? The construction of masculinity in men's magazines', in J. Sunderland and S. Johnson (eds), *Proceedings of the Language and Gender One-Day Conference*, University of Lancaster, February 1998. University of Lancaster: Centre for Language in Social Life Working Papers.

Benwell, B. (forthcoming) 'Have a go if you think you're hard enough: male gossip and language play in the letters pages of men's lifestyle magazines', *Journal of Popular Culture*.

Biber, D., Johansson, S., Leech, G., Conrad, S. and Finegan, E. (1999) *The Longman Grammar of Spoken and Written English*. London: Longman.

Bolinger, D. (1980) *Language, the Loaded Weapon*. London: Longman.

Boyle, R. and Blain, N. (1998) 'Sport as real life: media, sport, and culture', in Adam Briggs and Paul Cobley (eds), *The Media: An Introduction*. London: Longman. 365–76.

Brierley, S. (1995) *The Advertising Handbook*. London: Routledge.

Brown, P. and Levinson, S. (1987) *Politeness: Some Universals of Language Usage*. Cambridge: Cambridge University Press. (Abridged version appears in A. Jaworski and N. Coupland (eds) (1999) *The Discourse Reader*. London: Routledge.)

Butler, C.S. (1988) 'Politeness and the semantics of modalised directives in English', in J.D. Benson, M.J. Cummings and W.S. Greaves (eds), *Linguistics in a Systemic Perspective*. Amsterdam: John Benjamins. 119–53.

Button, G. and Lee, J.R. (eds) (1987) *Talk and Social Organization*. Clevedon: Multilingual Matters.

Carter, R. (1987) *Vocabulary: Applied Linguistic Perspectives*. London: Routledge.

Carter, R. (1988) 'Front pages: lexis, style, and newspaper reports', in M. Ghadessy (ed.), *Registers of Written English*. London: Pinter. 8–16.

Carter, R. and McCarthy, M. (1997) *Exploring Spoken English*. Cambridge: Cambridge University Press.

Carter, R. and Nash, W. (1990) *Seeing Through Language*. Oxford: Blackwell.

Chisnall, P.M. (1992) *Marketing Research*. London: McGraw-Hill.

Christie, F. (1990) 'Young children's writing: from spoken to written genre', in R. Carter (ed.), *Knowledge About Language and the Curriculum: the LINC reader*. London: Hodder and Stoughton. 234–47.

Cicourel, A. (1985) 'Doctor-patient discourse', in T. van Dijk (ed.), *Handbook of Discourse Analysis. Volume 4: Discourse Analysis in Society*. London and New York: Academic Press. 193–202.

Ciliberti, A. (1990) 'Instructions for use: a macrotextual and stylistic analysis', in M.A.K. Halliday, J. Gibbons and H. Nicholas (eds), *Learning, Keeping, and Using Language: Selected Papers of the 8th World Congress of Applied Linguistics*. Sydney, 16–21 August, 1987. Volume II. Amsterdam: John Benjamins. 299–313.

Clark, K. (1992) 'The linguistics of blame: representations of women in *The Sun*'s reporting of crimes of sexual violence', in M. Toolan (ed.), *Language, Text, and Context: Essays In Stylistics*. London: Routledge. 208–26.

Cohen, A. (1987) *The Television News Interview*. Newbury Park, CA: Sage.

Cook, G. (1992) *The Discourse of Advertising*. London: Routledge.

Coulthard, M. and Ashby, M. (1976) 'A linguistic description of doctor-patient interviews', in M. Wadsworth and D. Robinson (eds), *Studies in Everyday Medical Life*. London: Martin Robertson. 72–86

Cruttenden, A. (1986) *Intonation*. Cambridge: Cambridge University Press.

Crystal, D. (1987) *The Cambridge Encyclopedia of Language*. Cambridge: Cambridge University Press.

Crystal, D. (1996) *Rediscover Grammar*, second edn. London: Longman.

Crystal, D. and Davy, D. (1969) *Investigating English Style*. London: Longman.

Davis, A. (1995) *Magazine Journalism Today*. Oxford: Focal Press.

Delin, J. (1992) 'Properties of it-cleft presupposition', *Journal of Semantics*, 9: 179–96.

Delin, J. (1998) 'Facework and instructor goals in the step aerobics workout', in S. Hunston (ed.), *Language at Work: British Studies in Applied Linguistics*. Volume 13. British Association for Applied Linguistics in association with Multilingual Matters. 56–71.

Duszak, A. (1991) 'Schematic and topical categories in news story reconstruction', *Text*, 11 (4): 503–22.

Dyer, G. (1982) *Advertising as Communication*. London: Methuen.

Edelman, M. (1974) 'The political language of the helping professions', *Politics and Society*, 4: 295–310.

Eggins, S. and Slade, D. (1997) *Analysing Casual Conversation*. London: Cassell.

Ervin-Tripp, S. (1976) 'Is Sybil there? The structure of some American English directives', *Language in Society*, 5 (1): 25–66.

Fairclough, N. (1989) *Language and Power*. London: Longman.

Fairclough, N. (1992) *Discourse and Social Change*. Cambridge: Polity Press.

Fasold, R. (1987) *The Sociolinguistics of Society*. Oxford: Blackwell.

Ferguson, C. (1983) 'Sports announcer talk: syntactic aspects of register variation', *Language in Society*, 12: 153–72.

Ferguson, M. (1983) *Forever Feminine: Women's Magazines and the Cult of Femininity*. London: Longman.

Fisher, S. and Groce, S. (1990) 'Accounting practices in medical interviews', *Language in Society*, 19: 225–50.

Fowler, R. (1991) *Language in the News: Discourses and Ideology in the Press.* London: Routledge.

Fowler, R., Hodge, B., Kress, G. and Trew, T. (1979) *Language and Control.* London: Routledge & Kegan Paul.

Frankel, R.M. (1984) 'From sentence to sequence: understanding the medical encounter through micro-interaction analysis', *Discourse Processes*, 7: 135–70.

Freeborn, D. (1993) *Varieties of English*, second edn. Basingstoke: Macmillan.

Friedlander, E. and Lee, J. (1988) *Feature Writing for Newspapers and Magazines: The Pursuit of Excellence.* New York: Harper & Row.

Fromkin, V. (ed.) (1973) *Speech Errors as Linguistic Evidence.* The Hague: Mouton.

Fromkin, V. and Rodman, R. (1997) *An Introduction to Language.* Fort Worth, TX: Harcourt Brace Jovanovich.

Galtung, J. and Ruge, M.H. (1965) 'The structure of foreign news', *Journal of Peace Research*, 2: 64–91.

Garnham, A. (1985) *Psycholinguistics: Central Topics.* London: Routledge.

Geis, M. (1982) *The Language of Television Advertising.* London and New York: Academic Press.

Ghadessy, M. (1988) 'The language of written sports commentary. Soccer: a description', in M. Ghadessy (ed.), *Registers of Written English: Situational Factors and Linguistic Features.* London: Pinter.

Ghadessy, M. (1993) 'Thematic development and its relationship to registers and genres', *Occasional Papers in Systemic Linguistics*, 7: 1–25.

Goddard, A. (1998) *The Language of Advertising: Written Texts.* London: Routledge.

Goodworth, C. (1979) *Effective Interviewing for Employment Selection.* London: Business Books.

Gordon, K. (1993) *The Deluxe Transitive Vampire: the Ultimate Handbook of Grammar for the Innocent, the Eager, and the Doomed.* New York: Pantheon.

Graddol, D. and Boyd-Barrett, O. (eds) (1994) *Media Texts: Authors and Readers.* Clevedon: Multilingual Matters: Open University Press.

Graddol, D., Cheshire, J. and Swann, J. (1994) *Describing Language.* Milton Keynes: Open University Press.

Gray, M. (1992) *A Dictionary of Literary Terms.* London: Longman; Beirut: York Press.

Greasley, P. (1994) 'An investigation into the use of the particle well: commentaries on a game of snooker', *Journal of Pragmatics*, 22 (5), November: 477–94.

Greatbach, D. (1998) 'Conversation analysis: neutralism in British news interviews', in A. Bell and P. Garrett (eds), *Approaches to Media Discourse.* Oxford: Blackwell. 163–85.

Green, G. (1978) 'Discourse functions of inversion constructions', *Pragmatics Microfiche*, 3 (4), August: A3–A33.

Green, G. (1989) *Pragmatics and Natural Language Understanding.* Hove and London: Lawrence Erlbaum.

Grice, H.P. (1975) 'Logic and conversation', in P. Cole and J.L. Morgan (eds), *Syntax and Semantics III: Speech Acts.* New York: Academic Press. 41–58.

Halliday, M.A.K. (1985) *An Introduction to Functional Grammar.* London: Edward Arnold.

Halliday, M.A.K. (1989) *Spoken and Written Language.* Oxford: Oxford University Press.

Halliday, M.A.K. (1994) 'Spoken and written modes of meaning', in D. Graddol and

O. Boyd-Barrett (eds), *Media Texts: Authors and Readers*. Clevedon: Multilingual Matters: Open University Press. 51–73.

Halliday, M. and Hasan, R. (1976) *Cohesion in English*. London: Longman.

Halliday, M., MacIntosh, A. and Strevens, P. (1964) *The Linguistic Sciences and Language Teaching*. London: Longman.

Hartley, J. (1985) *Designing Instructional Text*. London: Kogan Page; New York: Nichols.

Henley, N., Miller, M. and Beazley, J. (1995) 'Syntax, semantics, and sexual violence: agency and the passive voice', *Journal of Language and Social Psychology*, 14 (1–2): 60–84.

Hennessy, B. (1989) *Writing Feature Articles: A Practical Guide to Methods and Markets*. Oxford: Heinemann.

Heritage, J. (1984a) *Garfinkel and Ethnomethodology*. Cambridge: Polity Press.

Heritage, J. (1984b) 'A change of state token and its sequential placement', in J. Atkinson and J. Heritage (eds), *Structures of Social Action: Studies in Conversation Analysis*. Cambridge: Cambridge University Press. 299–345.

Heritage, J. and Greatbach, D. (1991) 'On the institutional character of institutional talk: the case of news interviews', in D. Boden and D. Zimmerman (eds), *Talk and Social Structure*. Oxford: Polity Press. 93–137.

Hermes, J. (1995) *Reading Women's Magazines: An Analysis of Everyday Media Use*. Cambridge: Polity Press.

Heywood, J. (1997) 'The object of desire is the object of contempt. Representations of masculinity in *Straight to Hell* magazine', in S. Johnson and U. Meinhof (eds), *Language and Masculinity*. Oxford: Blackwell. 188–207.

Hodge, B. (1979) 'Newspapers and communities', in R. Fowler, B. Hodge, G. Kress and T. Trew (eds), *Language and Control*. London: Routledge & Kegan Paul. 157–74.

Hodgson, P. (1987) *A Practical Guide to Successful Interviewing*. Maidenhead: McGraw-Hill.

Hoey, M. (1983) *On the Surface of Discourse*. London: Allen & Unwin. (Reprinted 1991 by the Department of English Studies, University of Nottingham.)

Hughes, A. and Trudgill, P. (1996) *English Accents and Dialects, third edn*. London: Arnold.

Hughes, D. (1982) 'Control in the medical consultation: organizing talk in a situation where the co-participants have differential competence', *Sociology*, 16 (3): 361–73.

Hurford, J.R. (1994) *Grammar*. Cambridge: Cambridge University Press.

Hymes, D. (1962) *The Ethnography of Speaking: Anthropology and Human Behavior*. Washington, DC: Anthropological Society of Washington. (Reprinted in J. Fishman (ed.), *Readings in the Sociology of Language*. The Hague: Mouton, 1968.)

Jefferson, G. (1978) 'Sequential aspects of storytelling in conversation', in J. Schenkein (ed.), *Studies in the Organization of Conversational Interaction*. New York: Academic Press. 219–48.

Jeffries, L. (1998) *Meaning in English*. London: Macmillan.

Jones, H. (1996) *Publishing Law*. London: Routledge.

Jucker, A. (1986) *News Interviews*. Amsterdam: John Benjamins.

Klein, Marie-Luise (1988) 'Women in the discourse of sports reports', *International Review for the Sociology of Sport*, 23 (2): 139–52.

Kress, G. (1983) 'Linguistic and ideological transformations in news reporting', in H. Davis and P. Walton (eds), *Language, Image, Media*. Oxford: Blackwell. 120–38.

Kress, G. and Fowler, R. (1985) 'Interviews', in R. Fowler, G. Kress, B. Hodge and T. Trew (eds), *Language and Control*. London: Routledge. 63–80.

Kress, G. and van Leeuwen, T. (1998) 'Front pages: (the critical) analysis of newspaper layout', in A. Bell and P. Garrett (eds), *Approaches to Media Discourse*. Oxford: Blackwell. 186–219.

Labov, W. (1972a) 'The transformation of experience in narrative syntax', in W. Labov (ed.), *Language in the Inner City*. Philadelphia, PA: University of Pennsylvania Press. 354–96.

Labov, W. (1972b) 'Some principles of linguistic methodology', *Language in Society*, 1: 97–120.

Labov, W. and Fanshel, D. (1977) *Therapeutic Discourse*. New York: Academic Press.

Labov, W. and Waletsky, J. (1967) 'Narrative analysis', in J. Helm (ed.), *Essays on the Verbal and Visual Arts: Proceedings of the 1966 Spring Meeting of the American Ethnological Society*. Seattle: University of Washington Press. 12–44.

Leckie-Tarry, H. and Birch, D. (1995) *Language and Context: A Functional Linguistic Theory of Register*. London: Pinter

Leech, G. (1966) *English in Advertising*. London: Longman.

Leech, G. (1990) *Semantics*. Harmondsworth: Penguin.

Leman, J. (1980) 'The advice of a real friend: codes of intimacy and oppression in women's magazines, 1937–1955', *Women's Studies International Quarterly*, 3: 63–78.

Levinson, S. (1983) *Pragmatics*. Cambridge: Cambridge University Press.

Lewis, D. (1979) 'Scorekeeping in a language game', *Journal of Philosophical Logic*, 8: 339–59.

Mann, W. and Thompson, S. (1987) *Rhetorical Structure Theory: A Theory of Text Organization*. Technical report ISI/RS-87–190, Information Sciences Institute, University of Southern California.

Manoff, R.K. (1987) 'Writing the news (by telling the "story")', in R.K. Manoff and M. Schudson (eds), *Reading the News*. New York: Pantheon.

McCracken, E. (1993) *Decoding Women's Magazines*. Basingstoke: Macmillan.

McLoughlin, L. (2000) *The Language of Magazines*. London: Routledge.

McRobbie, A. (1978) *Jackie: An Ideology of Adolescent Femininity*. Occasional paper, University of Birmingham: Centre for Contemporary Cultural Studies.

McRobbie, A. (1991) *Feminism and Youth Culture: From Jackie to Just Seventeen*. London: Macmillan.

Messaris, P. (1997) *Visual Persuasion: The Role of Images in Advertising*. Thousand Oaks, CA: Sage.

Messner, M., Duncan, M. and Jensen, K. (1993) 'Separating the men from the girls: the gendered language of televised sports', *Gender and Society*, 7 (1), March: 121–37.

Mills, S. (1995) *A Feminist Stylistics*. London: Routledge.

Milroy, J. and Milroy, L. (eds) (1993) *Real English*. London: Longman.

Moens, M. and Steedman, M. (1988) 'Temporal ontology and temporal reference', *Computational Linguistics*, 14 (2): 15–28.

Montgomery, M., Durant, A., Fabb, N., Furniss, T. and Mills, S. (1992) *Ways of Reading*. London: Routledge.

Murcia-Bielsa, S. (1999) *Instructional Texts in English and Spanish: A Contrastive Study*. Unpublished PhD dissertation, Department of Modern Languages, University of Córdoba, Spain.

Myers, G. (1994) *Words in Ads*. London: Edward Arnold.

Nilsen, D. (1979) 'Language play in advertising: linguistic invention in product naming', in J. Alatis and G. Tucker (eds), *Language in Public Life*. Georgetown University Round Table on Languages and Linguistics, Washington, DC: Georgetown University Press: 137–43.

Ochs, E. (1979a) 'Transcription as theory', in E. Ochs and B. Schieffelin (eds), *Developmental Pragmatics*. New York: Academic Press.

Ochs, E. (1979b) 'Planned and unplanned discourse', *Syntax and Semantics, Volume 12: Discourse and Syntax*. Academic Press. 51–80.

Paris, C. and Scott, D. (1994) 'Stylistic variation in multilingual instructions', in *Proceedings of the Seventh International Conference on Natural Language Generation*. Nonantum Inn, Maine, June 1994. 45–52.

Prince, E. (1978) 'A comparison of WH-clefts and it-clefts in discourse', *Language*, 54 (4): 883–906.

Quirk, R. and Greenbaum, S. (1993) *A University Grammar of English*. Harlow: Longman.

Quirk, R., Greenbaum, S., Leech, G. and Svartvik, J. (1985) *A Comprehensive Grammar of the English Language*. London: Longman.

Roach, P. (1991) *English Phonetics and Phonology*. Cambridge: Cambridge University Press.

Ross, A. (1968) *Directives and Norms*. London: Routledge & Kegan Paul.

Sacks, H., Schegloff, E. and Jefferson, G. (1974) 'A simplest systematics for the organization of turn taking', *Language*, 50: 696–735.

Salkie, R. (1995) *Text and Discourse Analysis*. London: Routledge.

Sanders, J. and Redeker, G. (1993) 'Linguistic perspective in short news stories', *Poetics*, 22: 69–87.

Schiffrin, D. (1987) *Discourse Markers*. Oxford: Oxford University Press.

Schiffrin, D. (1994) *Approaches to Discourse*. Oxford: Blackwell.

Schiffrin, D. (1999) 'Oh as a marker of information management', in A. Jaworski and N. Coupland (eds), *The Discourse Reader*. London: Routledge. 275–88.

Searle, J.R. (1976) 'The classification of illocutionary acts', *Language in Society*, 5 (1): 1–24.

Short, M. (1988) 'Speech presentation, the novel, and the press', in W. Van Peer (ed.), *The Taming of the Text*. London: Routledge. 61–81.

Sinclair, J. and Coulthard, M. (1975) *Towards an Analysis of Discourse*. London: Oxford University Press.

Stubbs, M. (1983) *Discourse Analysis*. Oxford: Blackwell.

Stubbs, M. (1996) *Text and Corpus Analysis*. Oxford: Blackwell.

Swales, J. (1990) *Genre Analysis: English in Academic and Research Settings*. Cambridge: Cambridge University Press.

Talbot. M. (1992) 'The construction of gender in a teenage magazine', in N. Fairclough (ed.), *Critical Language Awareness*. London: Longman. 174–99.

Talbot, M. (1995) 'A synthetic sisterhood: false friends in a teenage magazine', in K. Hall and M. Bucholtz (eds), *Gender Articulated: Language and the Socially Constructed Self*. London: Routledge. 143–65.

Tanaka, K. (1994) *Advertising Language: A Pragmatic Approach to Advertisements*. London: Routledge.

Tanaka, K. (1998) 'Japanese women's magazines: the language of aspiration', in D. Martinez (ed.), *The Worlds of Japanese Popular Culture*. Cambridge: Cambridge University Press.

Tench, P. (1997) 'The fall and rise of the level of tone in English', *Functions of Language*, 4 (1): 1–22.

Ten Have, P. (1991) 'Talk and institution: a reconsideration of the "asymmetry" of doctor-patient interaction', in D. Boden and D. Zimmerman (eds), *Talk and Social Structure*. Oxford: Polity Press. 138–63.

Ten Have, P. (1999) *Doing Conversation Analysis: A Practical Guide*. London: Sage.

Toolan, M. (1988) 'The language of press advertising', in M. Ghadessy (ed.), *Registers of Written English*. London and New York: Pinter. 52–64.

Trask, L. (1993) *A Dictionary of Grammatical Terms in Linguistics*. London: Routledge.

Trew, T. (1979) 'Theory and ideology at work', in R. Fowler, B. Hodge, G. Kress and T. Trew (eds), *Language and Control*. London: Routledge & Kegan Paul. 94–116.

Tsui, A. (1994) *English Conversation*. Oxford: Oxford University Press.

Tuck, M. (1976) *How Do We Choose?* London: Methuen.

Turner, K. (1996) 'The principal principles of pragmatic inference: politeness', *Language Teaching*, 29: 1–13.

Van Dijk, T. (ed.) (1985) *Handbook of Discourse Analysis*. London: Academic Press.

Van Dijk, T. (1986) 'News schemata', in C. Cooper and S. Greenbaum (eds), *Studying Writing: Linguistic Approaches*. Beverley Hills, CA: Sage. 155–86.

Van Dijk, T.A. (1987) *Communicating Racism*. Newbury Park, CA: Sage.

Van Dijk, T.A. (1988a) *News Analysis: Case Studies of National and International News in the Press*. Hillsdale, NJ: Lawrence Erlbaum.

Van Dijk, T.A. (1988b) *News as Discourse*. Hillsdale, NJ: Lawrence Erlbaum.

Van Dijk, T.A. (1998) 'Opinions and Ideologies in the Press', in A. Bell and P. Garrett (eds), *Approaches to Media Discourse*. Oxford: Blackwell.

Vestergaard, T. and Schroeder, K. (1985) *The Language of Advertising*. Oxford: Blackwell.

Walker, R. (1992) *Magazine Design: A Hands-On Guide*. London: Blueprint.

Wardhaugh, R. (1998) *An Introduction to Sociolinguistics*. Oxford: Blackwell.

Waugh, L. (1995) 'Reported speech in journalistic discourse: the relation of function and text', *Text*, 15 (1): 129–73.

Wenner, Lawrence A. (ed.) (1998) *Mediasport*. London: Routledge.

Whannel, G. (1992) *Fields in Vision: Televisual Sport and Cultural Transformation*. London: Routledge.

White, C. (1970) *Women's Magazines, 1694–1968*. London: Michael Joseph.

White, P. (1997) 'Racism, hegemonic discourse and the news story: modelling genre in a cross-cultural, cross-discoursal training context'. Paper delivered at the Ninth Euro-International Systemic Functional Workshop, Halle-Wittenberg, Germany, 2–6 July 1997.

Williams, B. (1977) 'The structure of televised football', *Journal of Communication*, 27 (3), Summer, 133–9.

Williamson, J. (1978) *Decoding Advertisements: Ideology and Meaning in Advertising*. London: Marion Boyars.

Winship, J. (1987) *Inside Women's Magazines*. New York: Pandora.

Winter, E. (1994) 'Clause relations as information structure: two basic clause structures in English', in M. Coulthard (ed.), *Advances in Written Text Analysis*. London: Routledge. 46–68.

Wray, A., Trott, K. and Bloomer, A. (1998) *Projects in Linguistics: A Practical Guide to Researching Language*. London: Arnold.

Zwaan, R. (1991) 'Some parameters of literary and news comprehension: effects of discourse-type perspective on reading rate and surface structure representation', *Poetics*, 20: 139–56.

Index

Printed in the United Kingdom
by Lightning Source UK Ltd.
105761UKS00001B/160-204